C000082913

THE LIVES OF
TALLEYRAND

CRANE BRINTON was born in Winsted, Connecticut, in 1898. He received his A.B. degree at Harvard University, studied as a Rhodes Scholar at Oxford, and was awarded a Ph.D. there in 1923. Professor Brinton has been awarded honorary degrees from Ripon and Kenyon Colleges. He is now a Professor of History at Harvard, where he has taught since 1943.

In addition to *The Lives of Talleyrand,* Professor Brinton's major works include *English Political Thought in the Nineteenth Century* (1933), *The Anatomy of Revolution* (1938), *Ideas and Men* (1950), *History of Western Morals* (1959), and *The Fate of Man* (1961).

CRANE BRINTON

THE LIVES OF TALLEYRAND

The Norton Library
W · W · NORTON & COMPANY · INC ·
NEW YORK

Contents

Preface

TALLEYRAND'S lives spanned eighty-four of the most crowded years of French history, from 1754 to 1838; yet it is not mere length of years, nor even their rich content, that makes the singular of the noun inadequate here. Talleyrand prospered in societies and under forms of government so different that it hardly seems possible for one man to have done so many things with one life. To entitle a biography *The Lives of Talleyrand* is not, then, a mere conceit, but a faithful introduction to the facts.

I have not tried to fill in completely the historical background for Talleyrand's long career. The task would be too great; and, moreover, there are plenty of manuals of history in which the reader can take refuge. I have, indeed, tried not to be pedantically allusive; but one man's pedantry is another man's innocence, and I beg the reader's pardon in advance if I have misjudged us both.

I should also warn the reader that I have come to like Talleyrand, and to think very highly of him. I shall not mind very much if I am accused of trying to whitewash the old double-dealer. To many readers for whom I am sure I should, were I acquainted with them, have respect and liking, the following pages will undoubtedly seem at times flippant and cynical. For that I am genuinely sorry. But to get back to Talleyrand at all one has to brush out a whole nineteenth-century undergrowth of good intentions and pious hopes—as well as very unidealistic material struggles.

I like Talleyrand partly for the same reason I like La Rouchefoucauld, Robert Walpole, Pope, Voltaire, Chardin and Mozart, because he was part of a society too wise, too sober, too gifted with various skills, to mistake the Word for the Deed. I do not think I like him *because* he was—at times—a liar and a thief; nor, to be quite honest, *in spite* of his being—at times—a liar and thief. His thieving is to me at present pretty unimportant in a man who did so much that I regard as useful in this world. His lying—some of it—made it possible for him to do the useful things. Any extra lies are not very important. Had they been able to do what Talleyrand did at Vienna, I should personally have been glad to have had several thieves and liars assembled around the tables of Versailles in 1919. All this will shock many excellent men, as similar opinions have shocked such excellent men ever since ethical discussions have been recorded. Perhaps these readers will consider my preface as a stop-sign, and go no further? I am glad to spare their feelings, as I am sure they are glad to spare mine. We are not likely to get much further in the way of mutual persuasion than Socrates did with Thrasymachus several thousand years ago. And Thrasymachus was such a set-up!

I wish to thank Miss Martha Houser for suggesting the title of this book; Professor L. J. Henderson for arousing my first interest in Talleyrand, and for constant critical attention to the details and to the generalizations of this study; Professor Penfield Roberts for his customary kindness in all stages of its growth; Professor Carlton J. H. Hayes for invaluable editorial supervision, given at the busy close of an academic year; Professor Alfred Tozzer for supplying me with the amusing explanation of Mrs. Eddy in terms of her ancestry I have used as a sample of how *not* to begin a biography; Mr. Carroll Quigley for a description of Talleyrand's Letters in the Beauharnais manuscripts at

Princeton; Mr. and Mrs. Douglas Brown for reading the proofs; and—though such thanks seem to have gone out of fashion in our impersonal world of large publishing houses —Mr. W. W. Norton for going over this manuscript with an eye to much more than business.

CRANE BRINTON

Peacham, Vermont
July 1, 1936

THE LIVES OF

TALLEYRAND

CHAPTER ONE

"Plus ça change—"

I

CLIO used to keep a ledger in which all her characters were eventually enrolled either on one side as "good," or on the other as "bad." Like that angel of Leigh Hunt's who so handsomely made up for his erroneous first impressions of Abou Ben Adhem, she now and then transferred a name from one side to the other, and at times seems to have felt that some names belonged on both sides at once. But on the whole the ledger stood, solid and enduring. Of recent years some of Clio's attendants have announced rather loudly that the historian is a scientist, and that he should not apply the categories of "good" and "bad" to his subject matter. No chemist would think of writing about noble oxygen and vicious hydrogen. A close examination of the ledger, however, discloses the fact that many of the entries are in handwriting extraordinarily like that of some of the most loudly protesting scientific historians. The ledger itself, certainly, seems in no danger of lapsing. In the minds of the great body of literate and semi-literate people to whom some portion at least of the record of the past has life and meaning, historical figures are pretty confidently separated into sheep and goats. Scientific historians may complain that such a separation is not their business; conscientious historians may point out that human beings are much too many-sided for any such two-way classification to fit the facts of experience. Most men make no such reservations. Fama, rather than Clio, is perhaps after all the most important custodian of the records of the past. The great public can always tell a good man from a bad.

Charles-Maurice, Prince de Talleyrand, is irrevocably listed among the bad men. To Anglo-Saxons on both sides of the Atlantic he appears on the margin of their histories as a clever, corrupt, wholly unsentimental diplomatist. For Americans, thanks to Henry Adams, his name also flashes briefly and discreditably through the shocking incident of the X Y Z papers, where Americans first played so well their not unprofitable rôle of Babes in the Woods in the folk-drama of modern diplomacy. To Frenchmen, however, the name of Talleyrand is well and unfavorably known. Your man in the street—in the better streets—knows all about him; "Ah yes, Talleyrand. A wicked man—very intelligent, yes, but wicked. He served France well at Vienna. But he betrayed the Emperor—betrayed everybody in fact. He took bribes from everybody, whether or not he could give them anything in return. A clever man, a fascinating man, a very French intelligence, but completely unscrupulous. Alas, why are the wicked so much more interesting than the virtuous?——"

Clio herself has come, as she usually does, to acquiesce in the vulgar verdict. Talleyrand lived to be an old man and towards the octogenarian of the 1830's public opinion was not ill-disposed. The mere fact of long survival suffices to make most public characters lovable to their contemporaries. Voltaire and Queen Victoria, once well-hated, ended their lives in a cloud of incense. Talleyrand was a Grand Old Man in the days of Louis Philippe and Lord Melbourne. He had made too many enemies in his prime, however, and, as we shall see, he fitted too badly into the pattern of nineteenth-century judgments of value for this good repute to survive his death. Historians and biographers have occasionally praised his achievements, and more rarely, some phases of his character. The only important modern studies of Talleyrand steadily conceived and written in a friendly, admiring spirit are, however, the work of two Englishmen—the brief essay of Sir Henry Lytton Bulwer in 1868, and the admirable biography of Mr. Duff Cooper in 1932.

In France the evil reputation of Talleyrand was fixed for cultivated people by the publication in the *Temps* in 1869 of a series of essays by Sainte-Beuve, subsequently bound together in a single volume as *M. de Talleyrand.* Such, indeed, was the merited prestige of the writer as a subtle and sensible judge of character and of essentials generally that his opinion penetrated down into classes where cultivation may almost be regarded as ceasing. Sainte-Beuve was ill, distracted, and near his death, but these essays cannot be dismissed as the work of a man of failing powers. Most of Sainte-Beuve's great gifts are there—the quiet irony, never cheaply epigrammatic, the sense for the telling anecdote, the revealing gesture, the ability to reproduce the oneness of experience, undisturbed by such afterthought dichotomies as those between fact and theory, research and imagination. Some of his gifts are not pressed into service—notably his serenity, his detachment, his many-sided sympathies. Sainte-Beuve, however, is rarely at his critical best in judging his contemporaries; against Talleyrand he may quite conceivably have had some personal grievance not yet brought to light. From his bitter pages there finally emerges the Talleyrand of cultivated legend, the man supremely endowed with intelligence, charm, energy, placed by birth and training in a position to employ all three in the good life, actually misusing them in a life which, for all its external successes, was a bad life. It is, to quote the expurgated form of Napoleon's famous remark, the Talleyrand of "the silk stocking filled with mud."

In our own time, the late M. Lacour-Gayet has continued the attack on Talleyrand's reputation, this time from the convenient position of scientific history. A patient and thorough research worker alike among printed sources and the documents, he laboriously assembled four sizable volumes of what will no doubt long be the "definitive" life of Talleyrand. Lacour-Gayet, as a faithful disciple of modern French objective history, allows the facts to speak for themselves. That the facts should speak, as they seem to do, somewhat petulantly, and with the voice of a *savant* of the Third Republic, devoted to the memory of the great and good Napoleon, convinced that the conventional abstractions of a mildly positivistic ethics are reliably descriptive of human actions, distrustful of anything beyond the petty bourgeois world of official French scholarship—that, in short, the facts should speak with the voice of Lacour-Gayet need astonish only those who are quite unaware that in many quarters today "objective history" may well mean violently partisan history. For four volumes Lacour-Gayet, as prosecuting attorney, conducts an enquiry into the minutiæ of Talleyrand's life; in so far as any general impression emerges, it is pretty much the conventional nineteenth-century portrait of the clever, selfish, unscrupulous, time-serving diplomatist.

The Talleyrand legend is now firmly fixed, in content substantially the same both in its literary and in its popular forms. It would be difficult to effect any considerable change in the legend. None of the numerous groups contending for political power or literary prestige in modern France can make much use of Talleyrand. For the monarchists of all varieties he is ruled out by his active participation in the great Revolution. Moreover, in several of the more definite meanings of that Protean word "liberal," Talleyrand unquestionably was a liberal. The nationalists cannot use a man who signed away French territory at Vienna. For though Talleyrand held this terrestrial France very dear indeed, he could not, like the nationalist, worship in the abstraction, France, a flattering image of himself and God. Most middle-of-the-road Frenchmen are now, somewhat oddly, perhaps, great admirers of Napoleon. Talleyrand, who might otherwise not be unattractive to them, is ruled out by his abandonment of Napoleon. For the various Lefts of French life, Talleyrand is the cynical patrician. Moreover, many members of groups on the Left are, or wish to seem, anti-clerical ethical-society puritans devoted to a very abstract and very rigid moral code, and to be useful to such a group a man must have held publicly that Virtue is its own Reward, and behaved privately in a manner not too irreconcilable with such an adage. Talleyrand occasionally juggled with ethical abstractions in public, but his private life was pretty obviously not an echo of the Kantian categorical imperative. Not even the bright, if no longer exactly young, men of the *Nouvelle Revue Française* have chosen to exercise their modernity in the rehabilitation of Talleyrand. M. Jacques Sindral has given him a nagging, less flat and schoolmasterish than Lacour-Gayet's, inspired by the wisdom of modern psychology, seasoned with epigrams and full of rebellion against the *ce-qui-n'est-pas-clair-n'est-pas-français* attitude, but a nagging none the less.

All this is a pity, because a properly qualified Frenchman would be the best possible critic of the Talleyrand legend. No foreigner can cross the final threshold where something of so very French a person as Talleyrand is held from the rest of the world. Yet if the French will not try, there is some excuse for the heavy-footed foreigner's attempting the task. For, if in its main lines the legend seems immune from merely literary attack, there is always the possibility of trying to give a new meaning to the legend. After all, the facts about Talleyrand are, thanks to the diligence of Lacour-Gayet, as well-known as they need be. In most legends perhaps it is the facts themselves which are uncertain, contorted, unbelievable, as in the legend of St. Joan of Arc. In the Talleyrand legend the facts are solid enough as historical facts go; it is the interpretation put upon those facts that makes Talleyrand a legend, or at least a cliché.

Now the root of this interpretation is to be found in a notion which is no doubt perennial, but which in the nineteenth century obtained an almost universal assent from all sorts of men, a degree of assent unique, or at any rate rare, in recorded history. Briefly, the notion is this: that there is between men's words—particularly their more abstract words, like Liberty, Equality, Fraternity, or Tory Democracy, or the White Man's Burden—and their deeds an obvious and on the whole logical connection; and that therefore, given the Word, you have also given the Deed. This is, if you like, the intellectualist fallacy of the eighteenth-century Enlightenment. But the first few generations of the romanticists did nothing to destroy the fallacy. They simply piled upon it the emotionalist fallacy that certain human sentiments for which they had pleasant names, like love, pity, or the heart, determine directly this happy correspondence of word and deed.

Marx, Sorel, Bergson, James, Pareto, the Viennese psychologists—each has contributed something to our contemporary feeling that the foregoing beliefs really are fallacies. For us today this problem of the relation between men's ethical ideals, men's "guiding" abstractions, and men's actual conduct is certainly not solved, and probably needs re-statement and re-examination. Now all thought is in some sense abstract thought. The neat distinction between theory and practice is frequently too neat. You cannot build a stone wall without some recourse to theory, and rule of thumb is after all a rule. Farmer, engineer, poet, musician or politician all make use of the instrument of thought. We may, however, isolate that type of abstraction most common among moralists, preachers, reformers, philosophers and the like; which type of abstraction is embodied in such propositions as "all men are born equal," "all wars are unjust wars," and "the Nordic race is superior in virtue to all other races." Now in the great French Revolution, the National Assembly declared all men equal with respect to their rights—and then proceeded to draw up a Constitution in which men who paid a certain sum in taxes had the right to vote, and men who did not pay this sum had no right to vote. You may, if you like, call the members of the Assembly who approved *both* these measures "illogical," but you will not thereby get very close to understanding their action. The point is that for these men "Equality" was an ideal, an ethical principle, an abstraction of the type which, unlike a mere descriptive abstraction, *is not invalidated for those who cherish it if you show that logic or experience fails to fit it.* Many men quite sincerely profess such ideals, and not infrequently try to act in accordance with them; some few quite insincerely profess such ideals, and try only to avoid appearing to act contrary to them; others, more numerous than our grandfathers thought them to be, sincerely profess such ideals, and yet act in ways more or less evidently and logically contrary to them. No simple formula will cover the rôle played by these ideals in social and political life. It is enough for us here to realize the existence of these ideals, and to note that the relation between them and men's conduct here on earth is a complex one.

But if we think that our predecessors were mistaken in their too simple notions of the relation between good principles and good conduct, how can we accept their verdict as to the "goodness" and the "badness" of certain men? Now it happens that Talleyrand was one of the few articulate and conspicuous men of his time who obviously set little store by the abstract ideals most fashionable with his contemporaries; that, indeed, he went so far as to indicate by his own practice that he did not believe most men *could* practice what they preached. May it not be that he was finally listed among the bad men less for what he did than for what he failed to pretend to do? It is worth a moment's investigation to see how much of Talleyrand's reputation for evil can be explained by the particular definition of evil uppermost in the minds of his critics.

II

SOME of the things which Talleyrand did are things which a good many men of all times would agree must be classed as bad. He most certainly used public office to enrich himself. Most of what he did in this way was legal enough, or at least quite in conformity with the customs of his age and class. But he was, in good sound American, a grafter. He was quite unchaste, and though scandal has no doubt exaggerated the number of his mistresses and his bastards, one may apply here the remark made of the extraordinary number of witticisms attributed to him—"*on ne prête qu'aux riches.*" He was fond of good food and of good wine, and he enjoyed a little modest gambling. He was never crudely ostentatious, but he did like the life of a *grand seigneur* with its huge establishments, its princely expenditures, its costly moving about from town house to country house. To lead this life he had to have a great deal of money; he was, therefore, fond of money. He was proud, perhaps vain;

at any rate, lacking in Christian humility. He had a gift for self-dramatization, and indulged that gift to the full.

Put all these traits together and you have a total that might seem damning, a total that ought at least to explain Talleyrand's position on the wrong side of Clio's ledger. So many worthies, however, now safely ensconced in one pantheon or another have shown these traits that one is forced to conclude that they do not in themselves explain the Talleyrand legend. Danton, for instance, in the relatively short time he had available for the purpose seems to have peculated on quite as grand a scale as did Talleyrand. Yet Danton is one of the heroes of the Third Republic, the French George Washington. It is true that the warmest devotees of the Danton cult simply deny the patent facts of Danton's grafting, though, thanks to the late Albert Mathiez, these facts are in print for all to read. A few, like Herman Wendel, frankly find Danton's greatness transcends petty financial problems. Americans, it is well known, love a grafter no less dearly than a duke. As for sexual promiscuity, that, unless it turns towards the abnormal, is more often than not counted to a man's credit. It is certainly a fair working historical generalization that no great man is given a bad reputation on the score of sexual irregularities *alone*. Talleyrand was, indeed, in holy orders at the time when his love affairs were most varied and most numerous. This may well justify a good Catholic in condemning Talleyrand; most of those shocked by Talleyrand's conduct with women have, however, been good anti-Catholics, and from them condemnation comes with rather less grace. Voltaire was as much a hedonist, as hard-headed a business man, as vain, as fond of self-dramatization, as was Talleyrand. Now it is true that many Catholics and a few Protestant fundamentalists still have Voltaire's name on the bad side of their ledgers; but for the great public, Voltaire, though not unsullied, is still in the balance a benefactor of humanity, a great and good man.

One need not, however, limit oneself to examples from French history. Franklin, Washington, Jefferson, Hamilton, all display some of the traits that have damned Talleyrand. Occasionally mention of Washington's wealth and western land speculations, of Franklin's sex morals, of Jefferson's testy vanity, of Hamilton's entangling alliances with high finance, rise to the surface of American higher education. But the legends mention none of these matters, or gloss them over adequately. Why should the Talleyrand legend bring them out in such pitiless relief? There can be but one answer: because what men found ultimately unforgivable in Talleyrand was no one of these traits, nor even a combination of them, but something else.

Talleyrand's greatest sin, in nineteenth-century eyes, was his success—a success obtained in complete disregard of principles which the nineteenth century professed to regard as essential to success. He held high position under the government of Louis XVI, the absolute monarch, under Louis XVI, the constitutional monarch, under the First Republic, under Napoleon, under Louis XVIII, under Louis Philippe. One of the folk-tales about him relates how, as he took formal oath of loyalty to Louis Philippe, whom he helped to put on the throne of France in 1830, the King smilingly remarked that Talleyrand had sworn obedience to other masters in the course of his long life. "Sire," replied Talleyrand, "you are the thirteenth!" Now each of these governments save the first succeeded its predecessor with sufficient violence, or illegality, or both, to be commonly considered as revolutionary in origin. Talleyrand thus succeeded five times—or thirteen—in running with the hares and belling with the hounds, in passing from office under a discredited and defeated régime to office under a triumphant revolutionary régime.

Each of these governments had some sort of platform, announced to the world that it pursued a programme, held and defended and proposed to put into practice certain general principles, certain "ideals," if you like. In the language of the common man, each government "stood for" something. Again in the language of the common man, what these governments stood for might be summed up in certain stereotypes: Liberty, Equality, Fraternity; Stability; The Career Open to Talents; Legitimacy; The Rule of the Middle Classes. Since Talleyrand at various times gave public support to all of these clashing abstractions, it was clear to the nineteenth century that he hadn't *really* supported any of them. Talleyrand's unforgivable treason, in the eyes of later generations, was treason to those great moral and political abstractions by which men, like gods, assert—and thereby attain—eternity.

The peculiar function of political leaders, especially under popular governments, is often assumed to be the maintaining of these abstractions, these ideals, against the assaults of time and the flesh. That maintaining them hardly means more than repeating them is perhaps beside the point. Montesquieu's famous dictum, that virtue is particularly necessary in a republic, may mean no more than this: that in popular governments a certain permanence in accepted abstractions such as ideals, principles, ethical and political manifestoes like Bills of Rights, is essential to their stability. From this it follows that politicians under such governments must be "consistent"—that is, they must keep on repeating the same abstractions. In France and in the United States, for instance, it is almost fatal for a politician to change his principles, unless he can also manage not to change his party label. In England, where under popular government some of the habits and sentiments of feudal and monarchical government have survived, consistency is a virtue much less prized, and men like Peel, Gladstone, Chamberlain, and Ramsay Macdonald have made fairly obvious and public changes of principle. Even in England, however, a Gladstone found it convenient to show that he had been true to ethical abstractions even more lofty and valid than Party principles, and had therefore been morally consistent.

Now there are always some men who are by temperament, apparently, unable to set themselves aglow at the thought of Justice, Right, Virtue, Democracy, God, the Expanding Universe, and the innumerable train of similar abstractions current in this world. Indeed, some men are irritated by the presence of such abstractions, probably for a variety of reasons, one of which undoubtedly is that their *uncritical* use is an obstacle to certain kinds of thinking. Some men are irritated by other people's abstractions, but not by their own. Bentham was made most uncomfortable by the presence of such meaningless words as Justice and Right, and characteristically did not recover his serenity until he had invented Utility to take their place. Some of the dislike of common men for intellectuals derives from this source: common men prefer their clichés to the more finicky abstractions of the intellectuals.

Some of this dislike, however, has a different origin. Many men in all walks of life are at work trying to mould in a way that pleases them some refractory material—earth, bricks, men—and even, if they are poets, words. They resent the easy task of men who preside at the pleasant play of Absolute with Relative, who aid the Unmoved Mover to move. They resent it still more when the men who have spent their time at this play come to tell them how to do their work. Neither sort of man can be very tolerant of the other sort. Both exist in various mixtures in various societies. Some fields of effort are more markedly fit for one sort of man than for the other. The manipulator of abstractions would not, at least in so far as he devoted himself solely to the manipulation of abstractions, succeed at farming. On the other hand, the useful functions of priest, teacher, and journalist have been very successfully filled by men who apparently have been wholly unable to adhere for any length of time to the commonsense distinction between a fact and a theory. Politics can generally make use of both sorts of men. In the last century or so, perhaps the demand for manipulators of abstractions in politics has been greater than usual; certainly their rewards have been greater.

Talleyrand was not a manipulator of abstractions—*c'est là son moindre défaut*—except quite knowingly and quite hypocritically, for his own purposes. He was born without the feeling towards abstractions that makes a good metaphysician, and a bad one. He had, however, the desire to manipulate men, the desire for power, if you like, that makes for a political career. He had, as we shall hope to show, many other and by no means simple desires and capacities. But here we need only point out that he was devoid of reverence for abstractions. The nineteenth century, which in France began in 1789, was peculiarly reverent of abstractions. Had Talleyrand lived a century earlier, he would perhaps have had a career not unlike that of Cardinal Fleury, or at worst Cardinal Dubois, and, since he was an aristocrat, would have left a name not markedly discredited. But what could he do in his own time? He wanted power, and to have power he had, after 1789 especially, to have principles. The extraordinary accidents of French history between 1789 and 1830 made it necessary for him to change his principles if he were to retain his power. He changed them simply, as one would change clothes, and, for so public a performance, with amazingly little loss of dignity.

There are those, however, who do not regard principles as clothes. Principles are for them like marriage for a consistent Christian, made in heaven. To separate one's self from one's principles is an unholy form of divorce, and to assume new ones an impious adultery. To such men Talleyrand's career was a scandal. Some of them have written his life.

III

ONE might hope to write a life of Talleyrand "as it really was," to reproduce as exactly as possible an objective reality, to describe—and no more—what Talleyrand did and said. Unfortunately, one could not even write the life of a prizefighter in such a way. Biography is not a kind of photography—not even a moving picture. Beyond the simplest level of facts the human mind, even when it is trying merely to narrate or describe, is really forced to judge. Judgment may sometimes be made in terms of measurement, which is the ultimate goal of the sciences. In the study of masses of men the sociologist, and sometimes the historian, may be able to make this sort of judgment. In the study of a single man, the biographer can get no significant aid from mathematics or other sciences. He is forced to appeal to even older, and in these days less trusted arts—to processes akin to those by which men have decided that Bach's music is "good" and Carrie Jacobs Bond's music "bad," that *noblesse oblige,* that Frenchmen ought to wear mustaches, and—alas!—Talleyrand was a wicked man.

The immutability, universality, and possibly divine origin of such judgments are problems of lively interest to a good many people. We may be permitted to pass these problems over—a step which is, for the confirmed metaphysician, a somewhat patronizing solution of them. Actually it is nothing more than a frank statement that we choose to do what we can without them. These judgments, however, once made and recorded, become facts; and looked at as facts they offer considerable variety and range. The full extent of this variety and range is partly disguised by the fact that highly abstract terms like "good" and "bad" are commonly used to sum up whole series of concrete judgments of value. "Good" and "bad" as generalizing concepts have a degree of abstraction impossible of attainment by any scientific systematist. At the same time these words have the homely immediacy, the finality, the appeal to human emotions of all simple folk-words. To class Talleyrand among the "bad" is to put him in a class wider and more abstract than any phylum of the zoölogist, than any epoch of the geologist. It is also to make him more immediate and real to John Jones than any sub-sub variety of a species could be to Mr. Jones, and even, one suspects, to the zoölogical systematist himself.

It might be desirable to write biography without using any of these broad terms of appraisal. Unlike a life of someone "as he really was," such a biography would not be an impossibility. But to be intelligible, or at any rate interesting to ordinary human beings, all the varied concrete judgments of value contained in it would have to be bundled together somehow into more general and more abstract judgments. We could hardly hope to do much more than Bentham did, and write "useful" where others have written "good." To conclude, for instance, that Talleyrand's was the useful life of a bad man is to beg several questions, and in addition, to be very late Victorian.

The whole problem, indeed, hinges about an issue made clear at least as long ago as Aristotle's famous distinction between the good man and the good citizen. Talleyrand was a master technician. Over the course of a long life he employed his technical skill so to help make France and Europe more agreeable places for sensible men to live in. He used his gifts in the best interests of France and of Europe. If you still maintain that, since as a liar, a grafter and a libertine he was a *bad man,* he cannot have been a *good citizen,* there is nothing more to be said. You might, however, attempt to answer honestly this question, which is perhaps a bit more than casuistical: were you to face a surgical operation, would you rather have the operation performed by a mediocre surgeon unquestionably true to his wife or by a very competent surgeon proved guilty of adultery? A false dichotomy? Only, one suspects, in a fairer world than this one.

No, there is no other way out of it. We must attempt to write a life of Talleyrand in which he is finally classed as "good." Clio will certainly not thereby be moved to make a different entry in her ledger. Moreover, so bald an announcement will unquestionably give offense. It is not quite nice to announce your conclusion in your introduction. Science, induction, professional ethics are all against such a procedure. Fortunately, science itself provides a remedy. Everyone knows now that the inductive method does not consist exclusively in observing and piling up facts in an order implicit in the facts themselves. The searcher must start with an hypothesis, must know what he wants to ask of the facts. For us, "good" is to be a mere working hypothesis or conceptual scheme to tie certain facts together. It need, for the skeptic, be no truer than Ptolemy's conceptual scheme in astronomy. It is a means of selecting, arranging and working with the facts, of testing the results of these operations, and so of establishing certain uniformities and general relations. We shall, then, start with the hypothesis that, *in the sense which the word has in the fourth decade of the twentieth century to men educated in the traditions of the Western World,* the word "good" may be applied to the man Talleyrand as he appears in the records of history. There is no such sense, at least none upon which we can agree? Shame upon you! Who now is the cynic?

CHAPTER TWO

Priest in Spite of Himself

I

CHARLES-MAURICE de Talleyrand-Périgord was born at Paris on the second of February, 1754, of an undistinguished aristocratic family. Letters-patent issued by Louis XIII in 1613 mark the rise of the Périgordin family of Talleyrand into the group of court nobles from which there was soon to emerge the envied society of Versailles. The letters-patent of 1613 made clear that the Talleyrands were directly descended from the Carolingian Counts of Périgord. Skeptics, and even genealogists, have cast some doubts on the integrity of the links which joined the ninth-century Périgords to the seventeenth-century Talleyrands. Louis XVIII, with the fine malice so little suited to a constitutional monarch—or indeed to any monarch—used to say that the Talleyrands' claims were only one letter off the mark—"Ils sont *du* Périgord, et non *de* Périgord." What is certain, however, is that in 1754 the Talleyrands could look back upon at least three or four centuries of assured position in their own province of Périgord, and upon a century and a half of inclusion in the privileged group of nobles who surrounded the king. That group was a comparatively recent innovation built up by Richelieu and by Louis XIV from the more powerful and more conforming remnants of what had once been the feudal nobility. Charles-Maurice was born into a family as old as the hierarchy in which it held so high a place. There can be no more realistic a definition of aristocracy of birth.

The Talleyrands had been for several generations sound, worthy, and undistinguished servants of their king. The immediate ancestors of Charles-Maurice are as anonymous as dukes and counts can be—an anonymity to the ordinary historian as complete as the anonymity of their peasants or their servants. No La Rochefoucauld, no Turenne, no St. Simon disturbs the even mediocrity of the line. There is to be discerned in the Talleyrands no evident and recurring family trait, like the extraordinary physical vitality of the Mirabeaus. By the middle of the eighteenth century there is a pretty sure sign in the elder line of the lack of a very important kind of ability. The Talleyrands were, for their station, poor. No heroic or amusing spendthrift had, however, come to dissipate their fortune. They had simply been indifferent managers. Now the wealth of any French aristocrat of the old régime was derived primarily from two sources: the land, and the king, dispenser of pensions and patronage. The land, in a society where custom protected the peasants alike from efficiency and from oppression, could not be made to yield a great deal more to landlords. Rack-renting was inconceivable in most of France. The money from Versailles was limited in amount, and pretty well earmarked, in so conventional a society, for people with established claims to it. The king could not fling this money about him with the reckless abandon our Victorian historians loved to attribute to unconstitutional monarchs, or with the hopeful generosity of a New Deal. The claims of birth were at least as exacting as the claims of a modern bureaucracy, and tradition kept an even firmer hand on the budget than does a modern parliament. Now good hard work was necessary to maintain income from land at a steady level. Extremely able intriguing at Versailles, especially if the intriguer were young and charming, might divert an extra allotment of the king's money to a given family. The stock-market had, certainly, since the early eighteenth century, existed as a third and even more promising source of potential wealth, from which gentlemen were not excluded by the prohibition which closed to them mere vulgar trade. Not until Charles-Maurice, however, did a Talleyrand succeed in tapping this new source. Nor had any of the line shown exceptional skill at court intrigue, or exceptional diligence at estate management. The Talleyrands were poor in 1754, and poor partly, at any rate, because they were none too clever.

The rather naïvely Galtonian introductory chapter on heredity once so popular with biographers has gone out of fashion. The hero is in the best biographies no longer compounded out of ingredients furnished by convenient ancestors, though we find in a recent life of Mary Baker Eddy the confident statement that "the Abigail Ambrose in Mrs. Eddy gave birth to the radiant hopes of Christian Science, and the dark Earth-bound spirit of Mark Baker supplied the doctrine of malicious animal magnetism." Talleyrand could hardly have been very neatly derived from his ancestors by the most zealous practitioners of this not sufficiently forgotten art. His maternal grandmother had, by prudent management, saved her husband's estate from ruin, and had been able to give her daughter a most satisfactory dowry. His father's brother lived to be a Cardinal Archbishop, a post which he attained, as was fitting, rather by his virtues than by his intelligence. Talleyrand's physical inheritance was clearly sound. His ancestry was composed of sober, responsible, decent French noblemen, neither much above nor much below the level of endowment, as measured by distinction, common to their class. Of so-called aristocratic decadence, physical or spiritual, there are no signs. It would be encouraging, at least to some people, to be able to trace him back to a Gilles de Rais, or a Cardinal de Retz. But beyond the general soundness of his stock, nothing of importance can be established. What genes may have combined themselves into Charles-Maurice de Talleyrand-Périgord neither we, nor anyone else, can ever know.

The notion of heredity brings before the modern mind the notion of environment as naturally, and perhaps as profitably, as the notion of Heaven brought before the mediæval mind the notion of Hell. Talleyrand's later environment is clear enough. Unfortunately, the present fashion in psychology insists that the environment of infancy and childhood is of infinitely greater importance in moulding the man than is the environment of adolescence and manhood. And, though the old-fashioned biography used to dwell as lovingly and as unscientifically on childhood years as it did on blended inheritance, accurate and significant reconstruction of the earliest years of a great man is almost impossible.

One fact of probably the greatest importance for the understanding of Talleyrand is, however, clear in the record of his infancy. Nature and her confidant, Jean-Jacques Rousseau, had not yet begun their joint campaign against the iniquitous practice of wet-nursing. Charles-Maurice, as was the universal custom among French families who could afford the luxury, was at birth put out to a wet-nurse, and spent his infancy in a commoner's household in a Parisian suburb. His nurse one day carelessly left him lying on a table, from which he fell, injuring his right foot. She seems not to have noticed the injury until too late for correction by the crude surgery of the day. Talleyrand grew up with a deformed foot, which his enemies found it convenient to regard as an hereditary defect, obscurely but certainly tied up with spiritual defects. Special footwear made the deformity comparatively inconspicuous. Still, Talleyrand walked all his life with a noticeable limp, and could never do without a walking-stick. Participation in such fashionable pursuits as fencing or dancing was impossible, and riding was a rather awkward task.

The shame of this deformity seems not to have burned Byronically into Talleyrand's soul. Byron's lameness, which was much like Talleyrand's, may have affected his life and poetry in ways illuminated by modern psychological speculation. Not so with Talleyrand. His lifelong mental health is so obvious that even a psychologist ought to be able to see it. Compensation, inferiority complex, sublimation, and their variants explain Talleyrand not at all. This fact, of course, has not prevented writers from using them to explain him completely, nor will it prevent such explanations in the future.

The undoubted influence of this deformity on Talleyrand's career can be traced in less devious ways than the ways of modern psychology. With the death in infancy of an elder brother, Charles-Maurice became the heir to his father's rank and property. His future lay clear: apprenticeship in arms, still the only proper career for the eldest son of a great family; later, perhaps high position in camp and court, certainly a worthy life as servant of his king. The nursery accident closed forever to Charles-Maurice this essential military apprenticeship. Younger brothers were born, and grew up straight and sound. Both the Count of Talleyrand-Périgord and his Countess were conventional people, incapable of understanding their eldest son, and certainly incapable of adapting themselves to shifts of fortune. The Talleyrands had barely money enough to maintain their position at court. To an eighteenth-century French nobleman the solution actually adopted by the family was as fair, natural, and inevitable as, in almost all forms of ethical theory, it was unjust. Charles-Maurice was obliged to renounce his rights as an eldest son, and a younger brother was advanced to this position, and to the prospective command of a regiment under the gracious patronage of the king. With a thriftiness worthy of peasant stock, the Talleyrands then prepared Charles-Maurice for holy orders under the equally gracious, and even more generous, patronage of the Church. The accident to Charles-Maurice hadn't been such a bad thing for the family after all.

It was a very bad thing for Charles-Maurice. If there exists, or if there can be imagined, an ideal, or a normal, or a typical priest, then Talleyrand is as far away from that priest as logic or this world permits. He himself was aware of his lack of divine vocation from the first, and protested against his parents' plans. He was, however, even less disposed to rebellion and martyrdom than to the life of a servant of God. Moreover, to a fourteen-year-old French boy of noble family in the eighteenth century the idea of complete rebellion against parental commands was almost inconceivable. Charles-Maurice, on his graduation from the Collège d'Harcourt, where he had spent nine years as a resident pupil, was sent to his uncle, Coadjutor to the Archbishop of Rheims, under whose guidance it was hoped that he would take, not too reluctantly, the first steps towards the priesthood.

Lameness from an accident in infancy, a childhood passed mostly at an urban French school, deprivation of rights as eldest son in favor of a younger brother, forced entrance upon a distasteful career—all this sounds like a childhood about as unhappy as a childhood can be, short of starvation and physical cruelty. Most striking is the apparent absence of parental affection, at least in its ordinary manifestations in the intimacy of home life and in constant, loving care.

Now Talleyrand in 1816 wrote in his *Memoirs* a few pages about his childhood and youth which are almost our only source of knowledge of these years. In these pages the only light, agreeable touch is a brief interlude between his nurse's home and the Collège d'Harcourt, spent at the Périgordin home of his maternal great-grandmother, Madame de Chalais. Here he is moved at the pleasant memory of old days and old dignity, of the life of a great lady of the old, unquestioned nobility, the nobility who really were what Burke, Scott, Disraeli—and Talleyrand himself—insisted they must have been. The rest is gloom. Indeed, Talleyrand directly accuses his parents of neglecting him. "I am perhaps the only man of distinguished birth and belonging to a numerous and highly esteemed family who never enjoyed, for a week of his life, the joy of living beneath the paternal roof."

Talleyrand's hostile biographers, and foremost among them Lacour-Gayet, have insisted that the description of his childhood given by him in the *Memoirs* is essentially false. According to them, the old man was apologizing for a life which he knew most of his contemporaries considered at best as marred by many lapses, at worst as depraved. Seeking to put the best face on his conduct he said to his readers: "Of course I've done many things I oughtn't to have done. But what else could one have expected from a child who never came under the gentle discipline of discerning parental love?" Here, at the very outset of Talleyrand's career, we are beset with the confounding power of the legend Talleyrand himself did so much to create. The Machiavellian schemer, the clever diplomat, the master of lies, must always be lying. Whatever he writes in his *Memoirs* we may assume to be false from the moment we can conjure up any reason why our assumption of its truth should seem desirable to Talleyrand.

There is probably some justification in fact for Lacour-Gayet's view of Talleyrand's childhood. Men rarely write memoirs to make themselves contemptible in the eyes of posterity, and Talleyrand was a very good judge of what the romantic generations of the early nineteenth century would consider extenuating circumstances. The family was universally regarded in Victorian Europe and America as essential to the earthly salvation of the individual, and one who had grown up without benefit of family might be forgiven almost any sin. Yet to assume that Talleyrand is never sincere is to set up a good many problems that would not otherwise be problems; it is also a very good way to misunderstand him. It is almost as misleading to assume that, unlike all other human beings, he was incapable of self-delusion. He had undoubtedly to a minimum degree the power—or weakness—of confusing his thoughts and his wishes. But since such a confusion is as necessary to human life on this earth as is the air, we may take it that Talleyrand was not wholly devoid of it. In his later years he had grown very fond of his own immediate family circle. His gentleness with children is attested by many witnesses, and by some charming notes in his own hand. He was never, even in his youth, a man for nomadic or communal living, and as he grew older he became more and more fixed in a complicated and rather majestic domesticity. Looking backwards a half century from 1816, he may have read into his youth, and read in all sincerity, a sense of privation of this domesticity which he had hardly felt to that degree in 1766. Memory may blur or sharpen the outlines of the past; and in memory, the wish certainly is the father of the thought. The most diabolically detached intelligence cannot be superior to memory. Talleyrand's account of his own childhood reflects what, in 1816, he wished childhood could be.

Yet in the main the facts stand clear. The stay with the

nurse, the accident, the years as resident student at the Collège d'Harcourt, the resignation of his rights of seniority, the unwilling preparation for the priesthood—all these are facts confirmed by other sources than the *Memoirs.* They do prove that Charles-Maurice lived very little with his parents, though it is probable that his "not a week" is an exaggeration. Just why this was so is a problem that cannot be answered except by guess-work. He may have been a disagreeable little boy, very hard to get along with, and his parents may have taken the easier and wiser course in sending him away. His parents may have been unnatural parents, may have taken an unreasonable dislike to Charles-Maurice, may, quite humanly, have held his deformed foot against him. It is more likely that they were simply a rather dull but very occupied aristocratic French couple, engaged in a hundred unimportant but life-filling tasks which the care of a child would hinder, and that they sent him away for the same reason that many upper-class Americans send their children to a pretty continuous sequence of private schools and summer camps—to get rid of them. The monogamous family is an eternal fact in the history of Western man; but family life is no more uniformly patterned on an ideal than is the rest of life. Talleyrand had rather bad luck with his parents. He might have had worse; they neither beat him nor indoctrinated him. His singular freedom from devotion to abstract ideas may in part be explained by this parental neglect and by this unwilling priesthood. We never believe our teachers as we believe our parents. If later Talleyrand displayed so little of what the world calls faith, this surely is partly because his parents took so little care to bring about in him that suture between ideas and sentiments which is the structural basis of all faith.

Charles-Maurice went reluctantly to Rheims, where his

uncle sought to make a clerical career attractive to him by having him read the lives of such eminent clerics as Hincmar, Ximenes, Richelieu, and de Retz. According to the *Memoirs,* he was not convinced: "Youth is the time of life when one is most honest. I did not yet understand how one could enter a profession with the intention of following another one, assume a rôle of abnegation to follow more surely a career of ambition, go to the seminary to become minister of finance." But, he continues, he had no means of defense, he was alone, and subject to a resistless pressure all the more effective because it employed no threats, no violence. In 1770, at the age of sixteen, he entered the famous seminary of St. Sulpice in Paris. Nine years later, after passing through the earlier formal grades, and after extremely informal studies in theology at the Sorbonne, he was ordained priest at Rheims.

Those nine years were certainly not years of prolonged misery. Choiseul-Gouffier, school friend of Charles-Maurice at the Collège d'Harcourt, later a somewhat gentlemanly authority on the Near East, found him on the eve of his ordination in a desperate fit of weeping. Less worldly men than Talleyrand have, however, undergone a nervous crisis before taking the final vows that separate them from this world. There is ample evidence that by this time he had become fully aware that in eighteenth-century France a young aristocrat in holy orders by no means separated himself from this world. He became Monsieur l'Abbé instead of plain Monsieur, his costume commonly ran to somewhat more sober colors, and he ceased to be in danger of marrying a mistress. Otherwise the change was slight. Talleyrand had seen in practice that one could quite easily find through the seminary the way to salon, cabinet, and even boudoir.

He had, indeed, early found solace where he was always

to find the flattery, the little attentions, the anticipation of his wishes necessary to him even in success. He needed women as only a man not wholly unfeminine can need them. One might, and in a more perfect world perhaps one should, write usefully and honestly about Talleyrand without even mentioning his sexual relations. The most offensive form of the dogma that private virtues are essential to political success is that which insists that great statesmen must be faithful husbands or blameless celibates. To believers in this dogma, no love affair should remain decently buried. Concurring with them, and on grounds not methodologically so very different, are the Freudians and the emancipated generally, for whom sex has come to acquire the kind of immanence formerly attributed to God. Yet Talleyrand certainly learned much from women. The practice of love can only have confirmed him in his distrust of certain types of abstractions, and the negotiator of Vienna owed something to the successful lover. Moreover, Talleyrand's sexual promiscuity has, like his other moral failings, been grossly exaggerated by his enemies. He has nothing in common with the heroic Don Juan. In love as in the rest of life, he was quite unromantic.

The list of his reputed loves begins early. There is an improbable tale of a first affair on his entrance to the seminary at fifteen, a tale involving climbs by Talleyrand across neighboring roofs and visits to his cell by the young lady—aged fourteen—disguised as an errand boy. The first affair of which we have sure knowledge is less romantic, and is told quite frankly in the *Memoirs*. The lady was, by family pressure it seems, an actress in spite of herself, and had thus a common bond with the young man studying to be a priest in spite of himself. The *liaison* lasted two years, from Talleyrand's eighteenth year to his twentieth, in a good, sober French way, and no doubt did much to calm the young man's nerves and reconcile him to his fate. It was apparently easy enough for Talleyrand to slip away from the seminary to go to his mistress. Yet it seems unlikely that, even in those lax times, such a *liaison* should have lasted as long as it did without the knowledge of disciplinary officers of the seminary. One is obliged to conclude, as Talleyrand himself did in his *Memoirs*, that the authorities winked at the unecclesiastical conduct of so distinguished a neophyte.

Neither at the Collège d'Harcourt nor at St. Sulpice does Talleyrand's name figure on lists of prize-winners. He had none of the motives that ordinarily lead a boy to attempt to excel his fellows in the eyes of the masters who grade their work. But it would probably be wrong to say that he gained little or nothing from his academic training, and certainly wrong to conclude that he did nothing in all these years but play, or mope about, or pursue women, or otherwise prepare for the life of a *petit abbé*. Talleyrand certainly received a good classical education, and with it that command over written and spoken French which is still the enviable achievement of most French higher education. In later life he often dwelt on how much he received from his priestly education, and especially on how useful such an education could be as preparation for a career in diplomacy. The study of theology is an excellent training in the exact use of words which have for most men only very inexact senses. Theological word-spinning, if taken as an abstract exercise, is a good preparation for diplomatic word-spinning. Moreover, the Catholic Church of the eighteenth century had long put behind it any hope of hastening the second coming of Christ by the unduly literal application to this world of the teachings of His first coming. A Roman Catholic ecclesiastic turned diplomatist would not be bent by education, at any rate, towards the unworldly, idealistic diplomacy so well illustrated by the late Woodrow Wilson. There seems to be no reason to deny that Talleyrand learned at St. Sulpice much that stood him in very good stead at Vienna—patience, conciliatory manners, skill at dialectic, a sense of earthly limitations, an appreciation of the rôle of forms and ritual in human societies.

II

AT twenty-five, then, the Abbé de Périgord, ordained in the last of the major orders, was ready to take his proper place in French society. That place was, of course, with the aristocracy into which he had been born, and from which his priesthood was by no means an exile. Now a great deal has been written about this aristocracy. The French Revolution destroyed completely the way of life of French eighteenth-century aristocratic society, and though many of its members survived, and left their names to later generations, the society itself was never restored, was indeed incapable of restoration. Sentiments of varied kinds have fixed upon this dead society, and given it the life of lost causes. Talleyrand himself supplied one of the consecrated phrases—"He who has not lived in the years just preceding 1789 does not know the pleasure of living." Equally strong sentiments have fixed upon these aristocrats of the old régime and made them haughty tyrants, degenerate fops, witty and heartless sensualists battening on the labor of the lower classes. Ever since 1789, men have been at work to prove that the French Revolution was made necessary by the cruel tyranny of the upper classes, and by their wanton idleness. That the two accusations are partly in contradiction did not, of course, lessen the effectiveness of the whole indictment. Here again one cannot hope to alter such fascinating legends, nor to break down such convenient stereotypes. Yet, because in this society Talleyrand grew up, because in it, if anywhere, environment worked most effectively to mould him, we must make some attempt to describe this society with a decent regard for contradictions and complexities necessarily suppressed in legend and in stereotype.

The geographical focus of this society can easily be defined: Paris, with an extension to the already hardly more than suburban Versailles. No longer was Versailles, as it had been under Louis XIV, the center of fashion, art, and government. The court was important, but no longer isolated in the self-contained community of the palace. The definition of membership in this society is somewhat more difficult. Several groups, separated one from another by various caste distinctions, none the less combined to form a society not indeed homogeneous, but quite aware of itself as a group. In this larger group were all who set fashion in art and dress, all who wrote the books people read, all who provided scandal worth talking about throughout France, all who enjoyed the most evident riches, all who had the responsible and dramatic positions in the government. These people, though their really intimate social life centered in smaller circles, were on the whole in fairly frequent contact in café, salon, academy, or court. They formed a "ruling class" in many ways at least as self-consciously such as was the ruling class of Victorian England—and of almost as disparate social origins.

For this aristocratic society of the old régime in France was certainly no rigid caste determined by noble birth. The problem of just how rigid class distinctions really were in eighteenth-century France is a subtle one, and worth more dispassionate research than has yet been spent on it. But on the surface, at least, this society was recruited from men of most diverse talents, as well as from men of birth. The Abbé de Périgord had as intimate friends nobles like himself—the Count of Choiseul-Gouffier, the Duke of Lauzun, the Chevalier de Narbonne. But the names of those who enter any record of his life, the names most frequent in his *Memoirs,* include men of middle class, and even of peasant, origins: the Abbé Delille, a very fashionable and now very dull poet, an illegitimate child born of respectable middle-class parents; Barthès, famous physician from Montpellier, with a family background of doctors and lawyers; Panchaud, banker, of good Swiss burgher stock; Dupont de Nemours, founder of the princely American family of that name, himself partly of middle-class stock, partly of provincial Protestant nobility as puritanical and sober as the English Calvinist gentry; Rulhière, famous authority on Eastern Europe, son of a police inspector; Mirabeau, son of a marquis, but not unknown to the financial underworld; Chamfort, journalist and wit, who seems to have been the quite legitimate son of an Auvergnat grocer named Nicolas, but who found entrance to society easier for M. de Chamfort, natural son of an unknown father; d'Antraigues, a nobleman of connections even shadier than those of Mirabeau; the Abbé Barthélemy, *philosophe,* priest, of thoroughly middle-class origin; Louis, later Baron Louis, another bourgeois in holy orders, who was to escape them as completely as did Talleyrand himself; Turgot and Calonne, both members of that nobility of the robe which had for generations served the Crown in law-court and administrative office, a real *noblesse d'état;* Marmontel, another *philosophe,* son of a village tailor of pure peasant stock; d'Hauterive, later a diplomat of distinction and one of Talleyrand's most useful aids, wholly middle-class in origin, a lay professor with the Oratorians. There is no use prolonging the list. With people like these the Abbé de Périgord dined, talked, drove, lived.

Now it is possible that the aristocrats of birth regarded these middle-class men of letters, business men, and professional men as existing for their profit or amusement, like mistresses or lackeys on a rather higher level. It is possible that the small group of the Court nobility was so filled with pride, so utterly inaccessible at heart, however open on the surface, so completely in possession of the ultimate peak of the social pyramid, that ambitious lawyers, administrators, bankers, scientists, artists felt themselves balked by its existence. All the text-books point out that Voltaire was good enough to dine with a Chevalier de Rohan, but lacked the noble blood necessary to fight a duel with one. Another favorite tale explains how Barnave, the revolutionary leader, as a mere child came to hate the aristocracy when his respectable bourgeois mother was forced to vacate her box at the theatre in Grenoble to make way for the mistress of the Duke of Clermont-Tonnerre. It is, on the other hand, possible that much of this class-conscious hatred dates from *after* the Revolution rather than *before* it, that it is a part of the French republican mythology as George III and the Hessians are a part of our mythology. In the nineteenth century, even born aristocrats behaved the way a bourgeois public, guided or misled by romantic men of letters, thought aristocrats ought to behave. With our minds still influenced by Byronic patterns of aristocracy, we are likely to read back into the eighteenth century the notion of an aristocracy haughty, insolent, self-conscious, gracefully posturing, like a marquis in *A Tale of Two Cities.* Talleyrand was always recognized as a *grand seigneur;* and yet even his enemies agree that he was a singularly winning man, that he was able to adapt himself to all conditions of men—and women. Extraordinary self-control he did have, but not the aristocratic pride of a romantic grandee. It was said of Talleyrand that if, while one were conversing with him, he should receive a kick in the behind, one would never be aware, from any expression of his, of the indignity he had just suffered. He did, indeed, submit to much greater indignities from Napoleon, and without overt rebellion. Now a nineteenth-century aristocrat, unprotestingly kicked, simply ceases to be an aristocrat. The eighteenth-century aristocrat was perhaps more aware of hierarchies within hierarchies, of the rather elastic limits of social prestige.

To deny the existence of class-conscious social groups—Court nobility, country nobility, nobility of the gown, upper bourgeoisie, lower bourgeoisie, peasantry—in eighteenth-century France would be absurd. But the current view probably exaggerates the rigidity of these class lines, especially within the Parisian group we have described above as leading in fashion, art, business, government and conversation. The sharpness of the division between the old nobility of race and the more recent nobility of office-holders was certainly greatly overdrawn by nineteenth-century historians. Intermarriage in these groups—a pretty sure sign of absence of social rigidity—was so common that in many provincial centers like Dijon the two groups of nobles were genealogically indistinguishable. In the Parisian circles of Talleyrand, this distinction between *noblesse d'épée* and *noblesse de robe* was certainly not an ever-present reality. Noblemen like St. Simon, with his obsessions of rank, were exceedingly rare in the generation just preceding 1789. It would hardly be an equal exaggeration in the opposite direction to say that this group, into which Talleyrand was launched in his young manhood, was as heterogeneous in its origins, as indeterminate in its lines of precedence, as fluid in its organization, as encouraging to the career open to talents as any human society has been.

It is generally agreed that the ruling classes of eighteenth-century France were decadent. The word is not precise, and it is definitely dyslogistic. The old régime was, indeed, overthrown by the revolutionists. The particular society in which Talleyrand enjoyed the *plaisir de vivre* ceased to exist. To the nineteenth century, the old régime fell, not because of chance or because of the bare prevailing of slightly stronger social groups, but because it was weak and rotten. If only the dead die, then death may be in itself alone a proof of decadence. But we need subscribe to no such crude social Darwinism. Societies, like men, may be overcome in their prime. No problem in retrospective sociology is more interesting—and less near solution—than that of the instability of French society in the eighteenth century, or, as one used to put it, that of the "causes" of the French Revolution. The solution of the problem certainly depends on the understanding of the rôle of many mutually dependent variables, only one of which is the possible "decadence" of the society to which Talleyrand belonged. If we define decadence in a pretty broad way as unfitness to hold power, then an examination into the question as to how far this society may be called decadent will in itself provide a broad general review of the society.

Formalism, the tendency to prescribe rigid and often very complicated standards in guiding all kinds of human activities, has, in exuberantly romantic and nature-loving periods like the early nineteenth century, been taken as evidence of decadence in a given group or society. A too-successful imposition of laws and standards, it is claimed, suppresses vital elements of originality, produces a kind of atrophy in important organs of community action, leads to stagnation and decay. In the simple text-book view we have been brought up in, the society of the *ancien régime* can easily be shown to have been overcome by formalism. The absurd, endless etiquette of Versailles, the strait-jacket of the Alexandrine and the three unities, the minuet, the intricate coiffures of the ladies, the elaborate, necessary, and heartless love affairs, the formal play of wit and taste, the bundle of conventions—all this is obviously evidence of formalism. But it is a very incomplete choice of eighteenth-century aristocratic life. Elegant ladies—and gentlemen—were reading Rousseau and returning vicariously to Nature, honesty, tears, and the freshness of innocence. Another proof of decadence—the last inversion by which a worn-out and disillusioned society looks back wistfully and impotently at its lost youth? Theocritus and Alexandria? Certainly the spectacle of Marie Antoinette milking clean, gentle, and unquestionably contented cows in her thatched village at Versailles is of a piece with the rest of the conventional picture of decadence. This is dancing on the edge of a volcano, this is after-me-the-deluge, this is behavior of the kind God and Thomas Carlyle were unanimous in regarding as highly provocative of revolution.

Nowhere did this society more clearly display its lack of emotional depths, so runs the text-book view, nowhere was its disastrous preference for forms over realities more evident than in its love-making. Love was an elaborate game, which, to be sure, no one ever won, but which no one ever lost, either. In *La nuit et le moment* of Crébillon fils a gentleman suddenly appears in his bath-robe in a lady's bedroom, and eventually attains the lady's bed. One hundred and fifty pages describe their conversation, in neat, witty, very self-conscious French. It is true that the dialogue is now and then interrupted by action; but the participants seem even more interested in the dialogue than in the action, and they certainly never forget to be witty and polished. So right through the society. Love, natural, simple, instinctive in healthy societies had with these people come to be a jousting of the senses, but a jousting surrounded with all sorts of artificial rules to make it interesting. The head had conquered the heart, only to find that the body failed to respond satisfactorily to the sole command of the head. Formalism appears at its most ludicrous in the supreme experience of love.

One could follow this theme of the intellect as the grave of the emotions, and hence of all life, right down through all phases of human activity. Indeed, the generation of Wordsworth, Hugo and Heine found in it a simple formula to explain alike the inadequacies of eighteenth-century poetry and the destruction of the old French aristocracy. We are no longer fighting the battles of the Romantic Revolt, however, and we need no more accept this notion of the decadence of a formalistic, over-refined, impotently intellectual aristocracy than we need accept the parallel notion of a society rigidly fixed by distinction of birth. Nothing so much like Marie Antoinette at her play-village in the Trianon as Mr. Vincent Astor at the mile-long miniature railroad on his Rhinebeck estate. Nothing so much like Crébillon's *La nuit et le moment*—at a certain geographical and racial remove—as Schnitzler's *Reigen*. A proof that we are today as decadent as eighteenth-century Frenchmen, that decadence is endemic in modern society? Herr Spengler may regard our decadence as proven, but we may perhaps legitimately consider such details as the above as a challenge to our made-to-order views of the eighteenth century.

For the truth is that into this over-simple accepted picture of the eighteenth century has gone much confusion of æsthetic judgment and sociological analysis, cemented into a pretty effective whole by the natural interest of our grandfathers in justifying their revolt against *their* grandfathers.

Certainly we need feel no impiety in at least retouching the picture, especially as we need no longer fight our grandfathers' battles. Moreover, Talleyrand's own reputation for wickedness is partly derived from the reputed wickedness of the society in which he grew up. No whitening can attain him without splashing over a bit onto his environment.

The most important fact to be noticed in this now unacceptable picture of formalism and decadence is a confusion between art and sociology. The sociologist must be very wary of concluding, from the evident exhaustion of an art-form, the exhaustion of the society in which that art is practised. Painting, sculpture, architecture, music, literature and the minor arts are by no means simple indices of the condition of a given society. All art is a convention—the romantic poetry of Keats no less than the neo-classic poetry of Erasmus Darwin. Conventions wear out, and become thin and ugly, but new conventions, like new clothes, can be had by all but the very indigent. At any given moment in space-time, a cross-section of the arts will show conventions in various stages of wear, down to the "formalism" which shows them completely worn out. Let us agree that in the latter half of the eighteenth century lyric poetry was, in most of Europe, and certainly in France, quite worn out. So too were classical tragedy, baroque architecture (this is disputable) and formal metaphysics, whether derived from Descartes or from Locke. Yet no one will maintain that symphonic music was worn out—nor the novel, nor the writing of history, nor many of the decorative arts, nor even, as a blanket generalization, the plastic arts. Haydn, Mozart, Fielding, Gibbon, Voltaire, Sheraton, Chardin, Houdon—these are not names that suggest decay and death.

Nor can the difficulty be solved by the simple formula that the living art of the period has a middle-class origin, the dead art an aristocratic one. Artists and their audiences were recruited from the most varied social groups. Aristocrats admired Chardin, who was after all in the respectable Dutch tradition, as well as Watteau and Fragonard, wept with Rousseau as well as sneered with Voltaire, admired noble savages and despised French peasants, scorned superstition and avoided walking under ladders. No one can understand the late eighteenth century who sees its art as a battleground between text-book marshaled forces labeled "Old" and "New" or "classic" and "romantic." Its art is not all of one piece, nor of two pieces, but a complicated series of experiments made in an environment rather less hostile to artistic experimentation than most environments have been. A given individual might in a very short time find himself touched by very formal art, and by daringly original art.

Again, the assumption that the French aristocracy was decadent because it had nothing to do but amuse itself cannot be accepted without some modification. In the first place, many of the country nobility, and even certain of the court nobility, really did a good deal of socially useful work. Talleyrand's own description of his happy childhood stay with Madame de Chalais reflects an aristocracy more English than the text-books will have it. Madame de Chalais "took care" of her country people as the best English squires cared for their tenants. Names like La Rochefoucauld, Lally-Tollendal, Lafayette, all very noble names, suggest various kinds of seriousness and enlightenment and what seems nowadays a pathetic optimism about social problems rather than irresponsibility and loose living. In the second place, many aristocratic names are to be found in the roll of eighteenth-century men of science, jurists, historians, *philosophes*. Now, however faulty we may regard the methodology of the eighteenth century, especially in what are now called the "social sciences," we can hardly consider the men who pursued the search for truth and learning with such courage and energy mere idlers, unpleasantly decadent parasites. In the third place—and this is most important—an upper class can maintain itself only if it provides a pageantry for lower classes, a source of drama, of scandal, of soul-satisfying envy. Unless a great many other elements are changed so as to weaken the position of an upper class, the fact of spectacular consumption by its members must certainly be regarded as an element strengthening rather than undermining its position. Especially after 1789, the spectacle of Marie Antoinette seems to have disgusted more Frenchmen than it amused. At the present moment, the spectacle of Barbara Hutton seems to have amused more Americans than it has disgusted. The latter is more in the normal course of human nature, regardless of the comparative æsthetic value of the two spectacles.

Nor is even the witty, heartless, cynical habit of mind of the French aristocracy under Louis XVI a sure sociological indication of its approaching fall. In the first place, this habit of mind has been, like the social irresponsibility and reckless spending which are said to reflect it, greatly exaggerated. It seems possible that there may have been a certain amount of chastity among French noblewomen of the time, and even of fidelity to their marriage vows on the part of some French noblemen. After all, the highest in the land, Louis XVI himself, was as faithful to his wife as ever Mr. Gladstone was to his. But even granting that the fashionable attitude towards love was the attitude of the characters of Crébillon fils's *La nuit et le moment*—which is somewhat like saying that ours is that of the characters of Ernest Hemingway's *The Sun Also Rises*—even granting that love was only a game to the ladies and gentlemen of eighteenth-century France, we cannot assume that this is one of the reasons for their downfall. The essential thing is that people should fall in love, that they should find the game interesting. Whether love be regarded as a sport or as a religion has less importance for social stability, and even for ethics, than might at first appear. At any rate, the eighteenth-century aristocracy of France produced more children—sometimes known as the fruits of love—than does the twentieth-century democracy of France. The reasons for this difference are not intellectual? Quite so. But neither are the reasons for the downfall of the old régime. It took the nineteenth-century Thomas Hardy to decide that thought is a disease of the flesh; the eighteenth century was too healthy—and too thoughtless, in the romantic sense—to come to any such conclusions.

Mignet, the Orleanist historian of the Revolution, had a sounder appreciation of this society than most men of the nineteenth century. As permanent secretary of the Academy of Moral and Political Sciences, to which Talleyrand belonged, Mignet read in 1839 a tribute to the memory of the dead statesman which thus summarizes his early environment: "Intelligence was the true sovereign of the period. It had effaced everything without yet destroying anything. It had made authority more gentle, the clergy more tolerant, the nobility more familiar. It had brought people together without destroying class distinctions. It had introduced a flower of politeness and a charm of *savoir-vivre* into this old society—People were happy and confident, as they always are at times when revolutionary changes have as yet taken place only in the world of the intelligence, when only ideas have changed, when the decay of faith does not yet bring moral pain to anyone, when action is still purely ideal, and when enthusiasm for what is thought to be coming does not leave room for regret for what is being lost. It was in the midst of this time and this society that M. de Talleyrand lived, belonging to the school which had Voltaire for a master, sovereigns and great lords for disciples, the rights of the mind for a faith, and the progress of humanity for a purpose."

We are not, indeed, without certain clues to the weaknesses of this eighteenth-century French aristocracy. The conventional contrast between the French nobility and the British upper classes no doubt has some validity. While in Britain gentlemen from the plain Justice of the Peace to the Member of Parliament still shared in the responsibilities of government, in France an inefficient royal bureaucracy had displaced the nobility in important spheres of political life. French noblemen did enjoy privileges without returning services to the community. Yet only to the more confident sharers in the intentions of a just and avenging God will this fact in itself account for the destruction of the old French nobility.

This exclusion from politics, which was never complete, did help turn the younger and more ambitious French noblemen about 1750 towards that devotion to abstract political ideas which was their fatal weakness. Some, like Condorcet and Lafayette, became outright crusaders for the destruction of their own class. But even the more moderate were touched with a humanitarian faith which helped paralyze them for action in defense of their class. It is not that these noblemen were, in anything like a majority, skeptical, lazy, disarmed for the rude shocks of life by over-refinement, men lacking in virility. It is rather that these gentlemen, and especially the group centered at Paris and Versailles, had by 1789 become too little devoted to tradition, convention and form, too tolerant and open-minded, too ready to absorb newcomers, above all, not nearly stupid enough, to be a sound and successful ruling class. A touch of the fifth-century Spartiate, or of the nineteenth-century Tory duke would have helped them. They fell, not because they were wicked tyrants, not because they were decadent fops—for they were in the main neither—but because they were too kindly and too easy-going. Not until very late in the Revolution did they reply with violence to violence; and then they used violence unwisely.

It is probable that the kind of optimism and faith in Reason, Perfectibility and other abstractions we see in noblemen like Lafayette had more to do with the downfall of their class than had the kind of skepticism we see in noblemen like Talleyrand. Skepticism of a thorough-going sort has never yet penetrated to large numbers of people, even in a privileged class. Moreover, there is no evidence that true skepticism disarms for action, any more than there is evidence that it makes its entertainers acutely miserable. The *later* eighteenth century was, however, anything but skeptical. It had a religious belief in the natural goodness of men once they were freed from the shackles of convention, prejudice, custom and social institutions. Action founded upon such a belief is not likely to strengthen the position of individuals whose money incomes and indeed whose whole worldly life depends on existing social institutions. To the confounding of such innocent social theorists as utilitarians, positivists, Marxians and the like, it would appear that numbers of French aristocrats just before and after 1789 did found their actions on such a belief.

To anyone who has studied closely the last half of the eighteenth century in France, and especially the first years of the great Revolution, 1789 to 1791, it must be evident that chance, too, had a very large part in destroying the old aristocracy. Given anything like an even break in circumstances, and there would seem to be no reason why the French aristocracy, in spite of its bright young radicals, should not gradually have weathered its way through into the nineteenth century, much as did the English aristocracy. *The capacity of absorbing commoners—in Pareto's terms, the ability to maintain a circulation of the élite—it was beginning to manifest clearly in the late eighteenth century.* Even with a stupid man where an intelligent one ought to have been—on the throne—with bankruptcy, with Necker, with Lafayette and other liabilities, the revolutionary movement was not at first a menace to this society. War, the King's flight, the rise of the Jacobins, and much else had by 1792 made the fall of the aristocracy inevitable.

The Revolution made of the remnants of this aristocracy spared by war, disease, guillotine and emigration something astonishingly near—at least in respect to social rigidity—to what our text-book patterns declare it to have been *before* the Revolution. Frightened by the fate which overtook their fathers, the children who came back to France with Louis XVIII in 1815 foreswore their fathers' ways. Or, to put the matter sociologically, they set up a reaction determined by the extremes to which their fathers had carried faith in human perfectibility; they tightened up at just those points of behavior where their fathers had been loosest. For religious skepticism or mild deism they substituted a very ardent and rather too deliberately mystical Catholicism; for epigrammatic wit, wordy emotions; for tolerance and open-mindedness, a pretty consistent neophobia; for hope in science and learning, an obscurantist faith in misunderstood mediæval art and learning; for easy intercourse with all kinds of men, a self-conscious exclusiveness; in short, for a reasonably unassuming and tolerably real superiority, a very noisy and unconvincing assertion of a superiority no longer in them, as it had been in their fathers, unchallenged. The Revolution froze the aristocracy of France into all it had not been in the good old days. The Revolution did not, however, give it the supreme gift of all great ruling classes—the knowledge of when and how to use force. The White Terror was as foolish as the Red. The famous phrase about the returned Bourbons having learned nothing and forgotten nothing during their exile, though good Bonapartist propaganda, is bad history. Many a French nobleman forgot completely his old, Voltairean, hopeful, experimental self, and learned to be a good, class-conscious, persecuted, self-righteous, romantic, and intellectually obtuse Catholic gentleman of the new school.

Not so with Talleyrand. What was and is so often said of him, that he maintained to the middle of the next century the manners of a *grand seigneur* of the days of Louis XV, has full reference to more than social ease, dignity, the right turn of a compliment. Talleyrand carried over into a century which had largely lost it the intellectual detachment and resilience of the society in the last days of which he was brought up. At this point a distinction vital to the understanding of Talleyrand and of the eighteenth century must be made. The generation which had matured by 1750 had on the whole been brought up with a sound respect for facts, for the difficulties confronting the reformer, with a feeling for the complexities and subtle balances of this world. "Philosophy" was still a counsel of wisdom to the generation of Montesquieu and Voltaire. The generation maturing after 1750, on the other hand, commonly made of "philosophy" a very immature religion. The conviction that the task of ruling men can by the simple revelations of abstract reason be made into the almost automatic dispensation of ideal and all-satisfying justice is not to be found in Montesquieu and in Voltaire, but in Condorcet, Holbach, Mably and their peers. It was the *second,* not the *first,* generation of *philosophes* that went astray on the unattractive path of idealistic materialism.

Talleyrand was immune to the contagion that seized so

many of his fellow nobles. The society in which he was brought up had preserved, in spite of the inroads of abstract Reason, a good deal of the traditions, the tastes, the easy adaptabilities, the moderation, and sense for limitations, characteristic of the Augustan Age at its best in the early years of the century. Through all his shifts of allegiance, Talleyrand remained the representative of the very best of eighteenth-century civilization. This traitor was after 1815 truer to many of the traditions of his order than the loyalists who were so patently true to Throne and Altar. Adversity never drove him to take refuge in dogma.

The Revolution must have destroyed in him any old illusions, if, indeed, he had ever had such, as to the possibility of enlightening and perfecting the common man; but it did not force upon him new illusions as to the perfection and immutability of the aristocracy into which he had been born. He remained all his life an eighteenth-century gentleman. This is not to say that he remained utterly skeptical, impotent, in-, un-, or a-moral, a sort of Don Juan of the intellect. We have just gone to some trouble to demonstrate that this is not what is meant by an eighteenth-century gentleman. He did remain ever open to new ideas, distrustful of dogmas even when they were made beautiful by faith, skeptical of abstractions especially when they were made infectious by emotion, tolerant, moderate, earthly, always wishing to seem rather the talented amateur than the trained specialist, at home with general ideas which he never allowed to run away into the field of abstract ideas, witty, not too malicious, often indeed kindly, interested in everything, sure of nothing—but himself, and what he had learned from experience. Much of this is a heritage from the society of the early eighteenth century, some remnants of which survived even in the irresolute and hopeful society in which he moved as the Abbé de Périgord.

III

EVEN before he received the last of the major orders, Talleyrand had begun to enjoy the privileges of his position. In 1775, when he was but twenty-one, he received from the King the abbey of St. Denis de Reims, which brought him in a revenue of 18,000 *livres* a year. Estimates of how far a given sum of money would go in the past are somewhat arbitrary. This is $3,600 on a gold basis; actually it probably served the Abbé de Périgord as well as $10,000 a year would in Boston or Philadelphia today. Other sources of revenue were soon opened, among them the stock-market, to which he was initiated by the clever and realistic Panchaud. From this moment on, Talleyrand never lacked money, even in exile. As he had no parish, nor any important obligations towards his abbey, he was quite free to take his part in the varied life of Paris and Versailles.

He frequented the *salons* of the Comtesse de Brionne, of the Marquise de Brion, of Madame Grimod de la Reynière. In less respectable places, too, the Abbé soon acquired a reputation as a man of wit, an accomplished talker, an intelligent man of the world. One of the most familiar of the string of anecdotes which stretches down through Talleyrand's whole life relates how in these early days he was one of a group of bright young men in a gathering presided over by Madame du Barry. The rest of the young men were boasting of their conquests. Talleyrand was silent, and when Madame du Barry asked whether he had none to boast replied, "Alas, Madame, a sad thought occurs to me." "What?" "That Paris is a city in which it is easier to get women than to get abbeys."

There is no unanimity as to Talleyrand's *esprit*—except that he clearly had a good deal of it. The great public was always attributing to him wit in the form of the barbed shaft, the epigram. Those who knew him best assert that he rarely delivered himself of an epigram. Certainly he made no ostentatious show of firecracker wit; he was no Oscar Wilde, no Philip Guedalla. His success rested rather on an ability to talk naturally, easily, and with just sufficient art to avoid the commonplace, on a willingness to let others talk, too, on occasional striking flashes of originality, of fresh epithet or unexpected conclusion, and, of course, on appropriate, and never too frequent nor too noisy, touches of malice. Those who, after he had become famous, sought him out in the hope that he would put on a special show of his gifts for them, were almost invariably disappointed. Talleyrand was no professional wit.

His social and personal graces made him attractive to most women; his slight lameness seems rather to have enlisted their sympathies than to have repelled them. Talleyrand always had women, as he always had money. Gossip has probably not diminished the number of his mistresses. Yet at most periods of his life he seems to have been in love in something like the commonsense acceptance of the term—that is, his tastes and emotions were centered for relatively long periods on some one woman. In these early years, he was clearly most in love with Madame de Flahaut, through whom his history touches such diverse people as Gouverneur Morris and Napoleon III. Madame de Flahaut, wife of the Comte de Flahaut, was the daughter of a plebeian tax-farmer, brought up according to the best standards of Versailles, bright, lovely, and still young. Married to a man thirty-six years older than herself, she was not expected, in that society, to be strictly true to her husband. Actually her affair with the Abbé de Périgord, which continued after he became the Bishop of Autun, was conducted quietly enough, and with no great scandal. Gouverneur Morris knew all about it, but Morris was in love with the lady himself, and paid unsuccessful court to her.

In the *Memoirs* of our first Minister at Paris we get occasional amusing glimpses of the Bishop in situations far from sacerdotal. Everyone who has recorded himself on the subject—including M. de Flahaut's brother, as well as Morris himself—has assumed that Talleyrand was the father of Madame de Flahaut's son, born in 1785. This lad grew up to inherit the Flahaut title, to attain prominent position in the Napoleonic army, and to become, as lover of Queen Hortense of Holland, the father of that Duc de Morny who engineered the third Napoleon's *coup d'état* of December 2, 1851, and put a Bonaparte again on the throne of France. Of course, neither of these paternities can be definitely proved; but as such matters go, Talleyrand's in particular approaches the routine assurance of the old legal maxim, *pater is est quem nuptiae demonstrant.* The Revolution broke up this romance. Madame de Flahaut was widowed, and forced to emigrate. She married a nobleman of Portuguese origin, the Marquis de Souza, but he seems to have been an inadequate support. At any rate Madame de Souza poured out early in the nineteenth century a series of very bad sentimental novels. Talleyrand had nothing more to do with the mother of his child. This is usually put down as another proof of his heartlessness; if the lady had really grown to be much like her novels, it might be more justly put down as another proof of his good taste.

Talleyrand, though he liked to be thought an idler, actually contrived to do a good deal of serious work even in the pleasant surroundings of Paris and Versailles. One must, of course, constantly beware of finding Machiavellian calculation in everything Talleyrand did; yet it is true that, all moralizing to the contrary notwithstanding, the world does admire apparently effortless success and does not really believe apothegms as to the relation between inspiration and perspiration; Talleyrand, who knew pretty well what the world admired, always tried very wisely to retain as much of the world's admiration as he could. His great initiation into administrative work came with his appointment in 1780, at the age of twenty-six, as general agent of the clergy of France. The position might well have been a sinecure, and it is possible that he owed his appointment to his family name. On the other hand, he had already begun through his acquaintance with Panchaud his initiation into the business world, and it is thoroughly in keeping with his subsequent career to suppose that he secured the office for himself by the clever use of his social connections. The French clergy in the eighteenth century formed an enormously wealthy corporation which, unlike the French government of the time, was admirably organized and administered — at least for secular purposes. At quinquennial assemblies the clergy, through its delegates, took stock of its possessions, its income and expenditures, and its relations with the lay authorities. In the interval between assemblies, two general agents acted as finance ministers and budget directors for the corporation, supervised the collection and payment of the *don gratuit* which the clergy as a group paid the state in lieu of taxes, and acted as intermediaries between state officials and the clergy. Talleyrand's colleague was an Abbé de Boisgelin, who found the work little to his taste, and left most of the responsibility to Talleyrand. The post was a splendid opportunity for an apprenticeship in the business of governing—and an especially good entry into high finance. Talleyrand acquitted himself very well indeed, was rewarded by a substantial bonus from his grateful fellows, and found himself known as something more than a *petit abbé* of the salons.

He might, indeed, have got his bishopric with no better reputation than that of a *petit abbé*. The liberties of the Gallican Church had been won, and in practice this meant that bishops were appointed by the Crown as part of the royal patronage. The priesthood was a necessary qualification, but too close inquiry into the question of more apostolic qualifications was not commonly made. The corruption of the Gallican Church in the late eighteenth century has been much exaggerated by historians anxious to justify the Revolution by making the *ancien régime* vicious and corrupt enough to have provoked angels to revolt. Most bishops were unquestionably far better Christians than Talleyrand. Yet Talleyrand's bishopric is not indefensible. He was perhaps a better bishop than priest, for the bishop's work was in those days rather administrative than missionary, and Talleyrand was unquestionably a good administrator. It is sometimes maintained that Louis XVI, certainly a man of virtue and of good intentions, was shocked by Talleyrand's reputation as a man of the world, and that he long refused to permit his promotion. Only the dying wish of Talleyrand's father, long a faithful servant of the King, is said to have overcome Louis's scruples. There is no proof of this, except that Talleyrand hoped for, and intrigued for, a mitre at least three years before he got one. But the competition was keen, and it is not extraordinary that even a Talleyrand-Périgord was kept waiting—in comparative affluence—for three years.

In November, 1788, the Abbé de Périgord was nominated to the Bishopric of Autun. It was not a rich bishopric—a mere 22,000 *livres* of annual income. Talleyrand still had his abbey in Champagne, and now another one in Poitou was given him. Their combined revenue, with that of the bishopric, was 52,000 *livres*. By this time, Talleyrand's connections with the business world must have begun to bear fruit. All in all, he may have had, on the eve of the Revolution, an annual income equivalent to some $40,000 or $50,000 of American money of 1936. He was already, at thirty-four, a very rich man.

Early in January, 1789, Talleyrand journeyed to the little Burgundian town for his consecration, which took place very quietly indeed in a small chapel. His enemies and biographers have taken the occasion to suggest that the authorities wished to keep the whole scandalous matter as quiet as possible, and have added that Talleyrand himself wished the ceremony to be a private one because of his ignorance of the Roman Catholic liturgy. There may be something in both these suggestions, especially in the last. Talleyrand never achieved an instinctive command of his priestly duties. Yet the eighteenth-century Church in France had not yet, like the Church today, turned to large-scale ceremonies, vast public offices, and the other necessary methods of publicity in modern society. Autun would have been astonished had its new bishop been ordained in any very noisy fashion.

Autun, moreover, had an occasion for excitement much greater than the installation of a new bishop. In these early months of 1789, there was going on the first national electoral campaign since 1614. Louis and his advisers had tried in numerous ways to solve the financial difficulties of the government. As a last resort, they had decided to call together the old representative body of the realm, the Estates General, which had never been called by the absolute governments of Richelieu and his successors. Perhaps this new body could miraculously discover new taxes, or make possible a loan to which Frenchmen really would subscribe. The experiment had to be made. The Estates General were composed of three separately chosen bodies: the Clergy, or First Estate; the Nobility, or Second Estate; and the Third Estate, or Commons. The territorial unit of representation was the *baillage,* a mediæval local sub-division which had been the basis of the last election in 1614. At Autun the clergy of its *baillage* met and on April 2, by an overwhelming vote, elected their new bishop to represent them at Versailles. Talleyrand was one of the chosen group who were to make a constitution for France. At thirty-five he had attained a position from which he could enter high politics, could number himself among the rulers of France. No one of his house, worthy servants of the King though they had been for generations, had ever attained so high a position. This nobleman came to power through a popular revolution.

At the very outset of his political career, he was faced with a situation that was to be repeated, for him, indecently often: he could be loyal—that is, he could conform to the acts and sentiments of the particular group with which he had been associated—and be politically unwise; or he could be disloyal and be politically wise. Many great and good men have never had to face such a choice. Talleyrand was never naturalized as citizen of that fair world where Beauty is Truth and Truth Beauty, and where, since things equal to the same thing are equal to each other, to be loyal is to be wise. This harsh world from which he could not escape is perhaps too complicated for aphorisms; but in it, commonly, one cannot eat one's cake and have it. Talleyrand, forced to choose, was wise rather than loyal.

CHAPTER THREE

Revolutionist

I

FOR a time, indeed, it seemed that no one would ever again have to make unpleasant choices. Briefly, very briefly, in 1789 the boundaries of heaven and earth touched. No one in this post-war world of ours can understand, without a deliberate lift of the imagination, how like an evangel the first news of the French Revolution came to men nourished on the hopes of the Enlightenment. Had the German Emperor William II, somewhere about 1912, voluntarily abdicated in favor of a liberal republican government and had this government at once announced its intention of scrapping the navy and giving up all idea of conquest, hopeful young liberals throughout the West might have experienced a joyous sense of fulfillment like that shared by nearly all educated men in 1789. The great revolution of our time, however, was born of war and misery and has never seemed, even to its makers, wholly a thing of light and beauty. Nor is it easy to conceive a Russian Revolution in more cheerful circumstances. The last century has taken the bloom off revolutions. The violence which came later in the great French Revolution and in its nineteenth-century repercussions, the doubts fostered by the biological discoveries of the time, and by the growing movement sometimes called "anti-intellectual," as to the possibility of any rapid regeneration of the race, and the very fact that our only widely accepted notion of revolution, the Marxist, posits violence and suffering as an essential condition of revolutionary action, have combined to make it impossible for anyone today to expect the gentle miracles men thought they saw all about them in 1789.

The twelve hundred delegates who met at Versailles on May 4, 1789, were almost all determined that France should cease to be a "despotism," should have some sort of regularly assembled parliamentary body, and a constitution. Clergy and nobility numbered three hundred each; commons numbered six hundred, as a concession to the popular unrest. No decision had been announced on the crucial question as to whether the Estates should follow the traditional method of voting by Orders, when the clergy and the nobility could outvote the commons two to one, or the proposed new method of voting by individual deputies, when the six hundred commoners, re-inforced by the more advanced members of the other two estates, could easily outvote the conservatives. At the last moment, Louis decided to command the Estates to vote in the traditional way. It was much too late. These Estates had not been chosen to obey the King's commands. After a few confusing but dramatic weeks marked by the famous Tennis-Court Oath, when the commons swore not to disperse until they had given France a constitution, the King and his conservative advisers yielded, the twelve hundred deputies were merged in a single body, and that body became the National Assembly.

The commons had been able to win thus peacefully only because neither clergy nor nobles were unanimous in supporting the King. The electoral colleges which had chosen delegates for each order had, following the mediæval custom, drawn up *cahiers,* or petitions of grievances, which had really been platforms for the new parliament. Even in the clergy and in the nobility these *cahiers* had usually asked for some sort of constitution. Personal loyalty to the King had kept many of the two upper orders from resisting his command to organize in separate houses. In the confusion of motions and counter-motions with which the clergy busied itself during the stalemate over the vote by orders, Talleyrand is not very conspicuous. Nor was he among the first of the clergy to come straggling over from their own house to join the determined and triumphant commons in the new National Assembly. On June 24 a majority of the clergy—mostly humble *curés*—joined the commons; on June 25 more of the clergy, and forty-seven nobles, headed by the King's cousin, the unpleasant Duc d'Orléans, joined them; only on June 26 did Talleyrand, accompanied by du Tillet, Bishop of Orange, decide to risk the benches of the commons. On June 27 the King yielded, and ordered the remnants of the clergy and the nobility to join the commons in the National Assembly. Talleyrand had moved just in time to get the credit for siding with the advanced party.

Here, at least, his treason was slight. For in the mandate which his fellow-clergymen from Autun had given him, his course was clearly plotted: their representative was "to work for a charter which will maintain invariable the rights of all; to declare that henceforth no public act shall be the general law of the land save in so far as the people shall have solemnly consented to it; to consecrate the inalienable and exclusive right of the people to establish taxes, to modify, limit, or revoke them, to legislate as to their use; to establish the principles of sound popular representation."

Talleyrand, indeed, had drawn up his own mandate. But the cogency of his reasoning, the skill of his presentation, had won the almost unanimous support of the electoral body of the clergy of Autun. These first few weeks of revolution had frightened only the extremely timid, had tested the loyalty only of the fanatical feudal retainers of the King. Talleyrand was in the best of company in taking the side of the people. Lafayette, La Rochefoucauld, Orléans, Lally-Tollendal, Biron, Noailles, Mirabeau, Montesquieu-Fezensac, Sillery, the abbés Siéyès and Grégoire, were all members of nobility or clergy, and all were patriots. Some indeed were morally disreputable enough, but on the whole they were an honorable lot.

On July 14 the people of Paris, not unaided by radical politicians anxious to discredit the King, rose very effectively to protest against troop-concentrations going on in the region of Versailles and Paris. Their protest gave, not only to France, but to the world, one of the great symbols of all time—the fall of the Bastille. On October 5 and 6 the women of Paris began a bread riot which ended in a procession to Versailles, further rioting there, breaking into the palace, and bringing to Paris in virtual captivity "the baker, the baker's wife, and the baker's little boy." The royal family were soon followed by an assembly anxious to be in the heart of things. Paris was now the undisputed capital of France; and much of Paris had already decided that France must profit by the existing unrest and go far beyond the decent monarchy on the English model which had hitherto been the announced goal of patriots.

Even after these famous revolutionary "days" the experiment in constitutional monarchy was by no means doomed to failure. The fall of the Bastille and the march of the women on Versailles had indeed completed the separation between the less pliable of the old aristocracy and the rest of the country, and had begun the first emigration. But for most people these melodramatic events had seemed the end of an old era, the necessary winding up of years of civic irresponsibility and ignorance. Only a few, like Edmund

Burke, saw these disorders as a prelude to even greater disorders. There is no evidence that Talleyrand in 1789 foresaw 1792. He had an uncanny ability to guess right in a crisis. His abandonment of the clergy just one day before the King ordered that Estate to dissolve itself is in a way typical of his whole career. He was content to be right about the immediate future. Prophecy on too remote and too philosophical a scale never interested him. Talleyrand always took care not to be too right.

By the late autumn of 1789, the National Assembly had buckled down to work on the new constitution. Party divisions had begun to assume something like permanence. Parliamentary procedure had begun to seem quite natural to delegates untrained in the ways of representative government. Traditions are perhaps more easily manufactured than sentimental conservatives like to admit. Whatever else the National Assembly did or did not do, it most certainly established in its main lines—group or "bloc" party system, disorderly debate, reasonably efficient committee work, republican ritual—a French parliamentary tradition which has hitherto resisted fashionable forms of twentieth-century collectivism almost as well as the British or the American tradition.

In this quieter atmosphere, Talleyrand was a more effective and more conspicuous worker than in the hectic days when the Assembly was struggling to establish itself. In those first days strong lungs or a commanding stage presence were necessary for leadership, and a Mirabeau, who had bellows lungs and an impressively ugly strength, or a Lafayette, who looked commanding and virtuous in uniform as Commander of the Parisian national guard, took charge of the popular movement. Talleyrand was no orator. He could speak quietly and with authority before small groups, and in committee he was very effective. The Assembly listened to him well enough, especially on financial matters. Many of his speeches and reports show considerable skill in moulding phrases to catch the sentiments of his hearers—one of the essentials of all public speaking. But the power to move large numbers of men he did not possess. Morris says of him that he was good at *suaviter in modo,* but weak at *fortiter in re.* He lacked, for one thing, the physical necessities—a powerful voice and a kind of unbuttoned energy. He could never simulate an excitement he did not feel. All really successful oratory is portentous nonsense, and it is probably true that the most successful orators really believe their own nonsense. Talleyrand was wholly incapable of such belief.

The same gifts which had given him success as general agent of the clergy did, however, ultimately make him one of the leaders of the National Assembly. He was, of course, honored with its Presidency for the customary fortnight's term. There is no profit in following him in his daily comings and goings in the next few months. Little had really changed in his way of life. A few old friends had emigrated, but most of his pleasant circle were still around him. Madame de Flahaut was there, Narbonne, Biron, and Choiseul-Gouffier were still available for not too staid parties, and the almost legendary *danseuses de l'Opéra* were still to be had for such festivities. A little work could but add zest to so pleasant a life. The best way to estimate Talleyrand's rôle as a revolutionist is to see what kind of work he did in the National Assembly.

His chief labors were in the sober field of finance. Together with Mirabeau and Duport he worked hard at some solution of the financial problems which had brought on the Revolution. By October 10, he and his colleagues were clear that there was only one way out and on that day Talleyrand put before the Assembly his famous motion that the deficit be filled with the assets of the clergy. Here he seems to play a bit ostentatiously the part of a traitor. Why, among all the "patriot" leaders who must have prepared this motion in caucus, was Talleyrand chosen to take this first conspicuous step? He was chosen because the proposal for the nation to take over the property of the clergy would, if first moved by a member of the clergy, have an appearance of legitimacy, of originating in the best will of the clergy itself, that would help save the face of the Assembly. It is more difficult to explain why he lent himself to this proceeding. At first sight, it would seem that as a public character he stood to lose rather than to gain by an act that must seem to many a gratuitous assumption of a rôle unpleasant for anyone, indecent for a Bishop of Autun. Talleyrand may at this juncture have overestimated the strength of the revolutionary movement, and may have decided that he could hardly break dramatically enough from those of his old associates who had become reactionaries. It seems more consonant with his character, however, to assume that he took the step without any great illusions, simply because he had already decided that what he most wanted to do was to divest himself of his clerical character. Priest in spite of himself, he was perhaps beginning to see a possibility of ceasing to be a priest.

Talleyrand showed during the debates on this problem clear evidence of his gift for devising abstract formulas to satisfy his interests and his hearers' emotions—a gift he was to turn to such sovereign use at Vienna. "What seems to me certain," he declared, "is that the clergy is not a property-owner like other property-owners, since the property it enjoys (and which it may not sell) was given it not in the interest of individuals, but for the maintenance of its corporate functions." In other words, though you have as authors of the Declaration of Rights sworn to maintain property as an inviolate right, the property of the clergy really is not property. Even neater is a rationalization from another speech on the same subject: "Who really owns these lands? The answer can hardly be doubtful; the Nation owns them. . . . They were, indeed, given to the Church. Now, as we have already noticed, the Church is not merely the clergy, who form simply the teaching portion of the Church. The Church is the whole body of the faithful; and the whole body of the faithful in a Catholic land, can it be anything but the Nation?" The Nation is therefore not really confiscating anything; it is simply taking back its own.

The financial scheme based on the "return to the Nation" of the capital value of property really only "entrusted to the clergy as trustees" seems, as worked out by Mirabeau and Talleyrand and their helpers late in 1789, effective enough in principle. Talleyrand in his original motion insisted that the government must take over the payment of the clergy, and the support of such hospitals, asylums, and educational establishments as were of clear social utility. The profit to the government would come, first, from the suppression of needless monasteries, plural livings, wastefully large clerical incomes, sinecures, and unenlightened practices in general; second, from the use of the capital value of much clerical property to pay off the deficit. Once the new government got on its feet financially, it could pay the salaries of the clergy out of current income. In order to convert this land into the kind of asset which could be applied to debt reduction, Mirabeau proposed the famous *assignats,* the paper money of the Revolution, which, until the far more spectacular career of the German mark in our own time, was one of the stock bugbears of sound economists. Talleyrand, indeed, distrusted this paper money from the first. The *assignats* were, however, planned as carefully as such money has ever been planned.

They were not to be issued beyond the actual market value of the land on which they were based, and they were to be burned as soon as they returned to a government bureau in payment for the land. They were to be simply a means of paying the government's debts with the new assets furnished by the lands of the clergy. Paid to someone to whom the government owed money, a given *assignat,* after a little circulation, would fall into the hands of someone who wished to buy government land, would be paid back to the government, would be burned, and everyone would be paid and happy.

Actually this scheme of Talleyrand and Mirabeau may be regarded as the most important of the specific measures which made the Terror inevitable. The *assignats* were not burned up, and were not limited to the value of the lands confiscated. Paper money inflation brought high prices, breadlines, and sharpened the tension between the rich and the poor. The re-organization of the Church in France brought on conflict with the Papacy, and a religious schism which became a civil war. Inflation, civil war, foreign war —without these the Jacobin dictatorship of Virtue, commonly known as the Reign of Terror, might well have been impossible. Yet it is hardly fair to "blame" these later events on the framers of the earlier legislation. If blame is to have even the meaning of guilt in a court of law, its application to a given individual must rest on a firmer chain of cause-and-effect than any that can connect the Reign of Terror with specific individuals. Moderate revolutionaries like the Talleyrand of 1789 are in an embarrassing position before posterity, because they are always "wrong." To the conservative they will appear as essential links in the movement from good to evil, links without which the movement would never have got all the way to evil. To the complete revolutionist they will appear at best as futile half-traitors, at worst as men who fatally delayed the rule of the real children of virtue, and thus made the ultimate failure of the revolution possible. Your Kerenskys are dismal figures in any light. Many of Talleyrand's colleagues were doctrinaire moderates and many of their measures were mere blue-prints of an unexcitingly temperate utopia. But of Talleyrand's share in the legislation on the *assignats* and the property of the clergy, one can only conclude that it by no means puts him in a class with such moderates as Lafayette and Barnave. Talleyrand never assumed men to be better or wiser than they are; at most, we can say that at this time he may have assumed they would prove lazier and more mundanely selfish than, under Jacobin stimulus, they in fact proved for a few short months to be.

Talleyrand's most dramatic political act in these years came as a result of the legislative working-out of this problem of Church property. Since, as Talleyrand himself had admitted in his original motion, those parts of the clerical organization which could not stand the enlightened test of social utility had to be eliminated; since, therefore, the economic structure of the Church in France had to be reformed, the Assembly decided to go ahead and reform the Church in its entirety. Talleyrand did nothing to urge his colleagues to this extreme, though it is not evident that he did anything to stop them. This new legal foundation of the Catholic Church in France was called the Civil Constitution of the Clergy. Under it, the old dioceses were eliminated or made to coincide with the new political subdivisions called *départements*. Bishops and priests were chosen by the same groups of voters who formed the local electoral colleges. A substantial minimum salary for curates, and a maximum salary for bishops and archbishops, were set up. The Pope was to be notified of elections, but there was no pretense that he had a right to approve or disapprove. Dogma the Assembly fondly imagined it had left strictly alone. The Civil Constitution of the Clergy was just what its title implied, a purely secular arrangement on the part of the State to make possible the services of the Roman Catholic Church in the new France.

We can see more clearly than these eighteenth-century legislators, accustomed as they were to the Roman Catholic Church in one of its long periods of stability and repose, and in a period, furthermore, when many of its leaders had made numerous concessions to fashionable deism, when the Church was, so to speak, at its most worldly, we can see more clearly than they that the Civil Constitution of the Clergy could never be acceptable to a Church which for nearly two thousand years had proudly made its own distinctions between Cæsar and God. More particularly, however acceptable it might be to the humble *curés* whose earthly lot it promised to improve, it could hardly be expected to be welcome to the noble bishops and abbots whose power no less than whose wealth it did definitely destroy. In fact, an almost insuperable difficulty threatened to make the application of the Civil Constitution impossible. The revolutionary party wanted the new Church to be not a new Church at all, but the old—a kind of desire strangely common among less courageous revolutionists, and of irresistible appeal to most revolutionists who want to win over their less resolute brethren. The new institution must, then, appear identical with the old. But the Roman Catholic Church has, in the doctrine of Apostolic Succession, an unbreakable chain with the past. Our Lord laid his hands on Peter, Peter laid his on the bishops, and from them a living miracle has come down the ages. All bishops are ordained by bishops. But who would ordain the new constitutional bishops with sees outlandishly and unhistorically called "Bouches du Rhône" or "Saône-et-Loire," bishops appointed in the face of papal opposition, bishops chosen by miscellaneous electoral colleges to which free-thinkers, Protestants, and Jews were eligible?

The Bishop of Autun, fortunately for the Civil Constitution, was a bishop in full and undoubted possession of the gift of apostolic succession. He alone of the bishops of the old régime was politically available. Two other bishops—mere bishops *in partibus* who hardly counted—made up the canonical three, and on February 24, 1791, the constitutional bishops of the Finistère and of the Aisne were duly consecrated, and the Constitutional Church, as it came to be called, was born. A few months later Talleyrand was by papal brief suspended from his episcopal functions and excommunicated. He had, however, already resigned from his position as Bishop of Autun. Election as administrator of the department of Paris in January had given him a plausible excuse for announcing his intention of devoting himself wholly to secular affairs. It seems clear now that he had sent in his resignation several weeks before, as Bishop of Autun, he officiated at the consecration of the new Constitutional bishops. At the moment, this was not known, and the whole affair was so completely uncanonical that a detail here or there could hardly have affected the ceremony.

The Constitutional Church, pathetic hybrid of faith and moderation, was persecuted during the Terror with as much conviction as was the Roman Catholic Church, and after the Terror was quite abandoned by the State which had brought it into being. Well on into the nineteenth century remnants of the Constitutional Church preserved in hope their little spark of Apostolic Succession, but the movement never attained dignity or importance after 1795. In after life Talleyrand was rather ashamed of his part in the establishment of the Constitutional Church, and in his *Memoirs* presents the ingenious explanation that he was afraid that, if he did not by participation preserve the episcopal tradition, the Church in France would fall into presbyterian ways. In actual fact, Talleyrand had so far committed himself with the revolutionary leaders that he could hardly have refused a request which, in view of what he had been saying and doing for eighteen months, was not unreasonable. Moreover, he could hardly yet have been clear as to how complete the return to Throne and Altar would one day be. For the present, his main desire was to wash his hands of the profession into which his family had forced him. The consecration of the bishops he undoubtedly planned to make his last act as a priest. As a matter of fact, it *was* his last act as priest, though not his last act as a Catholic.

For the rest, Talleyrand's activities as a revolutionist were unspectacular, though they add up to a tidy sum. He worked on a new system of weights and measures which in the long run, and thanks to the work of many others, became the metric system. He reported in favor of the confirmation to Portuguese Jews of rights given them by the monarchy before the Revolution—no very great step, but enough to lay him open to attacks by very literal Christians. He warned the Assembly several times about the dangers of paper money, and had some very sensible and very modern words to the effect that the *assignats* are good as gold only as long as most people have confidence in the political stability of the government. His most substantial parliamentary work was a long *Report on Public Education,* 216 pages in the form in which, by order of the Assembly, it was reprinted. It is now a rather scarce item in booksellers' sales, but the whole report is printed in volume XXX of the *Archives parlementaires.* Talleyrand published very little, and this report on education is one of his longest and most ambitious essays. It is a good revolutionary document. The old chaotic educational system must go, along with the old abuses in law and government. Too long tyranny has battened upon ignorance. Our new government rests on the consent of the people; but this consent must be enlightened. Public education, now that we have established public order, must be our immediate concern. Then follows an orderly scheme for a centralized educational system very like the one finally adopted under Napoleon. At the head of this system will be an Institute composed of the best and wisest, and designed not merely to teach the very ablest of the youth of the land, but even more to serve as a spearhead to advance science and learning. Talleyrand lived to become a member of the Napoleonic Institute.

How genuine was Talleyrand's enthusiasm for "this new state of things, raised on the ruins of so many abuses," as he puts it in his *Report on Public Education*? Was he ever a real revolutionist? The legend refuses to Talleyrand any beliefs, any loyalties, any attachments. The legendary Talleyrand must obviously have become a revolutionist because he saw some immediate gain to himself in becoming one. Yet the bitterest idealist would hardly maintain that profit and sincerity never go together. Talleyrand also suffers from the tacit assumption made by so many of his critics that because he did not love abstractions he therefore loved nothing. No one could maintain that Talleyrand ever threw himself into the Revolution with the religious ecstasy of a true Jacobin, or with the milder, if even less practical, hope of a Girondin. Yet it does seem likely that he welcomed the Revolution sincerely, as promising to perpetuate certain ways of life to which he was attached. His participation may not be very noble, altruistic, idealistic or otherwise satisfactory to ethically exacting critics, but there is no need to assert that it was cowardly, mean, and selfish. There is no simple answer to the question: why did Talleyrand identify himself with the Revolution? We must attempt various answers.

No modern, living in an age when the great catchwords are supplied by the science of psychology, can avoid concluding that Talleyrand in these years was seeking to make up for the suffering his unwilling priesthood had brought upon his youth. However much he had adapted himself to his calling, the adaptation can hardly have been effortless, can hardly have failed to leave a mark on his sentiments. That he foresaw as early as 1789 a chance of sloughing off his orders seems very unlikely. We know that he was not embittered to the extent of wishing to destroy Church and Monarchy. But the Revolution offered some emancipation—as it progressed an ever-widening one—from his clerical limitations, and it did offer him a chance to avenge a personal wrong. Even more evident, and even more in accordance with the legendary Talleyrand—who is by no means wholly unreal—is the fact that from the very first the revolutionists were clearly the stronger party, clearly destined to prevail. Talleyrand was no man for lost causes.

More profoundly, however, the way of life to which he had been accustomed pushed him, as it pushed so many of the more intelligent and more ambitious young noblemen, towards revolution. Nowhere is the pervasive influence of Marx—and of facts, too—more apparent than in our modern assurance that no large upper-class group is revolutionary. But in that dawn of 1789, a large portion of the French aristocracy greeted with perfectly explicable joy what they conceived to be merely an extension and prolongation of the enlightened ways to which they were accustomed. Talleyrand was personally acquainted with some of the older *philosophes*. His group had come to congratulate itself on its emancipation from superstition, from prejudice, from tradition, on its attachment to innovation and common sense. To them, the Estates General was merely a proof that most Frenchmen were as enlightened as they.

Now what Talleyrand was brought up to regard as "abuses" he continued pretty consistently through all his political twistings and turnings to regard as "abuses." He was incapable of the kind of sentimentality to be found in Burke, sentimentality which made of any picturesque and inconvenient mediæval survival a sacrosanct refuge from vulgar innovators. To Talleyrand the diversity of weights and measures, the confusion of legal systems, the piling up of one local governmental agency on another, the welter of state finance, the obstacles to individual initiative, the premium on mere routine, the picturesque group-life of province, *pays*, town and village—to Talleyrand all this time-invested aggregate of the social habits of centuries was condemned by its inefficiency, by its inability to allow Frenchmen to get things done, to get rich, if you like. The Marxian would say—and he would not be wholly wrong in saying—that in spite of his feudal ancestry, Talleyrand belonged to the *entrepreneur* class, that his participation in the Revolution was the perfectly consistent act of a man who found in the old, honor-bound feudal society a limitation on his own gifts for commercial enterprise. Moreover, soon after the calling of the Estates General the more loyal, more sentimental, more "noble" of the privileged classes began to fear for what they most prized, their privileges and their standards. Very shortly the gap between reactionaries and revolutionists appeared, and the reactionaries were driven to exalt precisely those elements in the old régime Talleyrand most disliked. For Talleyrand to have joined the first *émigrés* in their flight from the France in which his own intimate friends were triumphant would have meant a more astonishing *volte-face* than any he ever accomplished.

Talleyrand's *Memoirs* pass very lightly over his part in the Revolution. He would have us believe that he very early saw the disastrous ultimate consequences of resistance to royal authority, and that he confined himself to a passive rôle in the National Assembly. Writing in 1816, he could hardly have expressed himself otherwise. But the record proves him to have been an active, if moderate, revolutionist. Nor are there lacking bits of evidence to show that he was not unaffected by the contagion of hope in the future, that he was not by any means as worldly wise and superior to enthusiastic belief in the efficacy of the new dispensation as he appears in his maturity. To Choiseul-Gouffier he wrote in 1787, "My friend, the people will at last count for something. If the king makes all the reforms he has announced his reign will be the most brilliant and the most useful of the monarchy. I have nothing else in my head these days." Apparently even Talleyrand at thirty . . . was thirty. More sober is a letter of October 9, 1789, to his friend the Comtesse de Brionne, an aristocrat already shocked into reaction and hatred for the new régime. He is trying to justify himself to this friend for his share in the Revolution. "One truth ought to be clear to you, and that is that the revolution now going on in France is indispensable under the conditions in which we live, and that this revolution will in the end be useful. . . . In this situation, it is essential to have a definite opinion, an opinion as courageous as circumstances exact. It is necessary to tear oneself from the narrow circles of intrigue and convention in order to consider wider relations and to envisage the new epoch to which we have come. To take half-sides therefore becomes a danger for weak men and a disgrace for those who think themselves strong." Therefore one must accept the Revolution frankly. The aristocrats have failed to take a determined stand. "They have not strength to follow the movement, they have vague aspirations to slow it down. We are perhaps not yet at the end of the evils to which this disposition, as childish as it is cruel, has brought us."

Yet Talleyrand was incapable of the religious devotion and intolerance of the complete revolutionary. He could not wear the Liberty Cap, worship the Goddess Reason, mouth Rousseau in the clubs, bellow out the catch-words of the Revolution, damn the "aristos" and the profiteering rich. He was a good actor, but only in certain classical parts. He must have failed in melodrama or in low comedy. It was fortunate for him that he did not try to take up the Jacobin cause, did not try to adapt himself to the violently revolutionary régime of 1792 to 1794. The Duc d'Orléans found that even as Philippe Egalité he could not live down his aristocratic past. The Bishop of Autun—even, as the ex-Bishop of Autun—must surely have come, like the Duc d'Orléans, to the guillotine.

It is not quite fair to Talleyrand to imply that he left France only because he knew he could not act the part of a Jacobin. He was, after all, a gentleman; even the phrase about the silk stocking filled with mud admits the silk stocking to have been real. Now at this distance we may perhaps feel that the benefits of the democratic Revolution of 1792–1794 outweigh its cruelties and its crudities. We may even admire it as singularly free from snobbery. But Talleyrand had been brought up in one of the most refined of societies, and, as we should say, "conditioned" to certain delicacies. He could no more have stood life under the Terror, even had he been in sympathy with the evangelical Jacobins, than an eighteenth-century Marquis could have danced the Charleston. The precise Robespierre did indeed wear his powdered wig and his knee-breeches in the midst of the deliberately unwashed mob of *sans-culottes*. But Robespierre was not born a gentleman, and he was born a special kind of pedant, insensitive at bottom to the outside world. Talleyrand was shocked by the excesses of the Terrorists. You may think he ought to have been even more shocked by the excesses of his own life—his broken vows, his venality, his treasons. But that cannot alter the immediacy of his own sentiments. Talleyrand left France, much as he loved it, partly because he had certain standards of conduct he could not maintain in France. He might, of course, have stayed and courted martyrdom. That alternative recommended itself to many good men; one would hardly dare say that it recommended itself to all good men.

Early in 1792 Talleyrand contrived to get himself sent on a diplomatic mission to London. France was on the eve of war with Austria and Prussia, and British neutrality was very desirable for the reformed monarchy. It might even be possible for the two "free" nations to stand together against the absolute rulers of Central Europe. Talleyrand's mission is still somewhat obscure. We do know that he was looked on with disfavor in an England already much influenced by Burke against the French Revolution, and that he left London for Paris in March without obtaining any encouragement from the English. Within a few weeks he was back again in London, this time in an anomalous position in the suite of Chauvelin, the somewhat unskilled minister sent over by the Girondin ministry of Roland. This mission at least secured from England a declaration of neutrality in the war between France and the Central European powers which began on April 20, 1792. But Chauvelin had public relations with the English radicals, and the French were even less popular with the ruling classes than a few months before. The attack on the Tuileries on August 10 brought the fall of the French monarchy. Great Britain simply refused to recognize the new French Republic; the old mission no longer had any standing whatever. Talleyrand had gone over to Paris at the very moment of the revolt of August 10, and seems at that moment to have concluded that, for the time being, he could do nothing in France. With the aid of Danton he secured adequate papers, and, ostensibly still on a diplomatic mission, left for London on September 18. He had stayed in Paris long enough to live through the terrible September massacres, when hundreds of priests and other suspects were butchered in the streets. Now, only three years after the hopeful beginnings of 1789, he was on his way to exile.

II

THE Russian, German, and Italian dictatorships have made the political refugee a familiar figure in our contemporary world. Once more, as in the last decade of the eighteenth century, large-scale political emigration has brought upon certain host-nations scattered and usually very voluble groups of the oppressed. The French *émigrés* among whom Talleyrand was now, in spite of his earlier disapproval of their course, forced to cast his lot, were less numerous absolutely than our contemporary exiles, but, especially because of their tendency to concentrate in certain towns, perhaps relatively more conspicuous in a world still unaccustomed to political heroics. London, where Talleyrand spent half of his four years' exile, was one of their points of concentration. Here they could supplement their uncertain incomes in all sorts of ways, for London was already a vast city, with opportunities for stock-broker and for dancing-master alike. Here they could re-establish some social life, with the hierarchies, jealousies, and backbitings necessary to social life. Here, above all, they could be comparatively inconspicuous and yet be very French.

Talleyrand's stay in England was not unhappy. To most *émigré* circles he was a blood-stained traitor, as guilty as Danton or Robespierre, a person to be ostracized until it should be possible to hang, draw and quarter him as he deserved. To English Tories—and all England but Charles Fox and his little band was now Tory—the ex-Bishop of Autun was a renegade to be cold-shouldered. Talleyrand was at least better off than his fellow moderate Lafayette, who had the misfortune to take refuge with the Austrians, and was promptly put into prison as a dangerous revolutionary. For rather over a year, he enjoyed the freedom of England, subject only to an occasional snubbing, a treatment to which almost any foreigner who stays in England long enough is liable. He had about him many of his fellow moderates, like him subject to the hatred of true royalists, and all the more determined to build in exile their own little society—Narbonne, Lally-Tollendal, Jaucourt, Madame de Staël, Madame de Genlis, and half a dozen others. Fox, Lansdowne, Romilly, and other open-minded English gentlemen welcomed these misunderstood Frenchmen and women. The Marquis of Lansdowne, in particular, kept open house at Bowood for a society which ranged from the philosophic Bentham to the port-bibbing Whig aristocrats. Here Talleyrand and his group were frequently entertained.

Just how Talleyrand managed to live during these years of exile is a problem no biographer has yet solved. In December, 1792, the Convention passed a decree confiscating his property and registering him as an *émigré*—that is, virtually, an outlaw. Regular income from France was thereafter impossible. He had been able to have his library shipped to England before this decree was passed, and the public sale of his books brought him in a certain sum of money. He must have taken with him from France some jewelry and other valuables, and he may have taken the precaution to transfer funds to London. Certainly he never came down to the bare bones of poverty. Even in America he was accompanied by his valet, Courtiade, who through a long life displayed a story-book devotion to his master. The most likely explanation is that Talleyrand maintained in London the connections with the new world of finance he had so effectively set up in France, that he was always *dans les affaires,* executing a commission here, profiting from a tip there. From his American sojourn we have several short business letters which prove conclusively that he was acting as commission agent for several English firms.

This pleasant life in England came to an abrupt end. In January, 1794, he was warned by the English police that he had, under the Alien Bill, five days to quit the kingdom. Appeal to the Prime Minister himself secured nothing more than a delay, and early in March he set sail for Philadelphia. Why should the hospitable and freedom-loving English so suddenly have turned out the persecuted foreigner? The Alien Bill—which much resembles the American Alien and Sedition Bills passed just a few years later—did indeed give the government pretty wide police powers of the kind not usually to be discerned in nice handbooks like Blackstone's. These powers were to be used against those Jacobin secret agents who, just as did Bolshevik secret agents a century and more later, in conservative imagination swarmed down like locusts on the rich lands of orderly countries. They did not, however, make it compulsory on the government to get rid of all foreigners. Talleyrand was much aggrieved. He insisted that fishing, and correcting the proofs of a novel, his chief occupations at the time, were in no sense activities dangerous to his majesty, George III. The most likely explanation of his banishment is that, since the English government was after all a government of influential personalities, some enemy of Talleyrand got the ear of an influential personality, and had him brought under the Alien Bill. Of enemies Talleyrand always had a good supply, and in the London of 1794, filled with royalist Frenchmen, there must have been many who bore a grudge against the man who was so largely responsible for *assignats,* confiscation of clerical property, Civil Constitution of the Clergy, and a good deal else. Talleyrand himself pretended, at least, to believe that Austria and Prussia, powers which, after the beheading of Louis XVI in January, 1793, had become allies of England in war against France, had requested his banishment as a well-known revolutionist. Finally, it is possible that some easily frightened Englishmen really did think Talleyrand, even though outlawed by the Convention, might also be in its pay. Melodrama, like all other forms of art, is also a form of life. Moreover, Talleyrand had certainly tried to keep himself in the good graces of the Republic even after he left France for the last time. A letter of his written to Lebrun, then Foreign Minister, in October, 1792, discusses plans for a French expedition to Ireland, speaks enthusiastically of English republicanism, and finds England ripe for revolution. We now know that by 1793 Talleyrand was quite out of touch with the rulers of France. But we need not be surprised if quite sensible Englishmen thought the ex-Bishop of Autun able to carry double-dealing to miraculous lengths.

In America, which was now almost the only part of the Western World open to him, he was rather unhappy. Talleyrand was incapable of really luxuriant unhappiness. The very unhappy suffer either physically or metaphysically—and since the amount of metaphysical pain a profound nature can undergo is infinite, whereas physical pain has definite limits as to intensity and duration, it is fair to conclude that the world's great sufferers are afflicted with metaphysical pain. Talleyrand had an excellent constitution, and was in these years in the prime of life; and metaphysics, with all its depths and consolations—and afflictions—was no part of his consciousness. In America, however, he was at least uncomfortable, and for many reasons.

He did not like the climate. He was accustomed to the cool damp summers of northern Europe, and therefore the first onslaught of a Philadelphia summer drove him to a northward flight which did not end until he reached Machias in Maine. He did not like the Philadelphian notion of what to do on Sundays. He did not like American cooking. Like so many of his nation, distinguished for its artlessness in financial matters, he found the Americans money-grubbing materialists. Like so many foreigners of all nations, he was unable to understand the rather subtle interplay of class distinctions in America, and, even though he spent some time in New England, came to the conclusion that ours was a levelling democracy constantly edging towards plutocracy.

Just before he left England, Talleyrand had written, "America is as good an asylum as any other; when one is taking a course on political ideas, it is a country that must be seen." It may seem rather extraordinary that he should have said of this country one hundred and fifty years ago about what M. Luc Durtain has just finished saying. Talleyrand's judgment is the judgment of hundreds of much more commonplace travelers since his time. Perhaps the clichés were truer then, since they were at least fresher? Perhaps their persistence is a proof that they correspond substantially to facts? This is hardly the place to engage in a debate that has already filled so many library shelves. When Americans hear Talleyrand's reputed remark to Barante,

"Don't speak to me about a country where I found no one who wasn't ready to sell me his dog," they may have some doubts as to its accuracy, but they recognize the statement itself as one of the permanent facts of life.

Our concern is with Talleyrand rather than with the history of the American national reputation. We must try and see how he came to entertain these opinions, and how they came to serve him. Now the United States in 1794 can hardly have been a comfortable place for a French aristocrat. Even in these days of open plumbing, electricity, and airconditioning not all Europeans will admit that the animal man is better off in America than in Europe. In 1794, America could not yet provide the consistently luxurious surroundings Talleyrand had been used to in France, and even in England. The frontier was at the back door of Philadelphia. Climate, cooking, drinking, were all trials. And in much of the America through which he traveled the comparative comforts of the seaboard cities had made little headway against pioneering crudities. Again, Talleyrand was forced to note what many a Frenchman has since noted: that, although we share many political ideas, and some political habits with the French, although we owe the countrymen of Lafayette our national independence, and although a few of us are capable of almost maudlin devotion to some atypical fragments of France, the plain truth is that most Americans dislike France and Frenchmen. He saw with equal clarity that, although we had just fought a war to free ourselves from England, even in 1794 most Americans liked England and Englishmen, and certainly would long continue in England's trade orbit. Talleyrand's patriotism was hurt by this knowledge, which was later to form one of the chief ingredients in his foreign policy as Minister of the Directory and of the Consulate. Nor can his pride have been assuaged in any way by the obvious contempt many of the Federalist ruling class had for the shocking French revolutionists, so different from our own gentlemanly Washingtons and Hancocks. President Washington, no doubt wisely, refused to get into trouble with the Jacobin régime in France by taking official notice of the presence of the ex-Bishop of Autun. Talleyrand, though not a sensitive man about such matters, was certainly not indifferent to them. It is, moreover, quite possible that the upright Washington was moved by personal even more than by political dislike, for Talleyrand's evil reputation was, thanks largely to his jealous rival, Morris, already widespread in American governing circles. Finally, Talleyrand's experience of American life, when not simply that of a foreign tourist, was chiefly with the commercial and speculating groups in Philadelphia and New York. Many of these late eighteenth-century business men were no doubt charming, cultivated men of the world. Talleyrand had a very high opinion of Hamilton, whose mind and character seemed to him on a level with those of the best European statesmen. He is reported to have been particularly astounded at Hamilton's resignation from the Treasury because he could not get along on his salary! But many of the business men engaged in the wild scramble for wealth in the new and now solidly bottomed republic must have been what Talleyrand thought they were—pushing money-grubbers, quite unaware of European standards of gentlemanliness.

Talleyrand saw a good deal of the United States north of Mason and Dixon's line, and traces of his passage appear in odd quarters. So much was the little village of Machias impressed by the coming of a prominent member of the National Assembly that a legend sprang up to explain his presence. Talleyrand, according to this story, was born at Lamoine Point on Frenchman's Bay, the child of a beautiful daughter of an exiled Acadian couple and a French naval officer. The mother having died, the boy was taken at the age of twelve to France, where he was brought up as a Talleyrand-Périgord. Naturally when he returned to America he came back to his mother's home and his birth-place. The story, which has attained the dignity of print in *The Old Farmers Almanac,* is, of course, pure fantasy. But it does show that even in America, Talleyrand was no obscure person. Another Maine tradition about him has been handed down for generations within the same family. Talleyrand was visiting the then head of the family in their home on the Kennebec, and took the occasion to make violent love to a pretty servant-girl. The girl indignantly rejected the corrupt European, but never forgot him, and long years afterward rejoiced at the news of his disgrace and retirement under the Bourbons.

An American incident or two emerges sharply from the usually impersonal pages of Talleyrand's *Memoirs.* He was traveling about with Beaumetz, a former deputy to the Assembly, like him a moderate, and a M. Heydecoper. "Once, in the heart of Connecticut," he writes, "after a long day's ride, we stopped at a house where the people consented to give us bed and supper. The food supply was fortunately better than we usually found in American houses. The family was composed of an elderly man, his wife, about fifty years of age, two grown-up boys, and a young girl. The meal consisted of smoked fish, ham, potatoes, strong beer, and brandy. The two young fellows, who were rather elevated, spoke of a journey they were about to undertake; they were going beaver-hunting for a few weeks. They spoke of their future expedition in such glowing terms that they aroused our interest and curiosity to such a degree that, after drinking a few glasses of brandy, M. de Beaumetz, M. Heydecoper, and myself, were dying to join them." They were therefore enrolled in "the brotherhood of Connecticut beaver hunters," but the sobriety of the morning brought a change of mind, and they continued their journey. Again, "on the banks of the Ohio, Mr. Smith possessed a residence known in the country by the name of *log-house*. The walls of it were formed by rough trees. The drawing room contained a pianoforte enriched with most beautiful bronzes. M. de Beaumetz having opened it, Mr. Smith said to him, Please do not attempt to play, for the man who tunes it lives a hundred miles from here, and he has not come this year." After this incident, Talleyrand enters an aside which explains much of his dislike for America. "I must be pardoned for dwelling at some length on America. I was so lonely when there, that many reflections, which would otherwise have found vent in conversation, now come rushing to my pen."

Talleyrand's finances are a bit less mysterious during his stay in America than they are for his stay in England. He did not hesitate to take advantage of the opportunities for making money afforded by this crudely commercial civilization. America, he thought, suffered from an over-emphasis on commerce and a neglect of agriculture, which with the Physiocrats he held to be the true basis of a stable society. But he did not waste his time preaching. He took part in various land speculations, then an easy source of profit for men with capital or connections. With Noailles, hero of Yorktown and the Fourth of August, with Omer Talon, with Moreau de St. Méry, exile and bookseller, he formed a little group of Philadelphian Frenchmen who put to good use their friendship with American capitalists like Robert Morris and Bingham. He also acted as correspondent for several banking and shipping firms. Clearly, his unhappiness in America was not due to poverty.

In the meantime, Robespierre had fallen, and one by one the old proscribed groups were amnestied by the repentant

Republic, no longer the Republic of Virtue. Talleyrand was after all no royalist. He had gone pretty far on the way to the Republic. Moreover, he had in the Paris of 1795 a number of faithful friends, most useful among whom was Madame de Staël, now back from England and become an important woman, whose intelligence made up for her lack of beauty, even in the pseudo-pagan society of the Thermidorean reaction. A certain amount of wire-pulling procured in September, 1795, the passage in the Convention of a decree striking Talleyrand's name from the list of outlawed *émigrés,* and permitting his return to France. Marie-Joseph Chénier, who moved the decree, made a speech which shows that the good old Republican terminology was still in fashion. "Republican by pride of soul and by principle," he said of the ex-Bishop of Autun, " 'tis to the heart of a republic, 'tis to the land of Benjamin Franklin that he has gone to contemplate the imposing spectacle of a free people." Talleyrand actually had found the spectacle anything but imposing. He was never squeamish about abstract truth, however, and he can scarcely have worried about returning to France under false auspices. He waited impatiently in Philadelphia for the coming of favorable sailing weather in the spring, and, after some delay, set sail for Paris via Hamburg and Amsterdam, to avoid danger from British ships. He arrived at Paris in September, 1796, closing a four years' exile.

Exile had not embittered him, had not made him a convert to any Cause, lost or won. Had he stayed away much longer, some of the lack of perspective common among exiles might have appeared even in his cool, detached views. Nor had he learned much in England and in America. He had touched lives like that of the Ohioan Smith too remote from his to help him much. He had been uprooted, not transplanted, and absorbed little from alien soil. Talleyrand was too good a Frenchman to feel the need of learning a great deal from foreigners.

III

TALLEYRAND returned to the Paris of the Directory, a city of immorality, vulgar wealth, and neo-classic smartness. Just as in the England of 1660, the swing of the pendulum had brought an ostentatiously loose society in place of a society keyed by force and by hope to an almost ascetic morality. The scandals of the Directory have not been overlooked by historians and their readers. Perhaps they have been looked into a bit too thoroughly. Only by contrast with Robespierre's Republic of Virtue do these years seem out of line with the general course of French history. Perhaps certain traditionally French qualities—quiet good taste, dislike of extremes, decent gaiety, unpedantic freshness—are not obviously present in the costumes of the period, in its literature and painting, in the hurly-burly of its balls and its routs. But no one who has felt at home in other parts of French history can feel that the Directory is altogether abnormal.

Certainly Talleyrand fitted with obvious ease into this society. He may have regretted the absence of some of the old formal decencies, but this was so much better than Pennsylvania! Here he found again his former vicar-general at Autun, the Abbé des Renaudes, who had long been an indispensable aide, one of the band of helpers who did for Talleyrand the sober digging, the editing and organization of his ideas, much as Dumont, Clavière, and others had labored for Mirabeau. He found Madame de Staël, more active than ever, and many other old friends like Hauterive, Montrond, and Ste. Foy, the first a steady worker and a great help to Talleyrand, the two latter amusing and not unintelligent men of the world, and in their way also very helpful. He found new men like Barras, member of the committee of five which under the name of the Directory headed the government. He found a very successful young general, Napoleon Bonaparte, and his charming creole wife, formerly a mistress of Barras. He found, in short, a society not in the least like that of the puritanical Jacobins of the Terror, with their absurd copy-book notions about civic and private virtue.

Here too he found the lady who later became his wife. Catherine Worlée was born of French parents in the Danish East Indies, and tropically mature, was at fifteen married to an Englishman named Grand, an employee of the East India Company. Madame Grand, as she was known among the English and French upper-class society where she pursued her calling, was thirty-five when she met Talleyrand. Her calling was prostitution, but of that special character and in that special class which our Victorian ancestors used to designate by the name "adventuress." She attained great distinction in her calling, and the list of her lovers is indeed a rôle of honor. It was begun in India by no less a person than Sir Philip Francis, probably the famous Junius of eighteenth-century letters and politics. There is a painting of her in her twenties by Madame Vigée Lebrun which has become one of the stock examples of eighteenth-century sentimentality, and which must be known to many people who have never realized that its subject became the Princesse de Talleyrand. She does not bulk large in Talleyrand's *Memoirs,* and there is no authentic account of how the two came together. Madame Grand had emigrated to England during the Terror, and though she had legal permission to return, was haunted by the idea that the police were watching her. According to an almost too circumstantial story, she was advised to go directly to the Minister of Foreign

Relations and establish the innocence of her stay in England. She went to Talleyrand in lovely distress, and stayed, but not in distress.

Talleyrand's entrance into the service of the Republic as Minister of Foreign Relations was the culmination of several months of active intriguing. Elected a member of the Institute in his absence, he took advantage of his membership to read before that learned body a *Mémoire sur les relations commerciales des Etats-Unis avec l'Angleterre* which was well received, and which brought his name again into public attention. He talked to the right people, and above all, he got Madame de Staël to talk to the right people. The upshot was his appointment as Minister of Foreign Relations, made in July, 1797, chiefly through the corrupt Barras, and against the bitter opposition of the one real Jacobin member of the Directory, the Alsatian Reubell. The ministers of the Directory were hardly more than its servants, high-class clerks under its complete control. But the Minister of Foreign Relations received a good salary, a splendid house in the Rue du Bac, and excellent opportunities for receiving personal gifts from foreign gentlemen desirous of getting something from the Republic. And a minister was still a minister, even under the Directory.

Neither now, nor later under Napoleon, was Talleyrand to enjoy anything like a free hand in the pursuit of his own policies. Most detailed criticism of what he did as Foreign Minister rests upon a false assumption that he had the power to have done otherwise. Yet in the *Mémoire sur les relations commerciales des Etats-Unis avec l'Angleterre,* in other reports and addresses, and in his letters, is sketched out in broad lines a policy which he succeeded in getting partly adopted in the early days of Napoleon's Consulate, and to which he consistently adhered in his later years. Talleyrand was no doctrinaire with ironclad schemes worked out in advance; on the other hand, he was no muddling opportunist with a contempt for long-range thinking. It is worth while here to consider the main outlines of his foreign policy—outlines which under pressure from his republican or imperial masters he was frequently obliged to alter or efface.

Talleyrand assumed with a naturalness which more awkward Anglo-Saxons ought to envy him, that a French diplomatist should work to make France powerful, prosperous, respected, and if need be, feared. Patriotism *is* enough to a surprising number of Frenchmen. They love their country with none of the uneasy feeling that they are being untrue to God, or Mankind, or Virtue so evident in many English, and even in Americans. They are thus not obliged to pretend that, in a higher and nobler sense, they are thereby being even truer to God, Mankind, or Virtue. There is an artlessness in much French patriotism, even when it is very noisy and ill-mannered. In Talleyrand one does not expect anything artless, but his apparent attachment to France almost attains that quality. He sought, then, to promote the interests of France. He certainly never maintained to himself, and only rarely to others, that the interests of France were always, in the inherent fitness of things, also the interests of mankind at large. He belongs fitly to the long line which goes from Richelieu to Clemenceau.

Talleyrand also loved peace. He wished France great and prosperous, but he identified greatness and prosperity neither with megalomaniac expansion at the expense of neighboring states nor with a bristling military devotion to physical force. Anything like the kind of doctrinaire devotion to peace nowadays summarized as "pacifism" was completely foreign to his temperament, and always seemed to him either ridiculous or hypocritical. The Emperor Alexander's pleasing visions, for example, as embodied in the

Holy Alliance, seemed to him utterly incredible except on the hypothesis that Alexander was both a fool and a rogue. Yet if you are willing to strip the word pacifist of its humanitarian and metaphysical connotations. Talleyrand was a good pacifist. He hated war and cruelty as Voltaire had hated war and cruelty, because they seemed to him absurd, barbarous, unworthy of cultivated men. His true peers are perhaps less Richelieu and Clemenceau, realists to whom success gave more than a touch of extravagance and desire for sheer expansion, than Fleury and Walpole, realists also, but soberly restrained devotees of the cult of stability.

Stability among the European states Talleyrand considered to depend on the working of the old-fashioned balance of power. Anything like a federal league, a European super-state, would have seemed to him fantastic—as it certainly was. In general, he tended to hold that France ought as a rule to side with England and with Austria, old established countries with a long tradition directed to the support of existing international arrangements, and to side against, or at least attempt to curb, Prussia and Russia, upstart powers whose recent record had shown that they would disturb these arrangements whenever opportunity arose, new powers with more to gain by change than the older powers. Here too, Talleyrand's position depends by no means on abstract theories. He was attracted to England and Austria by that conservative side of his temperament which shows in his love of ceremony, his admiration for established ease, for good manners and good sense. He disliked Prussians and Russians because both seemed to him ambitious barbarians, however well veneered with the Enlightenment they might be. Prussian sentimentality he disliked as the complement of Prussian brutality. Russian temperamental depths seemed to him merely a rather complete and unpleasant kind of intoxication.

Talleyrand's policy of friendship with England was one of his most fixed guide-posts. He had, under the Consulate especially, to follow the fashion and damn perfidious Albion. No servant of Napoleon's could have been openly an Anglophile. Here as so often, Talleyrand gave in before what seemed to him forces beyond his control, and swallowed pride and principles in a quite unaristocratic way. Later he could begin quietly to undermine Napoleon's position, and in the last years of his life, after the Bourbon Restoration, he could actually make his influence felt in bettering Anglo-French relations. Talleyrand really liked the upper-class Englishmen he knew so well, Englishmen who, like Charles James Fox, were thoroughly at home in the liveliest and lightest of continental societies. He did not know middle-class Englishmen, and he would doubtless not have enjoyed the tone of English society in the middle and later years of Queen Victoria as he had enjoyed it under William IV. He liked the way Englishmen went about politics, with not too much pretense at adherence to logical principles, or even to moral consistency. Here again he would not have been quite so happy in a later England where contempt for political theory had been erected into a political theory, and where Englishmen invariably did the morally correct thing. Yet Talleyrand's Anglophile policies were less the result of any personal liking for the English than of a reasoned conviction that France usually gained by coöperating with England. The two together could so obviously do what they wanted in Europe. England clearly had no wish to make territorial accessions in Europe. France, were she not ruled by a madman, would have no desire for such accessions. This could not be said of the powers of Central and Eastern Europe, both major and minor. England and France together, mature, civilized, economically advanced states, could act as policemen for the less civilized portions of the continent.

The most explicit part of Talleyrand's foreign policy, at least from 1796 to 1804, may still seem to conventional students of the subject quite inconsistent with the foregoing. He wished, as his report to the Institute, his attitude towards the Louisiana problem, and a good deal else shows, to attract the attention of Frenchmen from European to colonial expansion. The Americans, he is convinced, are bound for a long time to be an economic dependency of Great Britain even though they have ceased to be a political dependency. Emotionally, traditionally, in all the important little things that make social life, the Americans are English. France must not count on American gratitude for 1778 helping in 1798 to promote Franco-American trade or Franco-American political coöperation. Yet since it is precisely in this vast New World that the future greatness of the European races lies, England must not be allowed to monopolize colonial expansion. France, though she lost an empire in 1763, can start and rebuild another. Much of the world is still open to exploitation.

The trite criticism here would be that to attempt to rival England in the rest of the world while in close and active alliance with her in Europe is a most illogical policy. So it is, in a purely abstract sense. But the facts seem to be with Talleyrand. From the days of Wolsey on, England has decisively intervened against France whenever the latter was successfully aggressive on the continent of Europe. It is true that in these European wars world-empires finally became the stakes. But after 1815, France never seriously threatened to make European annexations; she did, however, build herself an empire second only to England's in size and wealth, and in Africa, at least, hardly second to

England's. There were stresses and strains, a Suez Canal and a Fashoda, but the peace was not broken. England would seem in the past to have opposed French expansion in Europe even more bitterly than she opposed French expansion outside Europe. There is no reason to declare *a priori* that Talleyrand's policy of sharing the world with England would have been impossible in 1800. Napoleon, who was in one sense an accident, made it impossible. After Trafalgar, France had either to contain herself, or to expend her energies on the suppression of peoples contiguous to her by land.

Talleyrand even then would have had France contain herself. But he was by that time the servant of a master more imperious than the Directory, a master for whom he clearly had, in the early days of their relations at least, the respect, even the admiring respect, men have for the more spectacular forces of nature—whirlwinds, thunder storms, hurricanes. Talleyrand's extraordinary gift of short-range prescience enabled him to see as early as 1797 that this brilliant young general Bonaparte, who had had such success in Italy, might be worth cultivating. He had written to the General in Italy to announce his entrance into the Foreign Office: "I have the honor to inform you, General, that the executive Directory has appointed me Minister of Foreign Relations. Justly conscious of the dangers and importance of my functions, I have need to reassure myself with the knowledge of how much help your glory must bring to the carrying out of negotiations. The very name of Bonaparte is in itself an auxiliary which must overcome all difficulties. I shall hasten to send you any advice the Directory may charge me to transmit; and Fame, which is your customary organ, will often deprive me of the honor of informing the Directory of the way in which you have carried out their advice." This flattery, seasoned as it was with a subtly ironical implication of the Directory's impotence, must have been very acceptable to the young general. To his letter urging Bonaparte to make a glorious peace, Talleyrand added a characteristic postscript: "As for the rest, trust to your own combinations; they will most certainly be marked with that quality of greatness and stability you give to everything you do."

The glorious peace was made at Campoformio in October, 1797. Austria was quieted with the cession of Venice, and the rest of the Italian peninsula was delivered over to France and the small group of Francophile "patriots" of Italian blood. Peace had earlier been made with Prussia and with Spain. The French Republic had now made peace with all its neighbors, save the English, who continued to defend the civilized world from the Red Menace of a regicide republic. Even the English were beginning to weaken. They had taken advantage of French penetration into Holland to seize, in the name of the dispossessed House of Orange, the very rich Dutch colony of Ceylon as well as the Cape of Good Hope, a useful station on the sea route to India. They had, once Spain had gone over to France, seized Trinidad and some other Spanish colonies. All in all, the Empire seemed to be in pretty good shape, and many Englishmen, who could not appeal to the still unannounced ideas of the still unborn Marx on Imperialism, began to wonder why they were fighting. Fortunately for England, such men were few, and after abortive peace negotiations at Lille, the English went on fighting without knowing why.

Yet the situation was pretty black for Bonaparte. England was the only enemy left, and to fight England you needed a navy—something of which Bonaparte was always disastrously ignorant. Italy was no field for a young man who could hardly do less than emulate Alexander the Great. In this emergency Bonaparte was saved from rusting away in idleness, or from a perhaps premature entrance into politics, by the Egyptian scheme. This scheme was certainly in part Talleyrand's. In July, 1797, he had read at the Institute a paper called *Essai sur les avantages à retirer de colonies nouvelles dans les circonstances présentes* in which he had recalled an old French project for the annexation of Egypt. But the matter had been in the air for years, and French agents had all during the century been far more active in the Levant than had the English. Talleyrand can hardly be considered responsible for Bonaparte's ill-fated Egyptian expedition. At most, he is but an element in a complex situation, the most important factor in which is certainly Bonaparte's own imagination and ambition, nourished with romantic notions of the East, with many a book of that exotic travel-literature so common in the prosaic century of all-conquering Reason.

As Foreign Minister, Talleyrand submitted to the Directory a report urging the Egyptian expedition, a report certainly drawn up by subordinates, and full of the virtuously republican missionary phraseology still popular in France—and elsewhere. France is to bring civilization to the languishing Egyptians. The expedition will not be expensive, considering what it will bring back to France. French trade will benefit enormously. England will be menaced in her communications with India. The expedition will thus really be a part of the war against England. The situation has certain parallels with current politics, and by a few changes in proper names and dates, Talleyrand's report might be submitted to Mussolini in justification of the Ethiopian adventure.

Talleyrand had certainly consulted with Bonaparte and with many others about the proposed expedition. He seems on the whole to have been favorable to it. It was a gamble perhaps, but Talleyrand, moderate and peace-loving though he was, was certainly no timid stand-patter unwilling to run any risks. If the expedition were successful, France would be greater, and ultimate peace with England certainly no more difficult to make. And the expedition had very good chances of success. Nelson and bad luck ruined it. The first might at least have been avoided, but Bonaparte himself refused to let the French fleet take to the safe shelter of the Ionian Islands. The French Admiral Brueys and his ships were caught by Nelson in the open roadstead of Aboukir, and annihilated in a battle in some ways more decisive than Trafalgar. Bonaparte was bottled up in Egypt with nothing left but heroics, upon which even Bonaparte could not live forever.

Lacour-Gayet finds here another one of Talleyrand's treasons. Egypt was under the nominal suzerainty of the Sultan of Turkey, and with Turkey France was at the time enjoying perfectly peaceful relations. The Sultan might be a bit surprised at the sudden armed descent of a friendly power upon his lands, and a very good French diplomatist at Constantinople would be necessary to prevent surprise turning to anger and a declaration of war. Talleyrand had come to a definite understanding with Bonaparte that he would resign from the Ministry of Foreign Relations and take on the task of pacifying the Sultan at Constantinople. Talleyrand was to depart as soon as the expedition got under way. He never left Paris, in spite of somewhat bewildered and complaining letters from Bonaparte. Aubert-Dubayet, the French Ambassador at Constantinople, had recently died, and at the crucial moment there was no one of first rank to represent the French cause there. But even had Talleyrand himself gone, he could hardly have achieved much. The most diabolically clever diplomat could not have disguised the open aggression of the Egyptian expedition. The Ottoman Porte at once declared war against France, and opened its resources to the English fleet.

Bonaparte never quite forgave Talleyrand for what he considered egging him on in the first place, and for subsequently failing to go to Constantinople to appease the Sultan. Lacour-Gayet here as elsewhere accepts Bonaparte's word as the law. As a matter of fact, Talleyrand was, like all the other ministers, the servant of the Directory—a fact which Lacour-Gayet himself expounds with some glee, as it helps to diminish Talleyrand's dignity and importance. He was far from free to go to Constantinople, even had he liked. The Directory was master of his actions, and in 1798 the Directory wanted him to stay at his post. There was unfinished work to carry out, work for which Talleyrand was better fitted than anyone else. This was the task of staving off war between France and the United States. One cannot prove it; but it seems more than likely that Talleyrand did not deliberately go back on his agreement with Bonaparte, but stayed in Paris to take care of the heritage of the XYZ affair.

The United States was experiencing during this particular World War of the 1790's what we have now come to consider its customary difficulties as a neutral power with an important overseas trade. Pinckney, Marshall and Gerry were sent by the American government to treat with the French about certain matters hinging on French violations of our neutral rights. Through intermediaries of Talleyrand, referred to as X, Y, and Z, they were told that negotiations could not be begun until the Americans had paid over what were clearly bribes, and subscribed to a loan directly profitable to the Directory. Now Americans have never been very effectively indignant over the vast amount of grafting, bribery, and log-rolling going on at home, but they are firm against such practices abroad. "Millions for defense, but not one cent for tribute." Adams, apprised of the evil doings in France, informed Congress of what was going on, and soon the American press was ringing in denunciation of the corrupt Messrs. XYZ.

Talleyrand at once wrote in the *Moniteur* an official disavowal of his subordinates, pointing out that no Foreign Minister could keep rigorous control over secret agents whose very success depended on a certain amount of freedom from such control, and insisting on his own innocence. As usual, he puts up a very reasonable case indeed. It is spoiled by the fact that many men higher up, probably even certain Directors, were involved. It is spoiled also by the fact that Ste. Foy, Montrond, and d'Arbelles, Messrs. XYZ, were his cronies, most intimate friends, and had long been his associates in various kinds of speculation from stock-jobbing to mild blackmail. Indeed, the extraction of "sweetness" from negotiators was an accepted fact of European diplomacy. The Americans were vulgarly and innocently applying the standards of the Enlightenment where they clearly had no place. Pinckney and Marshall, early disgusted, left for home, but Gerry stayed on in a somewhat anomalous position. Meantime Frenchmen and Americans were fighting on the sea with as much abandon as if war had been officially declared. The Directory did not wish an American war, especially now that, with Turkey up in arms, a new coalition of hostile Europe was forming against France. They insisted that Talleyrand, who had had personal experience with Americans, stay on and finish the negotiations so inauspiciously begun. Gerry had left Paris, but waited in Holland, where Talleyrand's agents eventually persuaded him of their good intentions, and Franco-

American relations were once more patched up, and assumed their normal status of a friendship based on mutual misunderstanding.

The Egyptian campaign was approaching its disastrous end. Italy, or at least certain Italian princes, had revolted against the little republics set up under French influence throughout the peninsula. The Ottoman Porte had declared war and soon Russia, Austria, Naples and other powers formed the second of the great coalitions directed against revolutionary France. The Directory, adequate but not popular, ran into a series of military misfortunes. Talleyrand, ever sensitive to the political future, resigned his position and returned briefly to private life. He had been much criticized by the petty squabbling groups who carried on the republican tradition. An adventurer named Jorry brought suit against him for false accusation, a suit without any foundation, but supported by the numerous enemies of Talleyrand. He was accused of not being a good Republican, of complicity with *émigrés*. Barras, still Director, had come to dislike him. In this summer of 1799, there was a general recrudescence of violent Jacobinism; clubs were formed again, and once more orators spoke with feeling of Liberty, Equality, Fraternity, instead of leaving these grand words in their proper status of ritual. Talleyrand was uncomfortable. There were storms in the air, and he had to withdraw to make his meteorological observations more precise. On July 20, 1799, his resignation was accepted by the executive Directory.

Five months later the Directory had fallen, and Talleyrand was preparing to return in triumph to the Ministry of Foreign Affairs in the rue du Bac. Once more, and in more than usually difficult circumstances, he had guessed right. Bonaparte, back from Egypt, where he had left the remnant of his army to die, had proved himself the strong man. By the successful *coup d'état* of 18 Brumaire in November, 1799, Bonaparte overthrew the Directory and set up a new republican form of government, the Consulate, in which the real power was centered in himself as First Consul. Talleyrand was not among the active participants in the *coup* itself, which got a bit out of hand when the legislators of the old system refused to depart at Bonaparte's request. The military Bonaparte could always rely on, and at last the legislators were forced out at the point of the bayonet. Talleyrand was no man for this sort of thing. But he had taken part in the preliminary intrigues which had brought Bonaparte and Siéyès, a political nostrum-maker of high reputation, together in the effective coalition that disposed of the Directory. He had used his numerous friendships to further the plot. He was soon to have his reward.

On November 22, less than a fortnight after the *coup d'état,* he received from the First Consul his appointment as Minister of Foreign Relations. He was back in office, and more firmly so than ever before. For the next fifteen years his story is inseparably bound up with that of the young man so soon to be known as the Emperor Napoleon. For the next seven years, he is the minister of Napoleon, the instrument of the latter's foreign policy. He is in office, but hardly in power.

CHAPTER FOUR

Bonapartist

I

TALLEYRAND had now for some ten years been a conspicuous figure in French life. Memoir-writers, letter-writers, journalists, essayists, all the array of scribes who draw up the crazy record of our civilization had had their chance to put something of Talleyrand on paper. Portrait-painters and caricaturists alike had been able to draw him. For another ten years he was to remain in sound middle age, physically at the point where senescence has not yet made intolerable inroads, and certainly no less conspicuous a member of the little group of Frenchmen deemed worthy of the immortality conferred by memoir-writers, letter-writers, journalists, painters and caricaturists. This is, then, as good an occasion as we shall find to attempt the paradoxical task of fixing him, a living person, on the printed page.

Some of the very best-known figures in modern history, especially where they have become objects of a cult, are present as concrete persons of extraordinary definiteness and fixity of feature in the minds of all of us. Washington, Lincoln, Goethe, Bismarck, Napoleon, Gladstone are parts of our sensory life, can be summoned before us by the mere shutting of the eyes. True, the choice of a single portrait, like the Stuart Washington, and even more the concentration upon traits which have proved useful as patriotic propaganda, no doubt explain the vividness of our mental pictures of these men. Now Talleyrand, if he has become a lay figure at all, has become such not as a hero but as a villain, and for reasons no doubt clear to sociologists and psychologists, we simply do not see our villains as clearly as we do our heroes. Had Talleyrand fitted better into the purposes of important groups in nineteenth-century France, someone—say a clever minister of education—would have singled out a good ennobling portrait, like the one Ary Scheffer did of him in old age, added a few appropriate tags, given it circulation in the proper channels, and in a short while the thousand agencies which distribute through society that portion of our social income commonly labeled "intellectual," "artistic" and the like, would have made Talleyrand a French folk-hero. As it is, Talleyrand in the flesh is as Protean and uncertain a figure as Talleyrand the *politique et moraliste.*

There are portraits enough of him, and in his prime. Gérard and Prud'hon, both court painters of the highest reputation in the Empire, painted him. Several prints and several anonymous drawings show us the Bishop of Autun and the Foreign Minister of the Directory. The trouble is that so few of these portraits look alike. Literary description is notoriously inaccurate and subjective, and one would give a good many bright, possibly even profound, phrases like that of Arnault, who described Talleyrand in 1789 as "an angel's face lighted with a devil's spirit," for a few details of the kind appearing on a passport.

Talleyrand was, we know, of about middle height, well-proportioned, with deformed right foot not especially conspicuous—indeed, the caricaturists make the *left* foot misshapen fully as often as the right. Neither in coloration nor in feature was he at all "Latin" or "Mediterranean." He was not indeed quite "Nordic" either, but he would pass muster in either England or Germany as a not eccentric national type. A snub nose, not undignifiedly snub, but just alertly *retroussé,* is the trait which most observers pick out, and which most portraits confirm. Prud'hon, however, in a very formal portrait of Talleyrand in the robes of a vice-grand-elector of the Empire, endows him with an almost Roman nose. Literary description—alas, all such description is inevitably literary!—gives him a sardonic mouth, a thin mouth turned up in a leer, a reticent mouth. Actually there is a portrait now in the possession of Count Stanislas de Castellane which shows a mouth almost cherubic, certainly full and appreciative of the world's delights. Upon bushy eyebrows all are agreed, and on the portentous bushiness they attained in the old man.

Talleyrand is, then, as his countrymen would put it, as difficult to seize *au physique qu'au morale.* His gift of being all things to all men has here served him ill. We cannot summon his image before us. It is clear that his features were not ill-formed, nor his frame ill-proportioned. Unquestionably, however, his interlocutors rarely had a chance to observe his features in natural repose. What gave Talleyrand a hold over most people he thought it worth his while to seek a hold over was his ability to bring out in his features, his voice, his bearing, the great intellectual and artistic gifts he undoubtedly possessed. He had the restrained animation which the century of Reason sought as its goal. The courtly virtues of politeness, moderation, sense of hierarchy, feeling for social ritual, he had acquired in his youth. And upon these formal virtues his free intelligence played, and brought them to life in a century and in a society which denied them. Talleyrand had that quality which many modern Americans have desired and sought for by the pathetic shortcuts of democracy, so that the squeamishly literate have no word left for it—not charm, not personal magnetism, not even sex appeal.

This intellectual animation of his features was all the more effective in contrast to the studied calm which he cultivated in repose. Talleyrand deliberately aimed at what we call a "poker face," and anecdote after anecdote shows how well he attained his aim. We have already recounted Murat's remark about the impassivity attributed to him in the hypothetical case of a very undignified kick. Napoleon once made him the butt of a passionate tirade in the presence of other dignitaries. The Emperor screeched and swore and grew purple with anger, real or assumed. Talleyrand's expression never changed. Only, when the meeting had broken up, and the Emperor gone, he turned to a colleague and remarked quietly: "What a pity that so great a man should be so ill bred!" This mask he no doubt deliberately made slightly cynical, certainly detached from the heat of the struggle, superior, aloof. He was well aware of the fact that, especially in practical affairs, the successful man conforms as much as possible to what people expect of him. One must not too openly defy eternal simplicities. A really shy movie star, a playboy Sanskrit scholar, a French Carrie Nation, or an open-hearted diplomatist are felt by the most eccentric of us to be contradictions in terms. Talleyrand's mask was assumed partly with a view to his profession. His rare—and studied—outpourings would be all the more effective in the conduct of negotiations in contrast with his customary, and equally studied, aloofness.

Beneath the mask there was probably no tortured soul. Talleyrand, said the historian Sorel, was the least romantic of men, and certainly he gave no sign of affliction over the problems of appearance and reality. But beneath the mask he, like all decent men, put on for public life, there was the much less mysterious and less mystifying man of domestic routine. Talleyrand, though he never attained legal fatherhood, was very much of a *père de famille.* The physical setting for his domestic life was indeed rather grandiose for the exercise of the simple virtues. As Minister of Foreign Relations he lived in a great *hôtel* of the old aristocracy, situated in the rue du Bac, with an interminable series of wax-floored *salons* ("one sees," said Talleyrand of a Napoleonic parvenu, "that he is not used to walking on *parquet*"), with a *cour d'honneur* and a Corinthian façade. Later he bought a town house on the rue St. Florentin, next to the formidable palaces which under the names of Hôtel Crillon and the Ministère de la Marine, still front the Place de la Concorde. Talleyrand's Paris home is today the *Hôtel du Baron Edouard de Rothschild,* a home quite fit for a millionaire. In 1803, Talleyrand acquired for a country estate the Renaissance château of Valençay in Berry, on the edge of the great Touraine region, and now, along with Chambord, Chenonceaux, Blois, Amboise and the rest, one of the places a tourist *must* see. Valençay was a princely estate, with outbuildings, park, farmlands, and Talleyrand lived on the scale of the great eighteenth-century Whig lords, a Bedford at Woburn or a Marlborough at Blenheim. The great gallery measured nearly two hundred feet in length; there was a *donjon,* a library of 15,000 volumes, a chapel.

Yet in all this lordly splendor Talleyrand found place for the simpler virtues of domestic life. In these surroundings, he unbent as much as he could unbend—say again, as much as an English duke could unbend. He liked a quiet game of whist, with old and familiar partners; he read a good deal, and rather on the serious side, history, memoirs, politics, travel; music and the plastic arts apparently did not greatly move him, though he preserved a gentlemanly awareness of what was going on about him in these fields. One of the more surprising anecdotes about Talleyrand tells how greatly moved he was by a first reading of Lamartine's *Méditations*, now consecrated in the text-books as one of the starting points of French romanticism. In general, Talleyrand's tastes were those of the age of Prose and Reason, and he had a temperamental dislike for violent innovations in the arts. But that surprisingly open mind of his could always be called on. Lamartine was no Dadaist after all, and furthermore the anecdote emphasizes less Talleyrand's emotion than his prediction that the young man would go far. He was quite right. In the art of eating and drinking he measured up to the highest standards of his race. An Anglo-Saxon visitor was greatly disappointed with the brilliant Talleyrand; he made no epigrams, destroyed no reputations, but commented at length, and in his visitor's opinion with a most disgusting air of seriousness, about everything he ate and drank.

He had a good deal of small talk, and in small gatherings would take part in the give and take of trivialities. But, unless he were with his most intimate friends, he said very little indeed and would keep silent for long periods, unless he were sure that what he said would be striking, memorable, worthy of the Prince de Talleyrand. Here again, many who met him casually in large gatherings were disappointed with his silences, his failure to live up to his reputation. At any moment, however, if he thought it worth his while, he could summon the nervous energy necessary to win people over. Queen Hortense of Holland met him at Mainz on his way to join the Emperor in Berlin, and wrote in her Memoirs, "I had often asked myself how M. de Talleyrand could be considered so clever, when he showed so little cleverness. For years I had seen him come into the *salon* at La Malmaison with a cold, nonchalant air, dragging his lame foot, leaning on the first chair he found, and barely nodding a greeting. Rarely did he say a word to me. At Mainz, on the contrary, he went out of his way to pay me attention. I was surprised, even flattered, for the attentions of a man who pays few attentions are all the more agreeable, and I am convinced that his great reputation as a clever man derives more from the little he says, and says very well indeed, than from anything remarkable he does. . . . The attraction which he possesses, and which is great, is due in good part to the vanity of others. I was caught myself. The day when he deigns to speak to you, he has already become amiable, and you are almost ready to love him, once he has asked how you are feeling." Her Majesty, born Hortense de Beauharnais, and not by nature majestic, perhaps reveals even more about herself in this passage than about Talleyrand. But it is an interesting confirmation of his ability to win people over.

Early in the new century Talleyrand began to take an annual "cure" at the modest watering-place of Bourbon l'Archambault. Here he appears at his most modest and simple, seems for a moment to have cast off the cares of office and even the need to pose. He would meet the local gentry, merchants, and professional men at the level of pleasant, natural intercourse, and do the things the other "patients" did. He was, for a time, a very good advertisement for the town, and the town was grateful to him. His name was cherished in Bourbon l'Archambault long after it had become, in most of France, a symbol of infamy. To the peasants on his estate, and to the townspeople of Valençay, he seemed more remote, though here too he left the memory of a kindly man.

By the far the most surprising thing in the record of Talleyrand's private life at this time is his marriage. In September, 1802, he was united, by purely civil ceremony, to his mistress *la belle Indienne*. Madame Grand had in 1798 secured a French divorce from her English husband on grounds of desertion. Talleyrand, after a good deal of tortuous negotiation, had obtained from Pope Pius VII a brief reconciling him with the Church, and another authorizing him to return to civil life. The canon law herein involved is extremely subtle. During the negotiations for the Concordat, the religious peace with the Papacy finally achieved by Bonaparte in 1802, the French had attempted to insert the clause: "Ecclesiastics who have entered the bonds of marriage since their consecration or who have, *by other acts,* notoriously renounced the ecclesiastical state, will return to the ranks of ordinary citizens, and will be admitted as such to lay communion." Talleyrand was certainly one of the prime instigators of this clause, though one can hardly accept Cardinal Mathieu's phrase, *la clause de Madame Grand,* as more than churchmanly malice. The traditions of the Papacy forbade acceptance of a clause which ran so evidently counter to the provisions of canon law. Priesthood is literally indelible, for the miraculous power the priest has of God is like God himself, beyond change. At most, papal dispensation can permit a priest to retire to private life, to maintain his miraculous powers in suspension. But this priest may do nothing to soil his sacred self. He may not marry. And as for a bishop! Pius VII therefore refused any blanket clause absolving all ecclesiastics no matter what their violation of their oaths had been, but as a special and extreme concession he did by pure grace pardon sub-deacons, deacons, and secular priests who had married or otherwise renounced their state. Regular clergy and bishops were not included in this grace. Talleyrand succeeded no better in purely private and personal negotiations. One by one the canon lawyers demolished the cases he had hopefully set up as analogous to his own, and confronted him with the fact, final certainly to the ecclesiastical temperament, that in the whole eighteen centuries of the Church's life on earth, no bishop had been permitted to return to lay life and to marry.

Just why Talleyrand should want to marry, and in particular to marry Madame Grand, is not wholly clear. The common explanation is no doubt substantially valid. The Consulate was a government dedicated with a good deal of display to the task of substituting law and order for the shocking, and much exaggerated, disorders of the Directory. Napoleon's seizure of power had, in years still so close to 1789, to be related somehow to Virtue, if not to Liberty, Equality, Fraternity. As a matter of fact, not even our modern dictators neglect the benefits of an alliance with Virtue; this is, as one might expect, particularly true of Germany and of the economic Calvinists of Soviet Russia. The Directory had certainly seen among the new ruling classes a good deal of fairly conspicuous flouting of the Ten Commandments, and especially of those Commandments regulating family life. The First Consul proposed to make the family lives of his officials a model for the country. Now Talleyrand's *liaison* with Madame Grand had been for several years an absolutely public affair, and Madame Grand commonly received at social functions in the rue du Bac. Already the wives of some of the new bureaucrats had cut her publicly, and protested loudly against this scandalous relationship. Madame de Rémusat asserts that Napoleon ordered Talleyrand to put Madame Grand out of the house, and only relented at Josephine's intercession. The two women were, indeed, at least as closely related as Judy O'Grady and the Colonel's lady. The First Consul made as a condition of yielding to Josephine that marriage integrate Talleyrand's household with the virtuous official society of the Consulate.

There are several reasons why Talleyrand might have

been tempted to put his mistress away rather than to marry her. He had not yet succeeded in getting papal consent to marriage, and it was already pretty clear he never would get this consent. Marriage might cut him off forever from the Church, and certainly would prevent his immediate reconciliation with it. Again Madame Grand, though lovely, *était de ces femmes qu'on n'épouse pas.* Moreover, she was edging towards forty. Talleyrand was always proud of his name, and he must have hesitated before conferring it upon a plebeian. He is silent upon the subject in his *Memoirs,* and we are again reduced to conjecture. But conjecture is not necessarily a faulty kind of knowledge; it is often better than some kinds of certitude if only we remember what it is.

Madame Grand was still very appetizing. In the famous portrait by Madame Vigée-Lebrun, though she appears conventionally sentimental, almost chaste, with eyes upturned to Heaven, Cupid's-bow lips, blond hair set off by delicate blues, suitably enraptured by the song she is about to sing, she is clearly one of Eve's daughters. There is a touch of the Greuze milkmaid about her; and the milkmaids of Greuze are among the most lewdly innocent—or innocently lewd—products of man's imagination. She was, it is true, extremely stupid, and in public, rather bird-like and silly. Stories of her lack of *esprit* are almost as numerous as stories of her husband's ample fund of it. The story that, asked where she came from, she would reply *"Je suis d'Inde"* (*dinde* is the feminine of turkey, and also slang for a very stupid woman), has a made-to-order sound. Even less likely is the anecdote which relates how Talleyrand told her that Denon, the famous traveler, was coming to dinner, and that he would leave one of Denon's books for her to read so that she might have something to talk with him about; how somehow or other Madame de Talleyrand got hold of the wrong book and read *Robinson Crusoe* instead; how she asked the astonished Denon what became of his man Friday! Horace Walpole tells the same story of an abbé thirty years earlier, a fact which rather lessens the likelihood of its being true of Madame de Talleyrand. If we need not believe all these stories, however, we must still believe that all the world was not wrong, and that the lady was not as intelligent as she was beautiful.

It seems likely that in 1802 Talleyrand was still very much in love. He would probably have preferred not to marry. But Napoleon's position was firm, and Talleyrand never left office when he could help it. He might have sent Madame Grand away for the look of things, and maintained a secret *liaison* with her. But Talleyrand had reached an age when such romantic goings-on would have seemed a most awkward and unpleasant labor. In fact, he had settled down to family life, and his habits were too well formed for him to give them up. Celibacy would have been impossible, and he is said to have rejected indignantly an idea of Napoleon's that he complete his reconciliation with the Church and accept a Cardinal's hat. Under the circumstances, he could hardly have hoped, as former Bishop of Autun, to marry a lady of noble birth. Moreover, if Madame Grand behaved the way such ladies are supposed to behave, she had long been suggesting the desirability of marriage; there is, indeed, some evidence that she had been quite articulate on the matter. There was no way out but a *mésalliance* and without any fuss he took that way out. Long afterwards, when he was very old, and, for Talleyrand, very respectable, his niece asked him why he had made this strange marriage. "I cannot really give you any satisfactory explanation," he replied. "It happened during a period of general disorder. In those days one didn't attach much importance to anything, neither to one's self, nor to others; one had no society, no family; everything was done with the greatest carelessness, through war and the fall of empires. You do not know how far men can go astray in the great epochs of social decomposition."

Catherine Worlée was soon to be much more than Madame de Talleyrand. Napoleon had in 1802 made himself Consul for life and in 1804 he took the last step, and became hereditary Emperor of the French. Soon a new aristocracy was created around the new throne—and very new most of it was. That the Duchess of Leipzig had once been a laundress all the world knows since *Madame Sans-Gène* was the hit of the hour. Certainly members of the old nobility were not numerous among the new. None were more conspicuous than Talleyrand, no more than the disinherited younger son of a count in the old régime, but in the new Prince of Benevento, a title taken from the Italian conquests of the French. As a special hierarchy of dignitaries of the Empire was also set up, Talleyrand became vice-grand elector, and as such not merely *altesse,* but *altesse sérénissime.* Abbé de Périgord, Evêque d'Autun, M. de Talleyrand, le citoyen Ch.-M. Talleyrand—even the "de" disappears in 1797–99—M. de Talleyrand again, and now *son altesse sérénissime* Charles-Maurice, Prince de Bénévent—a long roll, with more lives to come. The Princesse de Bénévent was delighted with her new title. Talleyrand himself was not unduly elated. Von Gagern reports a talk with him at Warsaw, in which he asked to be called *M. de Talleyrand,* and not *Votre Altesse,* and remarked about his official title, "I am less, and perhaps I am more."

Talleyrand never lost his pride of race. He was all the more consciously a Talleyrand-Périgord because most of his family held that he had done things no Talleyrand-Périgord could do. His mother and his uncle, the Archbishop of Rheims, remained obstinately *émigrés* even under

Napoleon. His brothers drifted back to France, attracted largely by the success of Charles-Maurice. Talleyrand's own aristocratic poise, and the reputation of his house, were the envy and admiration of the new nobility, who were always paying him court. Napoleon clearly valued him, among other reasons, because he served as a link between the new and the old, between Fointainebleau and Versailles, and because, so Napoleon thought, he might attract others of his kind into the imperial system.

With the new security and apparent permanence brought by Consulate and Empire, Talleyrand set to work to build firmly the fortunes of his family. Badly treated though he had been by his parents, handicapped by the impossibility, or, in view of Madame Grand's origins, the undesirability, of having legitimate children of his own, he still displayed intense family loyalty, and a strong desire to make the Talleyrands an even greater and more powerful family. He had great hopes for his nephew Archambaud, son of his younger brother Archambaud, who should have been head of the house. Archambaud died in 1808, unmarried. Talleyrand at once set about marrying off his other nephew, Edmond, younger brother of Archambaud. Thanks to the benevolent interest of Emperor Alexander of Russia, a very rich Baltic German heiress came to add wealth and distinction to the line. Dorothée de Biren, Princesse de Courlande, had set herself for higher game than a French count, even if he had great prospects. Her mother, the Duchesse de Courlande, was wholly won over by Talleyrand—she is, indeed, one of the innumerable mistresses gossip has given him. Dorothée yielded to the Emperor and her mother, and married Edmond in 1809. From that marriage is descended the present Duc de Talleyrand-Périgord, fifth of the line. This Duke was married in 1908 to Anna Gould, previously divorced from his cousin Boni de Castellane, also descended from Edmond de Talleyrand-Périgord and Dorothée de Courlande. Their only son, Charles-Jason-Howard de Talleyrand-Périgord, Prince de Sagan, died in 1929. In the male line, then, the elder branch of the Talleyrands is on the point of extinction, and the chances are that the family name will not survive the twentieth century. Charles-Maurice failed to perpetuate his family. He remains its one great man.

II

TALLEYRAND is one of the very few men of Imperial France not wholly overshadowed by Napoleon. So highly did Napoleon estimate him that at St. Helena he coupled his name with Fouché's and remarked that if he had only hanged the two of them, he would still be on the throne of France. The relation between the Emperor and his Minister of Foreign Relations was not simply an official one, but a personal one, a relation which at one time may almost have been friendship, and which over some dozen years, gradually became enmity. Talleyrand himself wrote in 1816, "I was fond of Napoleon; I was attached to his person notwithstanding his faults—when he first appeared on the scene of the world, I felt attracted towards him by the irresistible spell inherent to great genius. I was sincerely grateful to him for the favors he had bestowed on me. Besides, why should I fear to say it? I had shared in his glory, which reflected upon all those who assisted in his noble work." There is no reason to question the sincerity of this passage. The "noble work" was, of course, the building of an orderly, peaceful state on a firm authoritarian basis, something for which Talleyrand was longing in 1799; and which in the early years of the Consulate, with the Concordat, the Civil Code, the general pacification at Luné ville and Amiens, seemed well on its way to realization. Napoleon's scorn for political idealists, for doctrinaire devotees of abstract right, his skill in command, his ability to fire men with enthusiasm and energy without holding any Utopia, any Heaven on earth before them as bait, his ruthless pursuit of his own ends—all this commanded Talleyrand's sympathy and imagination. A great actor himself, Talleyrand could appreciate the somewhat different greatness of Napoleon as an actor. Nor was the young general's romantic exuberance distasteful to the sober, self-disciplined, aristocratic Talleyrand. The attraction of opposites, perhaps; the very wise have only the somewhat foolish to love. Talleyrand was at first attracted rather than repelled by the demonic, indecent energy of Napoleon, which he may well have hoped to confine to channels not socially harmful. We can, with our wisdom of after-the-fact, detect in the sound administrator of 1802 the megalomaniac of 1812, discern in the fumbling of the 18th Brumaire the stupidity of the Hundred Days. Talleyrand certainly saw through Napoleon sooner than most of his contemporaries. We need not be astonished that he had a moment of illusion. It was, perhaps, not an illusion. The Emperor may have been a being quite unrelated to the First Consul.

Napoleon, too, was fond of Talleyrand. The First Consul was as incapable of genuine metaphysical love or friendship as was his minister; both were, in conventional terms, selfish men. But Napoleon had a respect for unsentimental intelligence, and this he found in Talleyrand. He liked to be flattered, and to be skillfully flattered was an especial delight. To hear from Talleyrand after the battle of Marengo that "There has never been an empire unless it were founded on the marvellous, and here the marvellous is the true" was to receive a tribute from taste and intelligence as well as from ambition. Nor could the son of an impecunious Corsican lawyer be altogether indifferent to the fact that this praise came from a man whose ancestors had fought—at least in genealogical books—side by side with Charlemagne. Talleyrand wrote to the First Consul to thank him for restoring the Talleyrand-Périgord family property, for taking the family off the list of *émigrés,* and ended, "Permit me to borrow from the history of a celebrated friendship what a minister of Henry IV said to his master: *'Since I have been attached to your fate I have been yours, for life or death.'* " What usurper would not have been pleased at a comparison which put him on the level of the most beloved monarch of the legitimate line? Moreover, Napoleon had a full appreciation of Talleyrand's gifts as a diplomatist, and, at first, relied a good deal on his knowledge of European international relations and on his feelings for the European balance of power. Of Talleyrand's good faith he had no very high opinion; but as he told Cambacérès, "I know that he (Talleyrand) belongs to the revolutionary movement only through his misconduct; Jacobin and deserter of his own Order in the Constituent Assembly, his interest stands surety to us for him." Talleyrand indeed had no reason, in these years, to be unfaithful to his master.

That the relationship was at bottom one between master and servant seems undeniable; and since such was the nature of the relationship, it was bound to be impermanent. For Talleyrand was, to paraphrase his own words about his princely title, something more, and perhaps less, than a servant. As Napoleon's Minister of Foreign Relations, he never initiated any great measure in foreign policy. He carried out very ably indeed orders received from Napoleon. Often he was able, by intentional delay, to pare off some of the extravagances, exaggerations, impertinencies and simplicities from Napoleon's projects. For some years Napoleon's policies broadly coincided with Talleyrand's, and may indeed have been not uninfluenced by Talleyrand himself. Talleyrand wanted a peace that would set the European balance of power back in working order, with no nation so disgruntled or so elated that it would be tempted to upset that balance. The First Consul seemed not unwilling to attempt to secure such a general pacification. Talleyrand thought the energies of France might best be devoted to colonial expansion. The First Consul regained Louisiana for France, and nourished grand schemes for a French Empire which would bottle up the United States on the Atlantic seaboard. Even the soon revived struggle with England, though not consistent with Talleyrand's fundamental notions of French policy, might, it seemed, turn out well enough. As for the subsequent wars with Austria, Prussia, and Russia, not only were their fruits in Austerlitz, Jena, and Friedland most agreeable to any patriotic Frenchman, but the policy out of which they came was not too remote from the traditional French policy in Central Europe: *divide et impera.* Talleyrand could negotiate with German princelets much as Cardinal Richelieu had done—and with great private profit to himself. But by the end of 1807, the Great Empire was becoming so absurdly great that by no ingenuity could Talleyrand's policy be reconciled with that of his master. It is significant that when that time arrived, Talleyrand left the Ministry of Foreign Relations.

That was seven years after his re-entering the *hôtel* in the rue du Bac. He had soon picked up his duties at the point where he had left them off. The routine work of the Foreign Office was well done, and the higher permanent officials, especially Hauterive and La Besnardière, collaborated most effectively with their chief. The legend—which so often starts with Talleyrand as he wished to seem to be—has here gone to absurd lengths. Everything ever written or spoken by Talleyrand is claimed as the work of an underling. From the days in the National Assembly, when Des Renaudes, Chamfort, or an obscure person named Guilhe were all named as authors of the long report on education, Talleyrand had been accused of getting his work done by a group of *teinturiers*—"ghost writers," we should probably say. On his re-entrance to the Foreign Office, he composed a very sensible report on the organization of this branch of the government, a report which anticipates much modern discussion of the Civil Services, and which sketches a sensible plan for the education of experts in government. La Besnardière, of course, wrote *that* report. So with all of Talleyrand's work. But his ghostly crew must have been chosen with amazing care and luck, for they all write alike, and they all write very well. The truth is, of course, that however much Talleyrand owed to subordinates, the plan, the style, that part of his work that is art, is all his own. His desire to appear always the gentlemanly amateur—a desire prompted partly, as we have seen, by his knowledge that the world admires such amateurs, but probably also prompted by his own sharing of this admiration—this desire has been too freely granted. He really was a *faux paresseux*—a man who pretended to be lazy. The world has accepted the pretense.

Talleyrand's method of work did indeed give some appearance of truth to the rumors about his laziness. He never bothered with spade-work, but like any good executive, left such matters as fact-finding, digesting the opinions of others, and securing illustrative material to his subordinates. He spent relatively little time in his office, and was not an ostentatiously industrious person. He was careless about reading reports of subordinates, especially when they didn't interest him. But those who worked with him, those who observed him with seeing eyes, were clear that he worked very hard. He had a knack of seizing the essentials of a problem readily, and carrying the problem about with him, and returning to it at odd moments. Once his mind was made up, he would dictate four or five topics or heads, each one of which would suggest a line of investigation to clarify the problem, or hint part of a satisfactory solution. Finally, his subordinates would report back to him what they had made of these suggestions, and he would pretty completely outline in final form the report, despatch, or memorandum. The neatest phrases, the pregnant sentence or so that throws light on all the rest, are certainly Talleyrand's.

An even more important part of his work, of course, was dealing directly with individuals—the test and end of diplomacy. There can be no doubt that he distilled into this part of his work as diplomatist all his varied experience of seminary, church, *salon,* stock-market, academy and *boudoir.* Nor did he ever cease to learn about people, nor cease to train and exercise whatever in him gave him the gift of understanding and manipulating people. Like certain other forms of high art—dancing, for instance—this seems deceptively easy. Actually long hard work and a suitable natural endowment are as necessary for the great diplomatist as for the dancer. Talleyrand learned a lot from talking with all kinds of men and women. He learned perhaps quite as much from reading, for books may to a wise man be not a withdrawal from life, not distortion of life, but an incredibly effective extension of life. You must take a very, very transcendental definition of wisdom, if you deny that Talleyrand was a wise man. Certainly he was no man to subscribe to the romantic illusion that

Grau, teurer Freund, ist alle Theorie
Und grün des Lebens goldner Baum.

Talleyrand's department, whether he worked or not, at any rate ran smoothly and effectively and Napoleon's foreign policy found no obstacles, as that of the First Republic had found obstacles, in the stupidity and lack of training of its agents. Napoleon himself gave tardy justice to Talleyrand, for in the desperate days of 1814, when he was in retirement and Napoleon was trying to fight off the armies of the Great Coalition, fast closing in on Paris, the Emperor is reported as having exclaimed, "If I only had Talleyrand! He could fix things up for me even now." Talleyrand's services were, of course, dear. The period of the Consulate and Empire was the source of the great Talleyrand fortune, some of which has come down to the present, in a generation of international gentility where Talleyrand and Castellane money mixes agreeably with Gould money. Napoleon is said once to have asked his Minister where he got his great wealth, and to have received the reply: "I bought *rentes* just before the 18th Brumaire, and sold them just after"—a reply flattering to the bringer of law and order, and substantially true. Talleyrand was definitely an insider on this *coup d'état,* and gambled also during the negotiations with England in 1797. We have reasonably good proof that he managed those negotiations through his agent Maret so as to benefit from stock-market fluctuations as peace seemed nearer or further away. Napoleon himself rewarded his Minister directly and generously, and the emoluments of his ministry, his office of vice-grand elector, and his Neapolitan principality of Benevento together made a sum which served to meet current expenses. The methods which had failed so dismally with the virtuous Messrs. Pinckney, Marshall and Gerry were much more successful with other suitors for the favor of France. Talleyrand grew very rich from the devoted offerings of his German friends, who sought his intercession on their behalf in the new territorial arrangements in Germany. Even Livingston, the American who concluded the treaty of September, 1800, with France is said to have been obliged to conform to the customs of the time. The peace is reported to have brought Talleyrand 2,000,000 francs. His speculations in the market were not always successful, but he took his losses with the self-control of the born gambler. His gains far outnumbered his losses, however, and he had, as early as 1807, built up a princely fortune. It was a fortune built up by means certainly not compatible with the purest of Christian—or Buddhist, or Confucian—codes. It was built up indirectly, no doubt, out of much human suffering. But Talleyrand's methods were not those of fraud or downright thievery. Even on purely Christian standards, the Talleyrand fortune would compare favorably in its origin with the Astor fortune, or with what used to be the Kreuger fortune.

In the work of "reconstruction," the "noble work" which marks the first few years after the 18th Brumaire, Talleyrand had his full share. Actually much of the work was merely adding the final touches to the achievements of the National Assembly, the Convention, and the Directory, but the Napoleonic legend has had such success that even those who dislike Napoleon feel obliged to admit that he saved France from "anarchy" and destruction. Quite apart from the *clause de Madame Grand,* Talleyrand was directly interested in the Concordat, and, especially in very difficult preliminary stages, did a great deal to further the reconciliation between France and the Papacy. He managed from Paris the negotiations at Lunéville, which in 1801 brought peace with Austria, and those at Amiens, which in 1802 brought peace with England. The Lunéville settlement was hardly more than a confirmation of the earlier peace of Campoformio. Austria retained Venice, and was encouraged to look towards Balkan expansion. In Germany, or rather in the Germanies, Lunéville made evident to all the practical dissolution of the old Holy Roman Empire, and began a scramble for power in the reorganized Germany in which France had a deciding voice and from which Talleyrand gained a great deal of money. For over two years the Germans debated this consolidation of their territory, and when in 1803 by the *Reichsdeputationshauptschluss*—a name which in itself renders the deed important—the scramble was momentarily over, Germany had been reduced to some thirty-odd sovereign states instead of several hundred, and was ready for the further consolidations of the nineteenth and twentieth centuries.

On the whole, there was little in this peace of Lunéville to which Talleyrand could object. The British peace was less satisfactory to him. On the British side, it had been signed by Addington, Prime Minister by accident of parliamentary jockeying, and a man without prestige. England surrendered to France and to her allies all the world-conquests which the British navy had made possible, save Trinidad, ceded by Spain, and Ceylon, ceded by the Batavian Republic, as Holland was now called by these neoclassic admirers of Roman greatness. France was to give Malta, seized during the Egyptian expedition, back to the Order of the Knights of Malta. Talleyrand used to say that he would gladly have given Malta outright to the British, if he only could have had the signature of Pitt or Fox, instead of that of the insignificant Addington. He must have felt that neither the English Tories nor his master Bonaparte really meant to carry out the treaty sincerely. On paper, however, the Treaty of Amiens did bring the great rivals into some sort of equilibrium, and France had gained English consent to French ownership of Belgium and the Rhineland—something which we are told in the text-books is almost contrary to a natural law.

With the creation of the Legion of Honor, with the building up of a new hierarchy of civil servants, with the setting up of the new nobility and the marshals—in short, with the more obviously conservative aspects of Napoleon's work, Talleyrand seems to have been pretty much in sympathy. He did write to a friend that he found the new dignitaries of the Empire a bit ridiculous, and that the title *Altesse sérénissime* seemed ludicrous applied to the new Arch-Treasurer, Lebrun, who had been a consulting lawyer in Paris. "*Altesse,* which is a title emanating from sovereignty, doesn't even make sense—but it's done, and whatever is done, must be maintained. This should be the doctrine of all who are attached to the present government." There is a story that someone, clearly unaware that the Age of Reason was over, protested to Bonaparte that the Legion of Honor and the other dignities were but baubles. "But," replied the Emperor, "it is with baubles that men are governed." Talleyrand would doubtless have agreed with this, though he apparently took a good deal of care not to go on record as having committed himself to such Machiavellian *opinions.*

With the most Machiavellian of all the deeds of these earlier years of Napoleon's ascendancy, Talleyrand's name is very ambiguously connected. In March, 1804, a French raiding-party commanded by General Ordener violated the neutrality of Baden, seized the Duc d'Enghien, last scion of the House of Condé, and brought him to Paris, where, with hardly a pretence of a hearing, he was shot as the center of an *émigré* plot to assassinate the First Consul. It is now as certain as anything can be in the kind of historical investigation that must deal with plots, spies, and secret societies, that the duke was innocent—innocent, certainly, of any specific intention of procuring the assassination of Bonaparte, though no doubt involved in various cross-currents of *émigré* agitation. It is even more certain that the fate of the Duc d'Enghien discouraged further plotting against Bonaparte and that it cut off his supporters from any possibility of bridging the way to a Bourbon restoration. Napoleon, it was clear forever, now, was no General Monk. This act was, then, politically profitable to Napoleon, though it has ever since been condemned, even by Bonapartists, as a shocking violation of international and moral law. Napoleon with characteristic courage took the onus on himself, and save for a few petulant outbursts at St. Helena, steadily maintained that he was responsible for the death of the Duc d'Enghien. That would perhaps be enough for some people—lawyers, for instance—but certainly not for historians. Many of them, including Talleyrand's "definitive" biographer, have put much of the responsibility on Talleyrand. Lacour-Gayet quotes with approval Molé's judgment: "The Duc d'Enghien perished as the result of an intrigue of Talleyrand and Fouché, who sought to lead Napoleon on and put him in their power by a crime which would make him their accomplice and after which he could not reproach them with their past activities as revolutionaries." Even M. Jean Hanoteau, the latest historian to deal with the affair, writes rather ambiguously in his introduction to Caulaincourt's *Memoirs* of "Talleyrand and the real culprits." His tone leads one to suspect that he would like to have written Talleyrand and the *other* real culprits, but didn't quite feel he had support in the facts.

Talleyrand in the first draft of his *Memoirs* passes briefly over the affair, though not without achieving a caustic ending. "The assassination of the Duc d'Enghien, committed solely to assure the support, by putting himself in their ranks, of those whom the death of Louis XVI made fear any power not coming from themselves, this assassination, I say could not be excused or forgiven, and never has been; therefore Bonaparte was reduced to boasting about it." But in 1823 the Duc de Rovigo, who had in 1804 been simply General Savary, having been accused of complicity in the death of the Duc d'Enghien, published a pamphlet in which he accused Talleyrand of egging Bonaparte on to the arrest of Enghien. Talleyrand thereupon wrote an appendix, which appears in volume III of his *Memoirs.* He admits that, as Minister of Foreign Affairs, he wrote on March 10 and again on March 11 letters to the Baron von Edelsheim, Foreign Minister of the Elector of Baden, the first notifying him of the suspicious attitude of Enghien and his circle at Ettenheim and of another group of *émigrés* at Offenburg and the second quite simply describing the raid as a *fait accompli:* "The First Consul has thought it necessary to send two small detachments to Offenburg and to Ettenheim, there to seize the instigators of a crime which, by its very nature, puts those convicted of participating in it outside international law." He had, then, more to do with the affair than appears from the first draft of the *Memoirs.* But we have only the word of his enemies that he was more than an agent of his master Napoleon in the seizure of the Duc d'Enghien. There is very good authority for the statement that a council of government was held well before the actual seizure of the Duke, and that Talleyrand took part in that council. Cambacérès unquestionably attempted to dissuade Bonaparte from the contemplated raid on Ettenheim. There is no evidence that Talleyrand also attempted to prevent the raid. He was certainly not a cruel man, but there is nothing in his character that would make him recoil from a deed of violence if he thought such a deed politically profitable to himself and to France. Here indeed is the surest indication that his part was a passive one. He did not produce the famous tag—"worse than a crime, a blunder," but the implications of this epigram are thoroughly in accord with his own feelings about politics. We cannot know for sure whether or not Talleyrand urged the seizure of Enghien on Napoleon. Talleyrand and Napoleon are agreed that the initiative and responsibility are Napoleon's. Savary, Chateaubriand, Molé, and a good many other enemies of Talleyrand right down to Lacour-Gayet are agreed that the project owes its beginning, and a good deal of its carrying out, to Talleyrand. We can but choose. Perhaps Napoleon's weight might be allowed to swing the balance?

III

M. PIERRE Bertrand has published a volume of over three hundred letters written by Talleyrand to Napoleon from 1800 to 1809. Most of these letters are colorless enough, filled with the details of administration, and pretty much the kind of letter a good civil servant would write to a superior. In general, they confirm the fact that Napoleon regarded his Foreign Minister as a servant, and that Talleyrand had to adjust himself to the situation. M. E. Dard, however, in his recent book, *Napoléon et Talleyrand,* points out that the relationship was certainly a more equal one than tradition and Lacour-Gayet have insisted, and that Talleyrand was constantly fencing with Napoleon on important matters. There is one long letter, dated from Strasbourg in October, 1805, which forms a striking exception, and which may be taken as a starting-point from which the breach between the two men steadily widened. In this letter Talleyrand not merely ventures to advise the Emperor, but sketches a grand master-scheme of French foreign policy.

In 1804, the peace of Amiens had been broken. Who broke it is not here our concern. On the surface of things, neither the French nor the English had lived up very loyally to its provisions, and both sides—or at any rate important leaders on both sides—had long wanted war. England was supreme at sea, France on land. Direct contact between the two rivals was difficult, and for months the "war" went on quite harmlessly. Napoleon gathered a huge army at Boulogne, and on clear days the French could see the white cliffs of hated England across the Channel. But the "Army of England" stayed in Boulogne. In the meantime, Austria, discontented with her losses at Lunéville, worked on by British agents, was restive. The young Emperor of Russia, Alexander, was restive too; he had been none too pleased by the accession of a lawyer's son to the sacred name of "Emperor"; besides the balance of power was clearly destroyed by recent French gains. Napoleon's assumption of the Iron Crown of Lombardy as King of Italy was the last straw. England assembled still another coalition composed of Sweden, Russia, Austria, and England, and, with Napoleon himself taking active steps to bring on, rather than to avoid, continental war, the rest was easy. The European pacification achieved by the First Consul had not withstood a single year of the Empire.

What followed is one of the marvels of military history. With beautiful precision Napoleon swung his armies from the Channel and the North Sea until, with perfect synchronizing, they met between the Austrian General Mack and his capital, and forced his capitulation at Ulm on October 17, 1805. That same day Talleyrand, who had followed more slowly after his master, wrote from Strasbourg a letter based on the assumption of French victory. "When your Majesty left Strasbourg, one thing alone tempered my regrets. It was the certainty that your Majesty was marching to victory." France has, then, beaten Austria. What next? There are, says Talleyrand, four great European powers—for Prussia, raised to artificial heights by the genius of Frederick the Great, is not a first-rate power. These are France, England, Austria and Russia. France is the greatest of these, both in men and in money, but she is not sufficiently strong to stand against the three others. In general, Austria and England both touch upon French territory and French interests so closely that their natural tendency is to ally against her. Russia is quite likely to be drawn into such a system, leaving France only the alternative of alliance with Prussia, not in itself an adequate guarantee of peace. On the contrary, the last fifteen years have seen Europe in constant turmoil, with nothing like a stable system of alliances.

Talleyrand proposes that Napoleon treat Austria very magnanimously at the approaching peace conference. All physical contact between Austria and the new France—that is, old France with the Kingdom of Italy, the Left Bank of the Rhine, and Belgium—should cease. Venice should be taken from Austria, and made into an independent republic. Austria should give up her Suabian lands and the Tyrol, which should then enter into the French system of client-states. *But,* Austria should be made territorially greater than ever by annexing at the expense of Turkey the Balkan lands of Moldavia and Wallachia, Bessarabia, and northern Bulgaria. These lands are but nominally dependent on the Sultan of Turkey, and will fall away soon of their own accord if we do not hasten the process. Austria will thus face eastward in the future, instead of westward and southward; will therefore be the rival of Russia rather than the rival of France. *L'Autriche, ennemie naturelle des Russes, aura pour alliée naturelle la France.* France can then consolidate her hegemony in Italy, from which the

Germans will be forever excluded. England will no longer find allies on the continent, or will find only Russia, not in any way useful to her against France. Russia herself may well be discouraged by Austrian expansion in the Balkans, and turn instead towards the interior of Asia. Europe may then enjoy peace for a while.

This is the kind of scheme with which any amateur of diplomatic history may easily find fault. It assumes perhaps undue passivity on the part of the Sultan. It assumes that Prussia will forever—or for some time—remain a second-rate power. It is, of course, wholly unaware of rising "Nationalism" in the Balkans. It smells of eighteenth-century chancelleries, of other grand schemes of Kaunitz, Hertzberg, Alberoni, Belleisle. It assumes that Austria will, in 1805, forget Germany and Italy and turn to the Balkans. All this may be granted, but the plan is no less interesting as a piece of Talleyrand's mind. It shows how completely he belongs to that school of equilibrium politicians of the end of the old régime, which, thanks to the work of Srbik on Metternich, now appear as something quite different from the ogres of liberal tradition they once were. Talleyrand wanted peace, not nobly, perhaps, as doctrinaire pacifists want peace, but with all the force of his worldly and unheroic temperament.

Madame de Rémusat reports a conversation in which Talleyrand outlined his program for the Emperor very neatly: "Bring back religion, morals, order to France, applaud English civilization while restraining English political ambitions, fortify his frontiers by the Confederation of the Rhine, make of Italy a kingdom independent of Austria and *of himself,* keep the Tsar at home by creating that natural barrier which Poland offers; these should have been the eternal designs of the Emperor, and to these led every one of the treaties I signed." His plan in some ways is astonishingly like that which Bismarck carried through successfully during twenty years of peace. Bismarck, too, encouraged the Austrians to expand south and east into the Balkans, looked with favor on French colonial expansion, nourished Russian and Austrian rivalry in the Balkans, but only to the point where such rivalry helped tie each to Germany—maintained, in general, that extraordinary equilibrium between a thousand conflicting desires which the subtlest of mathematicians cannot yet express in a formula.

Bismarck's system—which is essentially Talleyrand's—depended for its success partly on the existence of extra-European lands of weaker or inferior peoples for which the great nations could contend, even more, however, on the existence of one powerful nation to direct and maintain this equilibrium, to keep the others scrambling not too desperately outside Europe, a nation content with its existing territory, content with its existing supply of such imponderables as "prestige," an umpire-nation, in short. To waive for the moment the important problem of the relation between what a nation wants and what certain statesmen want, it is clear that Bismarck, once he had carried through his three great wars, was content with the rôle of umpire. It is equally clear that Napoleon, once he had helped bring France to its "natural" boundaries—Rhine, Alps, Mediterranean, Pyrenees, Atlantic—was not in the least contented. Few outside France can accept Sorel's famous thesis that both as First Consul and as Emperor, Napoleon was really fighting a "defensive" war made necessary by the Director's policy of expanding France to the natural frontiers. The long road from Marengo to Moscow was not laid out as early as 1797, though even if it had been so laid out, Talleyrand's advice to give up the road entirely was surely no less sound. Napoleon, however, was no prosaic child of the eighteenth century, no devotee of Reason, Common Sense,

Golden Mean, no spiritual contemporary of Franklin, Voltaire, Walpole or Fleury. Napoleon was at least as mad as William Blake. Napoleon was Prometheus, Alexander, Cæsar, Charlemagne. Napoleon was, indeed, slightly beyond mere words, and we had better not join M. Elie Faure in the attempt to catch up to him with words.

Napoleon, though impressed with the clarity and the daring of Talleyrand's elaborate report, turned aside for grander schemes of his own. The victor of Austerlitz would have no petty eighteenth-century peace. "The order and the peace I dreamed of for Europe," as he later put it at St. Helena, would be imposed on Europe by universal conquest, a *pax gallica* even greater than the *pax romana*. Perhaps the First Consul had still operated within the traditional lines of French diplomacy, had really wished to make a peace resting on traditional balances; the Emperor had gone on to nobler, or madder, at any rate, more unorthodox, notions of what Europe should look like. The Emperor, like so many fighters, had his dream of peace. Napoleon the man of deeds would, by that well-known path along which extremes meet, join in the unachievement of universal peace the man of words, Woodrow Wilson. He did not even take part of Talleyrand's advice, and treat Austria magnanimously. Napoleon was not, in the moral sense, magnanimous; magnanimous from policy he did not think it worth his while to be. Austria was deprived of her Italian lands, despoiled of even more of her western lands than Talleyrand had advised, but far from being compensated in the east, was left shorn and humiliated; an example of the futility of rebellion against the new Charlemagne.

Talleyrand supervised the negotiations of this Treaty of Pressburg, concluded December 26, 1805. But from this moment may be traced the break between Talleyrand and

Napoleon. The master-servant relation could not have lasted. In the first place, Talleyrand, for all his ability to adapt himself to circumstances, and to other human beings seen as part of circumstances, was not made for a servant. He had much too much plain ordinary pride, or vanity, or self-esteem. That little grain of true Christian humility contained in the proud phrase *servus servorum Dei* was quite beyond Talleyrand's nature. Humility he never had. More important, Talleyrand's very accurate sense of what was politically probable warned him quite early that the Napoleonic Empire could not possibly stand. He was no man to follow a master through to the well-earned defeat. So much hero-worship has come into our awareness of Napoleon, and so many of our sentiments of loyalty are attached to persons rather than to abstractions, that Talleyrand's desertion of his master and Emperor somehow seems more shocking than his desertion of a republic embodied in the Directory. Myth has given Napoleon virtue, and denied it to the Directory. Moreover, even sober historians, being mostly men of books, have an admiration for the earth-rending Napoleon. Historians have treated Talleyrand's desertion of Napoleon as a major treason, his desertion of the Directory as a sound bit of wisdom. The two acts seem to be much of a piece.

Finally, it is not unlikely that Talleyrand broke with Napoleon for a reason which any sound moralist ought to approve. He had certain sentiments which put a positive limit to his shifting allegiances. We may well leave to more skillful casuists the distinction between altruistic and egoistic acts. The simple fact is that Talleyrand could not have pulled the strings of foreign policy in Napoleon's fantastic Empire, any more than he could have joined in the frenzy of the Terror. There are certain heights and depths, in life as in literature, from which he was wholly shut out. A

France which included Hamburg, Savoy, and the Illyrian coast had to him simply ceased to be France, and he had no idea of what to do with such a political monstrosity. The expedition to Moscow might as well, to him, have been an expedition to the moon. Talleyrand—and this cannot be too often repeated—was not an opportunist if by that word be understood a person wholly at the mercy of the immediate event, a person wholly without his own judgments of value, wholly given over to flux and chaos. He must not be denied that final human dignity, an awareness of the fact that "impossible" is a perfectly good word in any language.

The break between the master and the unwilling servant was not immediate. Talleyrand was not, indeed, ever in complete disgrace, and to the end preserved his position as an imperial dignitary. As an active member of Napoleon's official household, his last important rôle was played at the famous interview at Erfurt between Napoleon and Alexander in the autumn of 1808. Between Pressburg and Erfurt, the Spanish affair had come to a head, and it was Napoleon's attempted absorption of Spain that made Talleyrand feel he could not continue in office. He resigned on August 9, 1807, in favor of the colorless Champagny, and after the interlude at Erfurt withdrew into very comfortable private life, from which he criticized the Emperor as openly as one could criticize the Emperor and remain at large in France.

The Spanish affair is difficult to summarize in a few paragraphs. Talleyrand himself has recounted the devious tale as neatly as possible in the fourth part of his *Memoirs*. The government of Spain had, by 1807, attained a remarkable degree of incompetence. The King, Charles IV, was in the last stages of senile decay; in his prime he had been feeble of mind and body. The Queen was a determined and ignorant woman, who had made her lover, the handsome Godoy, first Minister of the Crown. Finally, the heir to the throne was the eldest son of the King and Queen, Ferdinand, Prince of the Asturias, a young man who illustrated the workings of heredity at least as well as any Juke or Kallikak. Godoy had been in power for some fifteen years, and had acquired the title of "Prince of the Peace" after the inglorious treaty between France and Spain at Basel in 1795. The King, completely ruled by the strong-minded Queen, let Godoy have free rein. The government services were shot through with incompetence and corruption, and with intrigue. The central intrigue of all, in 1807, was the rivalry between Godoy and the Prince of the Asturias. Godoy quite rightly suspected Ferdinand of attempting to persuade his father to dismiss his Minister, and of harboring the hope of subsequently procuring his father's abdication. Ferdinand just as rightly suspected the Prince of the Peace of wishing to set himself up as a real territorial sovereign somewhere, certainly in southern Portugal and, ultimately, perhaps, in Spain itself.

The situation would have tempted a less ambitious man than Napoleon. Spain was important for Napoleon at first because through it lay the road to Portugal, and Portugal was in perpetual alliance with England—an alliance still marked by the otherwise unaccountable taste of Englishmen for port wine. Through Portugal, England had an entrance to the continent and a splendid series of harbors through which to introduce English goods. By a secret treaty signed at Fontainebleau after Talleyrand's retirement from the Ministry of Foreign Relations, Napoleon and Godoy agreed on the partition of Portugal, the southern part of which was to go to Godoy, and on the granting of permission to send French troops through Spain to occupy Portugal. Napoleon, however, clearly was not disposed to stop there.

He characteristically decided that he had better have the whole of Spain while he was about it.

The intrigue was astonishingly easy and carried on at the level of a Hollywood melodrama. After all, the Spanish royal family and Godoy *were* at about the cultural level of Hollywood. Junot brushed on into Portugal, but Dupont with 40,000 men was sent into northern and western Spain, where he was welcomed by a population which believed he had come to overthrow Godoy and set up Ferdinand. The Prince of the Peace was disliked by the Spanish people, partly because he had misgoverned them—not in itself a new thing in Spain—partly because he had been too lucky. The Prince of the Asturias, on the other hand, was the great hope of the Spanish patriots, chiefly because he was the only obvious alternative to Godoy. When the French under Murat penetrated to Madrid, the Spaniards arose, overthrew Godoy, frightened Charles IV into one of his numerous abdications, and sought to make Ferdinand king. Murat, acting in close concert with Napoleon, refused to acknowledge Ferdinand and referred the whole matter to his master for settlement. Napoleon persuaded the Spanish royal family to entrust themselves to him as arbiter in a meeting to be held on French territory at Bayonne. Here he frightened Ferdinand into abdicating in favor of his father, and tricked Charles into repeating his abdication, this time in favor of Napoleon.

For the rest of the Napoleonic supremacy, the Spanish Bourbons were in virtual captivity. Ferdinand, his brother, and his uncle, by a rather neat stroke of Napoleonic malice, were kept at Talleyrand's château at Valençay, where their various unintellectual hobbies caused a certain amount of damage to the estate. Talleyrand recounts in connection with the stay of the princes at Valençay an amusing example of Napoleon's pride. He received while at Valençay the following note from the Emperor: "Prince Ferdinand in writing to me calls me his cousin. Try and make M. de San Carlos see that this is ridiculous, and that he ought to address me simply as Sire." Ferdinand's uncle amused himself in a mild affair with the Princesse de Bénévent, now older, sillier, and definitely flattered by royal attentions. Talleyrand had tired of his wife, and we need not believe that he was greatly hurt by her infidelity. Indeed, he later expressed himself as grateful to the Spanish prince for keeping his foolish wife from mischief. There was gossip, of course, and Napoleon was soon to make use of Talleyrand's rumored cuckoldry.

It was much easier to dispose of the Spanish Bourbons than to dispose of the Spanish people. Napoleon took advantage of the abdications he had gained at Bayonne to set his eldest brother Joseph on the throne of Spain. The throne had to be supported by French soldiers, and eventually by a campaign led by Napoleon himself. Ordinary Spaniards had long disliked Frenchmen, whom they regarded as money-grubbers, materialists, indecently enterprising and ubiquitous vulgarians incapable of appreciating Castilian dignity, faith, and sense of the hierarchical fitness of things. They rose against the French with the heroic contempt for the conventions and common sense we have since come to associate with nationalism, and especially with "oppressed" nationalism, and, aided by the English, who saw at last a foothold on the continent for their small but efficient army, began that Peninsular War which was for Napoleon the beginning of the end.

In the intrigues of Bayonne Talleyrand certainly had no part, and even Lacour-Gayet absolves him here. In the *Memoirs,* Talleyrand maintains that he sought to restrain the Emperor from the very beginning of the Spanish difficulties, and that the exact terms of the treaty of Fontainebleau, in which Napoleon and Godoy agreed to partition Portugal, were unknown to him at the time of its signing. Madame de Rémusat, not perhaps the most reliable of sources, reports a conversation with him at the time, in which he showed himself aware that Napoleon was intriguing with Godoy, and in which he disapproved such intrigues as discreditable, because of Godoy's bad reputation at home, and as dangerous, because their success would destroy any hope of a balanced Europe. Napoleon later accused Talleyrand of encouraging him at first in the Spanish adventure. Only after the first French reverses, said Napoleon, did Talleyrand begin to have his doubts, and when the enterprise was obviously failing, he began condemning it to all and sundry. This accusation is obviously false, because Talleyrand withdrew from active participation in Spanish matters long before the treaty of Bayonne, when everything was still going swimmingly on the surface; moreover, he began to criticize the imperial policy long before the peninsular crisis of 1811. Villemarest, a hostile contemporary biographer of Talleyrand, and a dismissed employee of his in the Foreign Office, quite acquits him of any part in Bonaparte's Spanish schemes.

It is not unlikely that in the *Memoirs* Talleyrand goes a bit too far in denying any participation at all in Spanish affairs. Early in 1807 he may have felt that Spain was a safer field for the Emperor's uncontrollable energy than Central and Eastern Europe, and he may have been less decided in his condemnation of the early negotiations that led to the Treaty of Fontainebleau than he later claimed to have been. Again those who support the Napoleonic view are the personal enemies of Talleyrand, notably Chateaubriand and Napoleon himself. Yet simply because they were his enemies, they are not necessarily lying. In the absence of proof one way or another, one may simply make conjectures; and it is not unlikely that Talleyrand did at least discuss Spain with his imperial master, as he had discussed Egypt with young general Bonaparte. To make Talleyrand primarily responsible for the Spanish adventure is, of course, even more ridiculous than to make him primarily responsible for the Egyptian expedition.

One thing is certainly beyond conjecture: by the end of 1808, not only Napoleon himself, but most of the inner circles of French political life, knew quite well that the Prince de Bénévent was opposed to French intervention in Spain. Yet in spite of the growing coldness between them, in spite of Talleyrand's resignation of his office, Napoleon entrusted him once more with a function of major importance. Napoleon had arranged a formal interview with the Russian Emperor Alexander at Erfurt in Germany, where he hoped to dazzle the Russians into complete acceptance of his plans for the annihilation of Austria and for the throttling of England by closing the continent to English goods. The rest of Europe would gather around the two Emperors; everyone of importance would be at Erfurt. Only Talleyrand had the necessary knowledge, the necessary skill and experience, the necessary connections with the old world of diplomacy to smooth the way for Napoleon's schemes. The Emperor thought he could still use Talleyrand. He used him once too often.

For Talleyrand employed the excellent opportunities of Erfurt to initiate his first definite intrigue aimed towards the downfall of Napoleon. For a year or two he had withdrawn a bit sulkily from politics, but hitherto he had not struck back at the Emperor. Now, in the midst of a great European congress, in the environment most suited to his talents, which always stimulated him to his best efforts, he began to work towards the estrangement of the two Emperors, who so recently at Tilsit had proudly divided the world between them.

Napoleon, as Talleyrand reports, "wished to dazzle Germany by his splendor." The little town of Erfurt was made the scene of an effort to impose French supremacy on Europe by relatively modern methods of showmanship—or advertising, to give it the right name. Napoleon brought with him the very best actors and actresses of France, Talma, St. Prix, Lafon, Mlles. Duschesnois and Raucourt, and gave before his guests the masterpieces of the French theatre. Erfurt was filled with uniforms; there were officers of every army, except the English, Napoleonic bureaucrats, princes, as sumptuously uniformed as any soldiers, grand dukes, noblemen of a dozen nations. Music, parties, dances, picnics, all beautifully stage-managed, succeeded one another day and night. Europe was impressed. This was better than the Field of the Cloth of Gold; this was better than Louis XIV and Versailles.

One suspects that Napoleon enjoyed this pageantry as much as Francis I had enjoyed his, that the meeting at Erfurt was called as much to please Napoleon as to achieve any specific political end. In so far as the meeting had an end, it was the fortification of Franco-Russian friendship by providing for the cession of Moldavia and Wallachia to Russia, thus shutting Austria out of the Balkans, by making clearer than ever that Napoleon was to be Emperor of the West, and Alexander Emperor of the East, by bringing the two into firm agreement to hold out against England. Napoleon was particularly anxious to have Alexander commit himself against Austria. With Talleyrand he discussed the whole matter before they arrived at Erfurt. Talleyrand ventured to hint that Austria could be France's friend against England, and that therefore she ought not to be too completely humiliated. Napoleon refused to listen, and taunted Talleyrand with being "pro-Austrian," and belonging to the ancient régime.

Arrived in Erfurt, Talleyrand succeeded in meeting Alexander in person almost every evening at late tea with the Princess of Thurn and Taxis, a most gracious hostess, and one not open to suspicion of harboring political intrigue. In these brief visits Talleyrand, as we learn reliably from Metternich, contrived to keep Alexander well informed of Napoleon's real motives, and furthermore, to suggest to the Russian Emperor the necessity of standing by Austria, and not permitting her extinction. Alexander, outwardly as much impressed by Napoleon's genius as he had been at Tilsit, maintained an attitude of respect for the Emperor of the French, enjoyed his entertainments thoroughly, arose in public and grasped his hand when at a performance of Voltaire's *Oedipe* there came the line

L'amitié d'un grand homme est un bienfait des dieux.

—and continued to refuse to sign Napoleon's projected agreement. Night after night Talleyrand and Alexander talked over their tea cups. Metternich and the Austrians took heart. A Frenchman had dared to oppose Napoleon. The Emperor, failing to understand Alexander's clairvoyant resistance, chafed a bit, and decided that the meeting had been successful enough. A very non-committal agreement was signed by subordinates, and the Emperors separated, apparently as friendly as ever, apparently more determined than ever to divide the supremacy of Europe. Actually, Alexander had seen Napoleon as somewhat less than a god; he had secured an agent of genius in Napoleon's own court; he had begun to feel sympathy for the plight of such fellow sovereigns as the King of Prussia and the Emperor of Austria, had begun, probably as yet quite unconsciously, his progress in devotion towards that peak for which Talleyrand popularized the magic formula—Legitimacy.

Talleyrand in his *Memoirs* rather boasts of his work at Erfurt, though he will not have it that he betrayed his master. He had seen Alexander, he writes, several times in private at Tilsit: "I saw him nearly every day at Erfurt. Our conversations were at first of a general turn concerning the common interests existing between the great powers of Europe: the conditions on which the ties, which it was important to preserve between them, were to be broken; the equilibrium of Europe in general; then, gradually, our conversations turned more particularly to the States whose existence was necessary for this equilibrium, especially to Austria. These conversations put the emperor in such a state of mind that the coaxing, the persuasion and the threats of Napoleon were a dead loss; and that, before quitting Erfurt the Emperor Alexander wrote in his own hand to the Emperor of Austria to reassure him with regard to the fears which the Erfurt interview had caused him. It was the last service I was able to render Europe, as long as Napoleon continued to reign, and this service, in my opinion, I was also rendering to himself personally."

Talleyrand's opposition to Napoleon was not too open and melodramatic, nor did it attain the intensity of true conspiracy until the allied armies were marching on Paris in 1814. The year 1809 did, however, witness a curious episode in French politics, the true significance of which will probably never be known. Napoleon had dashed dramatically from Erfurt to Madrid, like the dynamic executive he was. Talleyrand improved his master's absence by referring very disparagingly to the Spanish expedition, by salting his talk with rebellious epigrams. The Empire was not spiritually *frondeur*—at most it was *grognard,* which is very different—and Talleyrand's attitude caused some surprise. This became astonishment when, at a private reception, he appeared arm-in-arm with his old enemy, the regicide Fouché, Napoleon's Minister of Police. Several times afterwards the two were seen very ostentatiously together. Tongues wagged, and letters sped towards Madrid. Clearly two such Machiavellian characters had not come together for mere love. At very least a conspiracy must be afoot. Historians have ever since worried themselves over that conspiracy. Was it to restore the Directory? The Bourbons? Was it to put Murat on the throne? It is more likely that both Talleyrand and Fouché were afraid that the Spanish affair might end in immediate disaster, and that they wished to seem to have deserted the Emperor in time to act as king-makers, if necessary. But at most these conferences must have been a kind of re-insurance, a mere precaution. Neither Talleyrand nor Fouché were stage-plotters.

Napoleon heard the full details, and when he returned to Paris after having put Spanish affairs into a semblance of order, he humiliated Talleyrand in the famous scene of January 28, 1809. He assembled Cambacérès, Lebrun, Decrès, Fouché and Talleyrand, and after a relatively calm beginning, turned upon Talleyrand with a string of oaths and obscenities which those who have reported the scene do not dare repeat in full. Here, according to report, Napoleon addressed to his former minister the famous words "You're nothing but a lot of . . . in a silk stocking."[1] Here he announced that everyone knew the Princesse de Bénévent had cuckolded the Prince with the Duke of San Carlos. Here he accused Talleyrand of inspiring the murder of the Duc d'Enghien, of urging on the Spanish expedition. Napoleon's language is so exaggerated that it may have been dictated by cunning rather than by passion. He could show the world that a Talleyrand-Périgord must

[1] *Tenez, vous êtes de la merde dans un bas de soie.*

cringe before him, that the ablest intriguer in his realm wasn't even dangerous enough to hang. At any rate, the break was now complete. Talleyrand resigned his honorary post as Grand-Chamberlain, and retired to private life.

For several years he lived quietly, mostly at the rue St. Florentin, or at Bourbon l'Archambault, preferring to leave the Infants of Spain in possession of Valençay. He wrote a little, played a good deal of whist, and talked a very great deal. From Madame de Talleyrand he had gradually been alienated, but he did not lack feminine support in this semi-exile. With the Duchesse de Courlande, mother of his nephew Edmond's wife, he was on the most intimate terms, and he came to value highly her opinions. Another old friend was the Countess Tyszkiewicz, a wholly Gallicized Polish lady of the old régime, of whom he was very fond. He still retained his position as vice-grand elector, and took part from time to time in public ceremonies. It is likely that through his uncle, the old Archbishop of Rheims who had set him to reading about Richelieu and de Retz, and who was now in the household of the exiled Louis XVIII in England, he was in communication with the Bourbons. Napoleon suspected him of treasonous acts, and threatened several times to imprison him; at other times, especially in the critical years after Moscow, Napoleon importuned him to take over the Ministry of Foreign Relations again. Talleyrand had laid his plans too firmly to be disturbed. He gave no real hold to the Napoleonic police. He saw the future much too clearly to commit himself.

For common sense was revenging itself on Napoleon, as it has on so many a hero, so many a saint. The old Europe, under the not very deceptive guise of patriotism, was asserting itself against "the order and the peace" Napoleon was trying to bring it. The two Cæsars had quarreled in 1812, and Napoleon had made the disastrous march to

Moscow. As the Grand Army struggled back through snow and flood to Central Europe, the tributary states were encouraged to rise against the French domination. By 1813 the last and greatest coalition had been formed, and France found herself at war with all Europe, save for a few forlorn allies like Saxony and Denmark. At Leipzig in October, 1813, the French were beaten at the Battle of the Nations, and by the spring of 1814 Napoleon, for the first time in his career as general-in-chief, was fighting on French soil. In that marvelous campaign of 1814 he regained the desperate art of his first Italian battles, and for a while the miracle of a successful French defense seemed possible. Beaten back, the great nation seemed at the point of another Valmy, another Fleurus.

There are a dozen moments in these exciting months when it seemed that the Napoleonic Empire might be saved as a French if not a pan-European state. Now it was that Napoleon called on Talleyrand to extricate him from threatened disaster and Talleyrand refused. Waterloo was to vindicate Talleyrand's wisdom. Napoleon might have made peace with the allies in 1814, especially had he had Talleyrand to help him. That peace might well have left France her "natural boundaries." But it would have been a peace in which France was re-integrated into a complex European balance of power, into a European system not very different from the system that did after all emerge from the Congress of Vienna. Even now, it was clear to Talleyrand that Napoleon could never accommodate himself to that kind of Europe. A victory or two, if only in skirmishes, and he became again the Master of the World, determined to make no concessions, maniacally certain of his Destiny. The allied armies were too numerous, the allies, for once, united and determined. In more ways than one, these were not the days of Valmy or Fleurus. Europe had at last learned to work together. The bickerings, jealousies, and short-sighted purposes of the great powers in 1792 and 1793, which, even more than French heroism and republican virtue, explain French victories, were momentarily overcome. Before a united Europe, Napoleon might incarnate the great Revolution, Destiny, Providence, but for lay purposes he was just a French general leading a tired French army.

Defeated, Napoleon abdicated in favor of his son at Fontainebleau on April 6. The allies had other plans, and on April 11 the abdication was made unconditional. In the abstract, there were many possible solutions to the problem of who should rule France: another Bonaparte, a Bonapartist risen to success like Bernadotte, an Orleanist, a new Directory, a Bourbon. Even in the concrete, the restoration of Louis XVIII was by no means automatic. Alexander, who at this time prided himself on his liberalism, had grave doubts of the wisdom of bringing the revengeful *émigrés* back to power. In these critical months of the spring of 1814, the Bourbon restoration was prepared by the devoted labors of a number of people, not the least of whom was the Prince de Talleyrand. The old revolutionary had made his most astonishing leap, and was on the eve of his greatest successes as statesman, diplomatist, or, if you prefer, artist.

CHAPTER FIVE

Legitimist

I

SAVARY, the General Savary of the Enghien affair, now become Duc de Rovigo, and none too successfully attempting to fill Fouché's shoes as Minister of Police for Napoleon, tells in his *Memoirs* how one evening in February, 1814, he decided suddenly to call on Talleyrand in the rue St. Florentin. There he found the Prince talking to de Pradt, Archbishop of Malines, since the Russian misadventure in great disgrace with the Emperor. "This time there's no getting around it," said the Minister of Police as he entered the *salon*, "I've caught you conspiring." There followed laughter and embarrassment, and the conversation continued somewhat limply. Savary notes that their behavior convinced him that he had hit the mark, but that there was nothing he could do about it. The anecdote, confirmed by Talleyrand, certainly shows why Savary was not a good Minister of Police.

Conspiracy is perhaps a bit too melodramatic a word for one whose taste was always as impeccably Augustan as Talleyrand's. But as 1814 wore on, Talleyrand managed to gather together informally a group of distinguished, or at least conspicuous, men who were either in partial disgrace with the Emperor, or who were pretty obviously not the kind to die for their master. De Pradt, an ecclesiastic with ambitions towards diplomacy and high politics, was one of these. Napoleon had entrusted him with responsibilities during the Russian campaign, and had blamed him for failures. De Pradt was a garrulous fellow, with a yearning for greatness, or at least for acquaintance with the great, and, though not to be trusted with much of importance, might prove useful. Baron Louis, later the great financier of the Restoration, was another malcontent who frequented the salons of the rue St. Florentin. Baron Louis had during the old régime progressed in holy orders as far as the diaconate, but had found, under the emancipating force of Liberty, Equality, Fraternity, stock-jobbing more suited to his talents. He was willing to follow where profit led. Still another habitué of the rue St. Florentin was the Duc Emmerich de Dalberg, a South German noble who owed his dukedom to Napoleon, and whose family was to be illustrated in Victorian days by that enigmatic figure, Liberal, Catholic, European and English, John Emmerich Edward Dalberg Acton, first Lord Acton. Dalberg had received favors from Napoleon, but he was a Catholic and a German gentleman of the old school, and like Talleyrand, he did not believe that the new Charlemagne would succeed any better than the old in founding a lasting European Empire.

With Talleyrand's personal entourage, with his numerous friends among the great ladies of the old régime, to whom Napoleon was always a bounder, with other and less conspicuous malcontents, there was, more or less under Talleyrand's own control, a not inconsiderable political force. It seems now unlikely that he should have considered very seriously such alternatives to Bourbon restoration as a Bonapartist regency or an Orleanist crown. Yet this was a time for extreme caution. Napoleon might yet suddenly turn sane, and conclude a peace which would salvage his throne. Talleyrand seems not to have committed himself in writing, or indeed in any way. Yet he was certainly in touch with Bourbon emissaries early in 1814. Indeed, after his public disgrace with Napoleon he had been able to communicate with his uncle the Archbishop of Rheims, who was one of the little court at Hartwell House, the English residence of Louis XVIII. Yet as late as March 20, in a very confidential letter to the Duchesse de Courlande he could talk of a board of regency in which Napoleon's brothers would have a merely nominal power, and which he hoped would satisfy everybody. This surprising letter was probably meant to cover his tracks if anything went wrong. He never disdained any kind of insurance.

Definite contact with the elder branch of the Bourbons was established through the Baron de Vitrolles, a royalist gentleman of discretion and courage. There are tales of messages in invisible ink, of passwords and secret conferences. This much is clear and incontrovertible. Talleyrand and his circle sent Vitrolles to the headquarters of the allies in March, 1814, when it was clear that nothing short of a miracle could save Paris from military investment. Vitrolles asked the allies—and that almost came down to asking Alexander I—whether they would permit France to choose freely another form of government were the Emperor defeated. He clearly received encouragement, and it is possible that his visit in turn encouraged the allies to remain firm in their demand that Napoleon abdicate. Vitrolles then continued on to Nancy, where he met Louis's brother, the Comte d'Artois, and informed him that Talleyrand's group were willing to work for Louis XVIII, on condition that some sort of constitutional government be established. Artois disliked the conditions, but for once was too wise to turn the offer down.

In the meantime the allied armies were moving on Paris with a speed hitherto the monopoly of Napoleon. As a last wild gesture and proof of genius, Napoleon formed a plan to march around the allies' rear into Lorraine, rouse the garrisons of beleaguered towns, and turn on the astonished enemy. The enemy refused to be astonished, but continued straight towards Paris, brushing aside the sole obstacle, a small force under Marshals Marmont and Mortier at La Fère-Champenoise in the region which was to see the great battles of the Marne in the Four Years' War. On the morning of March 30 there were skirmishes just outside the gates of Paris. A council of the regency, in which Talleyrand as vice-grand-elector had a place, had already decided that the Empress and the little King of Rome should leave Paris for the comparative safety of Rambouillet. Talleyrand, as member of the imperial household, ought to have left Paris with the Empress. By a refinement of his fondness for re-insurance, which in another might seem timidity, but in Talleyrand is perhaps even more the artist's insistence on perfection, he and Madame de Rémusat contrived that Talleyrand should set out officially, coach and all, to leave Paris as a good Napoleonic official should, that he should attempt to leave by the gate at which M. de Rémusat commanded the national guard, that at that gate he should be turned back by "force of arms," and be obliged to return to the rue St. Florentin. If by a miracle—and in dealing with Napoleon no prudent man would quite discount miracles—Napoleon should suddenly appear to rally Paris and the army, then Talleyrand's failure to go to the Empress would be quite explicable. No need to assume that he had stayed in Paris in order to hand it over to the Bourbons.

That, of course, was just why he had stayed in Paris, and, no miracle intervening, that is just what he did. On the night of March 30, Talleyrand went to Marmont's *hôtel,* where arrangements were made for the surrender of Paris to the allied troops. Here he met the Russian Colonel Orloff, and charged him with a message to his master. Early next morning, Alexander sent his minister Nesselrode to Talleyrand's *hôtel,* where Talleyrand, Dalberg, de Pradt, Baron Louis and Nesselrode set to work and drew up a proclamation later given formal approval by Alexander, the King of Prussia, and Schwarzenberg for the Austrians. This proclamation was rushed off to the printers, and on April 1 was posted up all over the city. It announced that the allies refused to deal with Napoleon, that they would "respect the integrity of France as it used to be under her *legitimate* kings," and that the Senate was invited to meet and choose a provisional government.

Napoleon, clear that his final stroke of genius had been a flat failure, had ridden at full speed for Paris. He reached Juvisy, now in the southern suburbs of the city, in the small hours of the morning of March 31, and learned that the city had been surrendered. He returned to Fontainebleau, where he was later obliged to sign his abdication. Talleyrand had now nothing to fear from his former master. Alexander arrived in the late afternoon of March 31, and took up his residence in Talleyrand's own *hôtel* in the rue St. Florentin. Next day, as the proclamation had suggested, Talleyrand called the Senate together to set up a provisional government. This body, which had been little more than a part of the universal imperial bureaucracy, none the less contained about all there was of political distinction and experience left in the dying Empire. The Senate which responded to Talleyrand's call was, of course, a rump, rather more than half its membership having, through loyalty to the Emperor or through doubt, failed to reply to the summons. The Senate set up a provisional government of five, composed of Talleyrand, Beurnonville, Jaucourt, Dalberg, and Montesquiou, and charged them to present a project for a constitution and to carry on the task of administration. Talleyrand was the dominant figure in this government; the others were his familiars, his creatures.

The provisional government went from triumph to triumph. Marmont was worked on cleverly, his soldiers influenced by a proclamation calling them to be loyal to France rather than to Napoleon, "a man who isn't even a Frenchman." Marmont and his corps surrendered, and put themselves under the provisional government. Talleyrand was also hard at work—not even his enemies accuse him of idleness in these weeks—to get some sort of constitution drawn up for approval by the Senate. On April 6 the Senate unanimously approved a document to which Talleyrand had given the effective name of *Charte constitutionelle,* and which recalled to the throne as Louis XVIII the brother of the last Bourbon to reign in France. On April 12 the Comte d'Artois arrived from Nancy, and assumed the titular headship of the nation as lieutenant-general of the kingdom. Talleyrand refused, however, to hand the government fully over to Artois, and insisted that Louis would not be king until he had accepted the Charter. Louis had judged it safe to leave Hartwell House, and on May 2 issued from St. Ouen a declaration which embodied Talleyrand's Charter, and from which the Restoration may be said to date. Certain concessions were later made to Bourbon pride; the Charter was finally dated "in the nineteenth year of our reign"; it was "presented" by the free will of the sovereign; it was left vague as to the exact nature of ministerial responsibility. But substantially Louis XVIII came to occupy just about the place Talleyrand had designed for him.

The allies had also to be dealt with. Talleyrand as the leading figure in the provisional government is, on the French side, largely responsible for the convention of April 23 and the treaty of Paris of May 30, 1814, by which the purely French part of the general pacification was concluded. To our generation, with fresh memories of the Peace of Versailles, the terms granted France in 1814 seem of almost quixotic generosity. Thoroughly beaten, her capital occupied by enemy troops, France was actually permitted to retain some of her revolutionary conquests—Avignon and the Comtat Venaissin, a part of Savoy, a few bits of territory on the fringes of Belgium and the Rhineland: Haiti, already quite lost by a black revolt, the Ile de France in the Indian Ocean and two small West Indian Islands were taken away from her colonial empire. Foreign soldiers were to withdraw at once from French soil, and the French garrisons were to be restored. France paid no indemnity.

Only a Frenchman will argue that the French loss of Belgium and the Rhineland was an act of oppression towards France. The concert of Europe had never—except briefly and unwillingly in 1802—admitted the "natural frontiers" for France as part of a solution acceptable to Europe as a whole. By the new, and as yet unaccepted criterion of nationalism, Mainz, Cologne, Aix-la-Chapelle and Antwerp were hardly French cities; and the German and Flemish peasantries about them were even less touched by French ways than the inhabitants of the cities. Moreover, for twenty-five years France had seemed to play the villain in European politics; in Germany, in England, in Spain and in Italy, the common people had been roused to a fury against "Boney" and his minions. Frenchmen were hated in 1814 as Germans were hated in 1918. And yet thus hated and thoroughly beaten France was permitted to retain all lands of French stock, was allowed to build up her army immediately, kept many of the works of art stolen by Napoleon, and was not even obliged to pay a war indemnity. Well may Talleyrand write: "When I think of the date of these treaties of 1814, of the difficulties of all sorts I encountered, of the spirit of revenge which I found in certain of the men with whom I negotiated, and which I was obliged to combat, I await with confidence the judgment which posterity will make of these treaties." Or again, of the treaty of May 30, "France, by this treaty, remained great and powerful."

We need not here recall the terms of the peace concluded with Germany in 1919, nor can we here attempt a complete answer to the problem presented by the contrast between the relatively light terms which the beaten "aggressor" France received in 1814 and the very harsh terms which the beaten "aggressor" Germany received in 1919. The recent Four Years' War was even more popular and democratic than the last phase of the Napoleonic Wars, and it may well be that democracies are by nature more revengeful and less magnanimous than other forms of society. The hands of the diplomatists at Versailles were tied by their dependence on parliamentary majorities, perhaps even more by their commitments to press and people. Lively and voracious economic appetites were centered in 1918 on coal and iron, on merchant fleets and colonial enterprises, with far more intensity than the simpler economic appetites of 1814 were centered on land and peoples still predominantly agricultural. On the other hand, however strong popular hatred for France was in 1814 in Germany, England, Italy and the rest of Europe, the kind of men who treated at Paris—the kings and diplomatists of the old school—were brought up on French literature, spoke and wrote French, admired the old civilization of France, felt in most ways more akin to upper-class Frenchmen than to peasants and workers in their own fatherlands. They did not hate France as Clemenceau, or even Wilson, hated Germany.

And yet, though all this and much more can be said as

to differences in the general conditions surrounding the treaties of 1814 and those of 1919, there remains one simple fact: France was represented in 1814 by Talleyrand; Germany in 1919 by . . . Brockdorff-Rantzau. No one today will be likely to accept a Carlylean hero-worship as a suitable interpretation of history. Yet treaties of peace are surely among the less impersonal manifestations of social life, and only a very convinced Marxian or other metaphysician would be likely to maintain that the men who discuss and sign treaties have, *as individuals,* nothing to do with what goes into treaties. The treaties of 1814 at Paris might have been much the same had Talleyrand never lived —though this is unlikely; the treaties of 1815 at Vienna might well have been very different had Talleyrand never lived. For a full appreciation of Talleyrand's importance at this crisis, we shall have to follow him to Vienna.

II

ON May 13 Talleyrand was named by Louis XVIII Minister of Foreign Affairs, and once more entered as master the *hôtel* in the rue du Bac from which he had directed foreign affairs for the Republic and for Napoleon. He was the great man of the moment, and even Joseph de Maistre, an upright moralist of the best Catholic tradition, notes this. "There is a touch of Talleyrand," he wrote, "in everything that is done here. Such a man at the side of the King of France is a strange spectacle; but it seems clear that he has rendered great services to the good cause. The king will, then, have made use of the gentleman and the minister while leaving the bishop to God's judgment." As Minister of Foreign Affairs, Talleyrand would have the direction of French policies at the great European Congress which was to settle the infinite problems, territorial, dynastic, and economic, left by the withdrawal of Napoleonic governments from half Europe. Rather than attempt to pull strings from Paris, and perhaps also to get as free a rein as possible, Talleyrand decided to head the French delegation in person, and had no trouble securing Louis's consent. Dalberg, the Comte Alexis de Noailles, and the Marquis de La Tour-du-Pin-Gouvernet accompanied him as plenipotentiaries. The faithful La Besnardière came to do efficiently the kind of work the superior civil servant can do. Finally, Talleyrand, who could hardly envisage Madame de Talleyrand in the rôle, took along his niece by marriage, Dorothée, daughter of his great friend the Duchesse de Courlande, to act as his hostess. Dorothée, at the height of her youthful beauty, educated in the graces of old Europe, not untouched by the romantic intensity of the new, was a great success, and facilitated her uncle's work by her charm and her tact.

Talleyrand arrived at Vienna on September 23, 1814, and took up his residence at the *Hôtel Kaunitz.* This fortuitous linking of his name and that of the great Austrian chancellor who had made the Austro-French alliance of 1756, he writes in his *Memoirs,* seemed to him a good augury. He found his colleagues in diplomacy rather surprised and disappointed over the reception accorded the treaty of Paris. "They had just traversed countries that had been ravaged by war for many years, in which they heard, they said, but words of hatred and vengeance against France, for having overwhelmed them with taxes, and treated them with the arrogance of a victor. My new colleagues assured me that they had been reproached everywhere for their weakness in signing the treaty of Paris. I therefore did not find them very enthusiastic over the satisfaction to be derived from generosity, but rather disposed to excite each other about the pretensions they were to advance. Each was perusing the treaty of Chaumont which had not only tightened the bonds of an alliance destined to last for the present war, but had also laid down conditions for an alliance which should survive the present war, and bind the allies together even in the remote future. And, moreover, how could they make up their minds to admit to the council of Europe, the very power against which Europe had been in arms during twenty years? The minister of a country so newly reconciled, they said, ought to think himself very fortunate in being allowed to give his assent to the resolutions of the ambassadors of the other powers."

The prospect, as this last sentence clearly shows, was singularly like that which faced the German delegation at Versailles in 1919. Brockdorff-Rantzau was confronted with the results of an agreement among the Big Four—Wilson, Lloyd George, Clemenceau, Orlando—and obliged to sign a treaty he had never discussed. Even journalism was more dignified in 1814, and no one could possibly have coined a phrase like "the Big Four." But the parallel is numerically exact. England, Austria, Russia, and Prussia—represented chiefly by Castlereagh, Metternich, Nesselrode and Hardenberg—had already decided, before the formal sessions of the Congress were opened, to come to a private agreement, and to present France and the little countries at the actual Congress with that delight of the hard-boiled politician—the *fait accompli.*

The preliminary conferences of the representatives of the four powers of the Quadruple Alliance were by no means productive of easy agreement. The fact turned out very difficult of accomplishment, for reasons now familiar enough to the readers of text-books. The four powers had differing views of what should be accomplished, especially as regards Saxony and Poland. The official opening of the Congress, set for October 1, had to be postponed, and postponed again. Here Talleyrand saw his chance. He first consulted the representatives of the lesser powers, won his way into their confidence, pointed out that they had a common interest with France in preventing the dictatorship of the four powers of the Quadruple Alliance, and was rewarded by their unanimous support in his formal request that the Congress be opened. This was not the least of Talleyrand's miracles. France, the ogre, the devourer of small nations, had now become their protector!

The next step is critical. Here are Talleyrand's own words in the *Memoirs:* "The opening of the Congress was fixed for a certain day. That day passed; I entreated that another should be fixed in the near future. . . . A few replies, evasive at first, caused me to repeat my entreaties. I even went so far as to complain a little, *but was finally obliged to make use of the personal influence that I had fortunately acquired in the previous negotiations, over the principal personages of the Congress.* Prince Metternich, and the Count Nesselrode, not wishing to be disobliging to me, both had me invited to a conference at the office of the minister of foreign affairs." Once Talleyrand had been admitted to these conferences, the Quadruple Alliance, in its simple form, was broken up. He needed only a very small hold, and this was given him by the invitation he describes above. We are free to speculate as to why he received that invitation. Unquestionably his well-advertised negotiations with the smaller powers had alarmed the four allies. It would not do to let France become the champion of European freedom. Moreover, Metternich, at least, and to some extent Gentz, perhaps more influential on the Prussian side than any other man, were firmly convinced that a strong France was necessary to European peace, and that above all the Bourbon Restoration must not be made unpopular in France by saddling it with diplomatic defeat and disgrace. In a world made safe for democracy by the victories of 1918, the French and English democracies were not quite so considerate of the reputation of the Weimar Republic. Finally, we may not wholly discard Talleyrand's own explanation: he was on intimate terms with both Metternich and Nesselrode, he belonged, if you like, to the same caste, and they could not, as gentlemen, openly snub him.

Talleyrand had also secured a similar invitation for the Spaniard Labrador, for Spain was the most considerable of the other excluded powers. They arrived at the appointed place, and found Castlereagh apparently presiding, with Nesselrode, Metternich, Hardenberg, Humboldt as representatives, and with Gentz acting as secretary. The protocol of preceding meetings of this group was on the table, and Talleyrand asked to see it. His alert eye hit upon the word "allies," and he had his hold. As he recorded it in his *Memoirs* written only a year later, he said something like the following: "I declared that *allied powers* and a congress in which powers that were not allied were to be found, were in my eyes very little able to arrange affairs loyally together. I repeated with some astonishment and even warmth, the word *allied powers*—'allied,' I said, 'and against whom? It is no longer against Napoleon—he is on the isle of Elba—it is no longer against France; for peace has been made—it is surely not against the King of France; he is a guarantee of the duration of that peace. Gentlemen, let us speak frankly; if there are still *allied powers*, I am one too many here.' "

And yet, he continued, my presence here may be very helpful to you all. France needs nothing, asks for nothing, and is in this crisis singularly disinterested. Moreover, the very presence of France here in this European assembly is a notice to all the world that the bad old days of revolt and anarchy are ended, that the new Europe will maintain the decencies of the old. For the Bourbon dynasty is a living link with the good past. "I want nothing, I repeat it, but I bring you a great deal. The presence of a minister of Louis XVIII *consecrates here the principle upon which all social order rests.* The first need of Europe is to banish forever the opinion that right can be acquired by conquest alone, and to cause the revival of that sacred *principle of legitimacy* from which all order and stability spring." To exclude France from important decisions would mean that the allies were not, after all, maintaining sound principles, defending legitimacy. It would mean, as Talleyrand clearly implies, but wisely fails to say outright, espousing unsound principles, it would mean *that the allies were the real revolutionists!*

If ever an argument based upon the manipulation of abstractions was wholly unanswerable, this is such an argument. The allies had said much too loudly and often that they were aiming to restore the good old days to be able now by any possible twist or turn to reply to Talleyrand. The plenipotentiaries looked uncomfortable, and Talleyrand hastened to make their surrender easy. He recognized, of course, that so large an assembly as the whole Congress could not possibly deal with serious problems, could not possibly get through its business efficiently. Those now present in conference had been quite sound in realizing that small groups must do the essential work of the Congress. But some means of distributing and classifying business could be found which would not wound any of the powers present at the Congress. The means suggested by the representatives of the four powers would never do. Talleyrand had now to prevent the establishment of a committee of six, composed of the four allied powers, France, and Spain, in which France and Spain might be outvoted four to two. Talleyrand suggested therefore the formal opening of the

Congress, which would proceed to deal with special problems by the organization of a number of special committees on which all interested parties would have representation. Various obstacles were brought up, and, as Talleyrand reported in a letter to his King, someone mentioned the King of Naples, meaning, of course, Napoleon's brother-in-law Murat, who had kept his army intact, and was trying very hard to preserve his crown by some sort of arrangement with the powers. Talleyrand, as representative of Louis XVIII and Legitimacy, could not appear to support a "usurper." He dismissed Murat in a phrase of the blandest impudence, "Of what King of Naples do you speak? We do not know the person you mention."

It may be doubted whether Talleyrand really thought he could attain his aim of making the Congress a genuinely deliberative body, in which the great and the little powers would share alike. What he had done by his brilliant performance at the conference described above was to put France on an equal footing with the other great powers. Henceforth no private conferences of any importance could take place without French participation. The real work of the Congress, however, was most certainly done in such conferences. For the rest, in a phrase of the Prince de Ligne which the movies have made commonplace, the Congress danced.

Talleyrand's success would hardly have done more than aid the prestige and consideration of France had the four powers really been united. His great achievement was to exploit and increase their disunion to the point where France came to hold a balance between conflicting pairs—Prussia and Russia on one side, Austria and England on another—and could therefore positively influence the actual decisions arrived at. The differences between the allied powers were almost as numerous as the specific problems they faced. We can trace more clearly Talleyrand's course in the complicated negotiations of the next few months if we confine ourselves to the two crucial problems on the solution of which the possibility of peace depended, the related problems of Saxony and of Poland.

One of the great difficulties at Vienna was to find actual territory to be carved up, according to immemorial custom, among the victors. The principle of Legitimacy, so skillfully kept in circulation by Talleyrand, prevented not only the partition of French territory, but even the happy distribution of pieces of the Empire Napoleon and his relatives once held: Spain, Italy, Holland, the Rhineland, the Kingdom of Westphalia. The Bourbons had to be restored in Spain and Naples, the House of Orange in Holland, the Hohenzollerns in Central and Western Germany, the Hapsburgs in Germany and Italy. Not only could these legitimate rulers not be deprived of their lands; most of them felt strongly that they ought to be compensated for their years of martyrdom by a positive increase in territory. No convenient "mandates" as in 1919 were possible, for practically all available overseas possessions were already in the hands of Great Britain, and Great Britain was the most victorious of victors in 1814, and did not even propose to restore to the virtuous and legitimate House of Orange the Dutch colonies of Ceylon and the Cape of Good Hope, taken from the miserable pro-French Batavian Republic. In Germany, it was clearly impossible to go back to 1789, and restore all the princelets and free cities of the old Empire; but central and western Germany barely sufficed for the appetites of Hohenzollerns, Zähringens, Wittelsbachs and other good German houses, which simply had to be fed. Belgium had to go to Holland as compensation for the loss of her colonies, or the principle of Legitimacy would be lamed beyond the powers of even a Talleyrand to restore it.

Three available bits of territory there were, however. The Rhineland, which had belonged chiefly to the three spiritual electors of the old Empire, the Archbishops of Mayence, Treves and Cologne, was already earmarked for Prussia. The Wettin family in Saxony, a prosperous and considerable state, had forfeited their rights to the blanket coverage of legitimacy by staying loyal to Napoleon just a bit too long. Only England, of course, had never compromised with the Emperor. One of Talleyrand's most effective sallies was in reply to a remark of Alexander's about the King of Saxony, "who," the Russian said, "has betrayed the cause of Europe." "That, sire," replied Talleyrand, "is a question of dates." Dates are, however, facts and dates were against Saxony. As for poor Poland with its *liberum veto,* its turbulent diets, its elected monarchs, it had perhaps been illegitimate in 1789? At any rate, Poland was in 1814 a problem rather than a nation, and having been completely partitioned in the eighteenth century, could obviously be re-partitioned without offense to international law. Napoleon had made a half-hearted attempt to restore Poland in the shape of the independent Duchy of Warsaw, taken mostly from parts of Poland that had fallen to Prussia in the great partitions. This much at any rate was available.

Now Prussia wanted the whole of Saxony, and Russia wanted the whole of Poland, or at very least the whole of the former Duchy of Warsaw. Both these territories were contiguous to the states which wanted them, formed natural additions to their lands. The Austrian Chancellor, Prince Metternich, who had in the last years of the war gained a very important position in Europe, and who was, with Alexander, the most conspicuous of the leaders at Vienna, was opposed to such an aggrandizement of both of Austria's powerful neighbors. The rivalry between Prussia and

Austria had been only in the most superficial way stilled by the common war against revolutionary France. That Prussia should add Saxony to Silesia no Hapsburg minister could in peace accept. Russian aggrandizement hurt Austrian pride less, but Talleyrand, true to his old principles, kept pointing out to Metternich that Austria's future lay among Slavic peoples, and that Russia must not get so powerful as to bar the way eastward. Some Englishmen were all for splendid isolation, for allowing the continental powers to settle the dog-fight among themselves. Castlereagh, however, was by no means of this school. He had caught from Pitt, perhaps, a rather premature attack of that Russophobia which was so profitably to afflict most nineteenth-century English statesmen. Towards Prussia he was inclined to be rather sympathetic, however, and to feel that Prussian annexation of Saxony, besides punishing a disloyal king, would help keep Prussia a strong make-weight against Russia.

Here, then, was a situation which made Talleyrand's work, if not easy, at least possible. Russia and Prussia wanted something which Austria was determined they should not have. England, though not hostile to Prussian claims, was definitely hostile to those of Russia. Obviously it was England that needed to be egged on, and Talleyrand accordingly turned first to the conversion of Castlereagh. Prussia, he insisted, is trying very hard to set herself up as head of a united Germany. "One can thus be persuaded that if Prussia succeeded in annexing Saxony, and appropriating for herself isolated territories on one side and another, she would form, in a very few years, a military monarchy very dangerous for her neighbors; and nothing, in this supposition, would serve her better than a great number of enthusiasts, who, under the pretext of seeking a mother-country, would create one by the most fatal upheavals."

There is 1871 foreshadowed for you, two generations ahead! Sentimental nationalism, especially outside of France, seemed to Talleyrand a disguise for reasonably old ambitions among established ruling groups. It has long been the custom to say that men like Talleyrand and Metternich "misunderstood" and "underestimated" nationalism. "Distrusted" and "feared" would of course be more accurate.

Now Castlereagh held views of the necessity of a European order based on traditions much like those of Talleyrand and Metternich. To persuade him that Prussia might disturb that order was well on the way to winning him over. In a special memorandum on Saxony, Talleyrand added a detailed study of the past, present, and probable future relations between Russia and Prussia, and concluded that, far from counterbalancing one another, Prussia and Russia, by the mutual sympathies of their rulers, by their common interests, by their unconflicting ambitions, would be likely to stand together, just as they were now doing. Much else, including Alexander's parading of his doctrinaire liberalism, helped to convert the Tory Castlereagh. Converted he was, however, and by the month of November the lines were being drawn more clearly every day: England, Austria and France on one side; Prussia and Russia on the other.

Alexander made several attempts to win over his fellow-guest at the Erfurt teas of the Princess of Thurn and Taxis. Talleyrand describes several interviews with Alexander in his letters to Louis XVIII. Politely, but firmly, and always in the name of the eternal principle of Legitimacy, Talleyrand turned down the Emperor's rather erratic proposals. At one point, Alexander frankly proposed a bargain at the good folk-level of a horse deal. "Listen. Let us strike a bargain. Give way to me on the question of Saxony, and I will do the same for you on that of Naples. I have given no promise there." Talleyrand replied that the annexation of Saxony to Prussia would be the extinction of the legitimate Wettin family while the return of Naples to the legitimate Bourbon rulers would mean merely the extinction of the usurper Murat, and that therefore one could hardly use the term bargain. "It is impossible for your Majesty not to have the same wishes with regard to Naples as ourselves."

All through November and December, beneath the surface amenities of the great Congress, a thousand intrigues were intertwining ever more firmly, until war itself seemed a possibility. In a letter of January 4, 1815, Talleyrand was able to announce to his King the consummation of a formal alliance between France, England and Austria, the specific purpose of which was to prevent, if necessary by force of arms, the annexations of Saxony by Prussia, of Poland by Russia. "Not only is France no longer isolated in Europe; but your Majesty has already a federal system such as fifty years of negotiations held out no prospect of gaining. France is acting in concert with two of the greatest powers, three states of second rank, and soon will be acting with all the states that follow other principles and other maxims than the principles and maxims of revolution. She will in reality be the chief and soul of this union, formed for the defence of principles which she has been the first to inculcate." All this, writes Talleyrand, is clearly the work of God. After God, he lists four "efficient courses" of this change. Louis, too, was a good son of the eighteenth century, and was probably not offended when his Minister added a postscript to the labors of the Deity.

"My letters to Prince Metternich and Lord Castlereagh and the impression they produced.

"The hints dropped to Lord Castlereagh relative to an agreement with France.

"The care I have taken to quiet his suspicions, by showing,

in the name of France, the most perfect disinterestedness.

"The peace with America, which, by getting him out of his anxiety on that side, has left him more free to act, and has given him more courage.

"Finally, the claims of Russia and Prussia, . . . advanced in a conference between their plenipotentiaries and those of Austria. The arrogant tone taken in this shameful and preposterous document so wounded Lord Castlereagh that, forsaking his habitual calm, he exclaimed that the Russians were claiming to lay down the law, and that England would accept it from no one."

Talleyrand knew his English. They could not be moved nearly so well as Germans by appeals to generalizations like Legitimacy, but they would always be roused to opposition by the spectacle of tyranny and "laying down the law." They liked to feel, too, that they were acting cautiously and soundly, wholly unromantically. Talleyrand was quite right in thinking that the Treaty of Ghent with America—a treaty of which he remarked, "it hurts the honor of neither party, and will consequently satisfy both of them"—prepared the way for Castlereagh's adhesion to an alliance which might well provoke another war.

Before this united front of France, Austria, and England, Russia and Prussia, after a certain amount of blustering, gave way, and the Saxon and Polish questions were duly settled by compromise. Prussia received a good bit of Saxony, but the Wettins kept the throne of a state which included Dresden, Leipzig and Chemnitz, and which remained one of the more important of German states. Russia received most of the Grand Duchy of Warsaw, which became the constitutional Kingdom of Poland, with Alexander as its king. But most of the Prussian and Austrian booty of the original partitions remained in Prussian and Austrian hands. The other major questions were settled along lines not too displeasing to Talleyrand. In Naples his policy was completely victorious. Murat unwisely picked a quarrel with Austria, moved his army, and was easily put down. Ferdinand of Bourbon returned to a kingdom which was to provide good useful scandal to liberals until in 1860 it was finally merged in that triumph of the liberal spirit, the Kingdom of Italy. The House of Savoy was strengthened by the addition of Genoa, a step which greatly pleased Louis XVIII. The French were not happy over the union of Belgium and Holland, but Talleyrand felt that time would be favorable to the French desire for an independent Belgium, since French retention of Belgium was apparently quite impossible. Time was favorable indeed, and perhaps more speedily than Talleyrand had hoped. For his last important act in European politics was to help make possible an independent Belgium in 1830.

Talleyrand has been criticized for permitting the aggrandizement of Prussia. We can now see clearly enough that Prussia emerged from the Congress immensely strengthened by her gains in the Rhineland and on the edges of Saxony. Talleyrand was certainly far from unaware of the possible danger to France from Prussian greatness. It is, however, asking too much of his political prescience to expect him to foresee and prevent Bismarck and Sedan. At the Congress he firmly withstood Prussian claims to Luxembourg and Mainz, and seems to have realized that, if Prussia were kept from absorbing all Saxony, she could not possibly be kept from the Rhineland. As between the Rhineland and Saxony, common sense in 1815 dictated the abandonment of the Rhineland, never well-organized, and the maintenance of Saxony, one of the important German states, and one readily available for the traditional French policy in the Germanies: divide and rule. Moreover, Saxon Leipzig and Chemnitz seemed in 1815 industrially far more important than the Rhenish towns. Again, we cannot blame Talleyrand for not anticipating the Essen of the Krupps. That a united Germany would menace France he saw, however, with singular clarity. He wrote Louis from Vienna on October 17: "German unity—that is their cry, their doctrine, their religion, carried even to fanaticism, and this fanaticism is shared by princes actually reigning. Now this unity from which France had nothing to fear when she possessed the Left Bank and Belgium would now be a serious question for her. Besides, who could predict the consequences of the eventual outbreak of a mass like Germany, when her component parts bestir and blend themselves as a whole? Who knows where the impulse thus given would stop?"

Professor H. E. Blinn has recently maintained that Talleyrand's failure in the Italian negotiations at Vienna was "pronounced." It is true that Murat's downfall came about in a way Talleyrand had scarcely planned, and that Austria by the treaty retained Lombardy-Venetia and a hegemony over Italy. But Talleyrand's policy was not anti-Austrian, and though he would have preferred to have the Austrians out of Italy, there are no signs that he thought this a major point. What he did think most important for France to obtain in Italy—the strengthening of the House of Savoy, the re-establishment of the Queen of Etruria, and Murat's ejection from Naples, together with the restoration of the Bourbon Ferdinand IV—had all been obtained by the summer of 1815. Talleyrand may have been lucky, may have reaped where others sowed, may have an inflated reputation because of the simple fact that he was always successful. No doubt Babe Ruth hit many lucky home-runs. But as baseball is still too undignified for even the social historian, no one has yet prepared a short scientific paper to prove that someone else hit most of the Babe's homers—or that, as a matter of fact, they were mostly foul balls.

Napoleon's return from Elba hastened the work of signing what had to be signed, but on the whole the Hundred Days had no effect on the settlement of Vienna. It had an effect, though less than a contemporary of the Versailles settlement might expect, on the treatment of France. Again Talleyrand labored hard to convince the victorious allies after Waterloo that to punish France was to punish the legitimate Bourbons. Legitimacy was still a powerful argument, but it could not wholly save a nation which had just given proof of its devotion to illegitimacy and usurpation. Bonaparte was sent to St. Helena instead of to the adjacent Elba; and on November 20, 1815, the second treaty of Paris set France back, generally speaking, to the boundaries of 1789, instead of those of 1792, which she had retained at the first treaty of Paris. The Saar and Landau ceased to be French, along with some fortresses on the new Dutch frontier, and Savoy. Seventeen fortresses were to be garrisoned for five years by allied troops, and an indemnity of 700 millions of francs was laid upon France. Most of the famous art treasures, left her in 1814, were now taken away. In spite of a good deal of talk, Alsace-Lorraine remained in French hands.

By the time this treaty was signed, Talleyrand was out of office, and the unpleasant task of assuming responsibility for its provisions fell upon his successor, the Duc de Richelieu. Talleyrand's greatest diplomatic achievements were finished. It is worth while to stop a moment here and consider the means he used in this consummation of his art.

Broadly speaking, Talleyrand's method in this crisis of 1814–1815 was to play upon the sentiments of his "opponents" in such a way that there were activated in them sentiments on the whole beneficial to France, sentiments stronger than the sentiments harmful to France with which they entered upon the negotiations. Now the sentiments harmful to France may be summarized briefly: a feeling that France was guilty of starting the war and was responsible for its length and intensity, and that therefore France ought to be punished; a simple but strong hatred for Frenchmen and France, not unmixed with envy, especially evident among the Prussians and Italians; a hatred mixed with contempt, especially evident among the English; a dislike for Bonaparte either as a revolutionary, the "Child and Champion of Jacobinism" or as a tyrant who had put an end to the fair promise of "Liberty, Equality, Fraternity"; a feeling that the France of Louis XIV and of Napoleon was a perpetual menace to European stability, that France was the preponderant state in Europe, and therefore the preponderant danger, and that she ought to be made as weak as possible; a feeling that France was a nest of radicalism, and that this radicalism might spread to Europe unless repressive measures were taken. Many other sentiments are also discernible among the allies, but these should suffice us. A desire to annex as much territory as possible we may assume to have animated every major ally, but this is rather a permanent and wholly concrete appetite, like the urge, instinct, drive, *libido,* or what you will which some psychologists discern in the individual. Such appetites can be more or less satisfied, but they cannot, like sentiments, be greatly modified by appeals in words to other sentiments.

What Talleyrand did was to employ the word "Legitimacy" *to convert these same sentiments to his own uses,* to uses which seemed to him, and which must seem to any reasonable observer, favorable to the interests of France. Some few other sentiments he did evoke, and play upon, but on the whole—and this is the reason for his great success—he made no attempt to *alter* deep-seated sentiments he found existing. What he did was to persuade men moved by these sentiments that they had mistaken the best means of satisfying them. France was guilty, and should be punished; of course, but how better punish revolutionary and Napoleonic France than by blotting out twenty-five years, and restoring the France of 1789? But your guilty France was revolutionary and Napoleonic France, and, now that you have restored the Bourbons to their heritage, to diminish that heritage by annexations and indemnities would be to punish the innocent. Moreover, what you really hate and fear on this earth is a revolutionist, a Jacobin. A "Jacobin" was to conservatives in 1814 what a "Bolshevik" became to such people in 1918. Europe must stand together, Talleyrand's argument continued, not so much against France as against what you may if you like call the "French" idea, Liberty, Equality, Fraternity, an idea all too widespread in England, Germany, Austria, Italy, in all Europe. The best way to resist bad new ideas is to make good old ideas popular. Let us then do all we can to support throne and altar, obedience, law and order, moderation, conservatism. Let us set up in opposition to revolutionary abstract ideals one of our own—Legitimacy. Let us bring Louis XVIII back to the throne of St. Louis.

And now, suppose you ask from defeated France indemnities in money, cessions in land? Surely you do not propose to weaken the principle of Legitimacy by despoiling a legitimate king, the *rex christianissimus,* in fact? What an example to revolutionists of all lands, to these men to whom nothing established is sacred, to see kings behaving like revolutionists, and actually *usurping,* like a Bonaparte, property of one of the oldest and most respected of royal families. On the contrary, you should take especial measures to strengthen the King of France, if you really are afraid of revolutions. Bourbon France is a guarantee of European peace and order. To punish Bourbon France would be, for Guelf England, for Romanov Russia, for Hohenzollern Prussia, for Hapsburg Austria, positively suicidal. Or, to put the formula in its most baldly intellectual form: you have agreed in 1814 to go back as far as possible to the situation in 1789: Louis XVIII must then in 1814 rule as nearly as possibly over a country as large and as prosperous as that over which Louis XVI ruled in 1789.

This, then, is Talleyrand's theme. He modifies and adapts it to men and circumstances in ways which show his artist's subtlety. He does not, like a popular song-writer, repeat his theme endlessly in the same form, but like the skilled composer, develops a dozen variations. Alexander of Russia, for instance, plumed himself on his liberalism, the product of an education in the later and radical forms of the eighteenth-century Enlightenment. In the critical days of March and April, 1814, when Talleyrand was "conspiring" to bring back the Bourbons, he had to convert Alexander. For this purpose, he dwelt less on Legitimacy than on the fact that in the proposed *charte constitutionelle* there would be embodied the really sound principles of the French Revolution, that the Bourbons would, like Alexander, be "liberal" monarchs. We have seen how he found other ways of working on the sentiments of Lord Castlereagh, product of a ruling class filled with sentimental dislike for logic and therefore not wholly convinced by the logic of Legitimacy. The sturdy, insensitive, and revengeful Prussians he found it much harder to deal with. The Junkers were not afraid of revolution in Prussia, and they were inclined to believe they could show the rest of the world how to deal with revolutionists. Yet he early turned his attention to the one exception in the Prussian delegation, von Gentz, a political thinker much influenced by Burke. The good impression he made on Gentz at the critical conference at Vienna in October, 1814, was very valuable.

Here as elsewhere, the question of Talleyrand's sincerity arises, and here as elsewhere its solution will depend on how one feels towards him. Certainly he did not, in any simple sense, believe what he said. Legitimacy as an abstraction, as something to love, as an object of faith, meant little to him. To Madame de Staël he wrote from Vienna, "The successes of Bonaparte were not the only detestable thing about him, but it was his principles which were horrible and which ought to be forever repudiated by Europe," and then, after some lighter touches, it is true, "Adieu: I don't know what we shall achieve here; but I can promise you a noble language." Yet in 1814 Talleyrand had at least come to set a very high value on the stability of the European political and economic system, and we may say that Legitimacy was in pleasant correspondence with many of the specific purposes Talleyrand held dear.

There has been some tendency of late years to lessen the importance of Talleyrand's rôle at Paris, and especially at Vienna. So great an authority as Professor Webster, though he is careful not to carp at Talleyrand's fame as Lacour-Gayet constantly does, none the less clearly feels that Talleyrand was rather less than a magician. Certainly we cannot today deny that impersonal forces had made the situation in 1814, and that Talleyrand did nothing contrary to Nature. Indeed, his greatness lies in the fact that he attempted nothing unnatural, that he, rather than the allies, took advantage of "fixed and immutable" material conditions. The metaphysics of historical determinism need not here detain us. Probably the fall of empires is as much determined as the outcome of a football match. But to us who do not share the omniscience of divinity, the success of a given football team seems to depend ultimately on the calibre of its players. After a certain point, diplomatic negotiations, at least in the old days, were a game in which the most skilled players commonly won. War, politics, geography, ethnology, and of course in a very special sense economics, established limits within which the diplomatist must work. Those limits have no doubt narrowed in modern times; in 1814 they were still fairly wide, and even in 1919 they had not quite shrunk to nothing. Now Talleyrand, judged by his work in 1814–15, was clearly a star. No one can read the letters to Louis XVIII printed in Part VIII of the *Memoirs* without realizing that he is, even if vicariously, following at close range and in detail the perfection of a given sort of human activity. Of course, one is free to feel that the whole performance, though like the work of a tight-rope walker, it requires great skill, is lacking in nobility and dignity. One is also free to feel that Talleyrand, as much as any shirt-sleeved diplomat, is a mere puppet in the hands of God, Providence, or Dialectical Materialism. Talleyrand, himself, never tried to argue his opponents out of their feelings.

One last word on the inevitable comparison between 1814 and 1919 still seems necessary. Granted, as we have already done, that conditions had so changed that in 1919 neither allied nor German diplomats had anything like the range of action men had at Vienna, granted that the German delegation found themselves virtually prisoners at Versailles, yet let us suppose the German delegation led by a man of Talleyrand's calibre. Two great arguments, singularly like those Talleyrand used in 1814, were available for German use: Wilson's own distinction between the Hohenzollern government and the German people, with the new republic ready to enter into the European democratic system; and, even more important, Communism, Bolshevism, as a first-class spectre. Brockdorff-Rantzau never succeeded in breaking into allied counsels as Talleyrand did in Vienna. When he replied to the dictated terms of the Allies in the spring of 1919, he did indeed point out that no more harsh conditions would have been imposed on a Hohenzollern Germany, but he also insisted that Germany was not solely responsible for the war, and in general took a virtuous and ineffectively idealistic position. Even so, Lloyd-George was frightened by the German reply, and one cannot resist the impression that some Machiavellian strokes by the Germans on the theme of the Communist menace might have furthered a better peace. A German Talleyrand in 1918–1919 certainly could not have secured a "just" peace: not even the most ardent of our present-day defenders of the Vienna settlement, however, maintain that Vienna was a "just " peace. They do maintain that Europe after Vienna was far more stable than Europe after Versailles, and it is hard to see how the most optimistic of our contemporaries can deny that they are right. A German Talleyrand in 1918–1919 might well have procured terms which would have given the Weimar Republic, and hence Europe, a much greater degree of stability. And a stable—or at any rate rather less unstable—Weimar Republic might have thrown off Hitler as the Third French Republic threw off Boulanger.

But this, you say, is even more nonsense than most history in the subjunctive? A German Talleyrand is inconceivable, for all Germans are by temperament metaphysical idealists, and take themselves and Virtue far too seriously to play well the cynical game of diplomacy? Well, national character is not quite as simple as every-day symbolism makes it. Who shall say that Kant, William II, and Hitler are better Germans than Frederick the Great and Bismarck?

III

TALLEYRAND was held in Vienna by the final formalities of the treaties until June 10, 1815. As long as Napoleon was in power in France, he could only lie low. Fortune was with him again, however, and on June 18 Waterloo opened the road to France. He at once went to the side of his exiled King, who had left Ghent and was following in the wake of the victorious allied armies towards Paris. Talleyrand shared with Metternich the sensible opinion that it was extremely unwise for Louis to re-enter his kingdom so obviously under armed foreign protection. At an early morning interview with his sovereign at Mons which found both men in bad humor—neither were habitually early risers—Talleyrand insisted vigorously that Louis ought to go to the second city of his realm, Lyons, a royalist center untouched by invasion, and there set up a provisional government with no foreign taint. After the allied armies had left, the King could return to Paris. Thus many French patriots, who had rallied to Napoleon as the unsullied defender of French glory, would not find support of the returned Louis XVIII too galling to their national pride. Louis was impatient and in a hurry to get back to Paris, and he dismissed Talleyrand with the advice to go to Bourbon l'Archambault and try a cure.

This is the first trace of the break between Louis and his minister which was to send Talleyrand shortly into the unwanted ease of retirement. Louis never could bring himself to a warm liking for his renegade servant, could not forget that Talleyrand had shared profitably in the life of Directory, Consulate and Empire while he was an obscure country gentleman in Hartwell House. In view of what he went through, Louis had maintained an intellectual balance, a rather lazy sense of reality amazing in an *émigré*. But he was after all a Bourbon and a gentleman, and he could not be expected to love Talleyrand. Nor was he wholly above jealousy; and the letters Talleyrand had sent him from Vienna were indices of a capacity and an ambition in his minister not altogether heart-warming to a sovereign. He would use Talleyrand as long as necessary, but he would not hesitate to drop him as soon as possible.

He still had use for the Prince. King and minister made up their early morning quarrel, and the court continued on to Paris. At Cambrai, in French territory, Louis issued a declaration for which Talleyrand was partly responsible, admitting that he had made mistakes. "My government was likely to commit certain errors; perhaps it has committed them. There are times where the best intentions are not a sufficient guide, when, indeed, they sometimes lead astray; experience alone could tell; it will not be wasted." At the council which discussed this declaration, the King's brother, the Comte d'Artois, had a lively passage with Talleyrand because of this confession, which Artois regarded as beneath royal dignity. Here Talleyrand comes out clearly as a constitutional royalist, as, relatively speaking, a man of the Left. From this position he never really withdrew, and this, even more than the loss of Louis's favor, meant that he could not get on with a Chamber in majority Royalist.

Meanwhile in a Paris deserted by the beaten Emperor another unscrupulous and successful politician, who shares with Talleyrand the contempt of all good Victorians, had constituted a provisional government. Fouché, however, was a regicide, a member of that Convention which had martyred another Louis. He ought to have been even more objectionable to Louis XVIII than Talleyrand, who had wisely emigrated in the worst of the Terror, and was innocent of royal blood. Fouché had, however, accomplished a feat more difficult, because of the extremes thus brought together, than any of Talleyrand's political *volte-faces,* and had actually wormed his way into the confidence of the extreme royalists of the Faubourg St. Germain, who were persuaded that he was the only man in France able to protect them against the Jacobins. Louis was forced to negotiate with Fouché, and ended by taking him into the first ministry of the second Restoration. Talleyrand in his *Memoirs* writes of this as a most unhappy choice, and appears duly scandalized by the spectacle of a regicide minister of Louis XVIII. At the time, there is no sign that he protested. The careers, temperaments, and abilities of the two men were too much alike for them to be anything but rivals and enemies, and neither is really fair to the reputation of the other.

In this first ministry, formed on July 9, Talleyrand was President of the Council and Minister for Foreign Affairs. Fouché, still known by his Napoleonic title as the Duc d'Otrante, was fitly enough Minister of Police. Baron Louis, Pasquier, and Jaucourt, in Finances, Justice, Interior and the Navy were intimate friends of Talleyrand, and made his ministry a very personal one. During its life of ten weeks Talleyrand was in fact, as Prime Minister, head of the French government.

This experience was too short to afford a fair test of Talleyrand's ability as head of a government. His cabinet fell for reasons beyond his control. And yet it seems likely that his abilities had by this time—he was now in his sixties—been a bit too specialized in diplomacy to allow him to shift to the conduct of a cabinet, and to the manipulation of a large popular Assembly. For one thing, his reputation, which probably helped him in diplomacy, where villainy is expected if not condoned, certainly made it almost impossible for him to command the sentimental allegiance of a political party. Moreover, he had come, in the long conduct of his department, to expect obedience from his collaborators. The kind of devoted help he had from men like La Besnardière and d'Hauterive he could not possibly expect from a Fouché, a Gouvion St. Cyr, a Richelieu. He had been used to negotiating with opponents; he could not negotiate with colleagues. In actual practice, he was a somewhat vain and overbearing Prime Minister. Under more favorable circumstances, his undoubted gifts of tact and understanding of men's sentiments might have permitted his development as a great political leader. Yet one doubts it. At least under parliamentary government, a great political leader needs a better stock of illusions than Talleyrand was ever able to accumulate.

Talleyrand's brief ministry did render some services to France. For one thing, it saved the *pont de Jéna,* which bridges the Seine at the point where now stands the Eiffel Tower and where lately stood, on the other bank, the unmourned Trocadéro. The allied armies had occupied Paris after Waterloo. The Prussian Blücher wished to blow up this bridge because it commemorated a battle which the invincible Prussians had somehow lost. Wellington, who had learned better than this on the cricket fields of Eton, was able to take the first steps to stop Blücher from blowing up the bridge. Talleyrand, who had perhaps always known better, was able to head him off completely by the simple expedient of re-naming the bridge the *pont de l'École militaire.* As he himself remarks, this was "a designation which satisfied the savage vanity of the Prussians, and which as a play of words, is perhaps even a more pointed allusion than the original name of Jena." The incident, insignificant enough, is fit to stand for a good deal more in Talleyrand's life and in a world which persists in giving the lie to those hopeful souls who think men do not really quarrel over words. Why, asks the moralist, should a grown man wish to blow up a bridge because of a *name?* The answer, though the moralist may not accept it, is surely that the name is connected with, and indeed serves to arouse and maintain, a very strong sentiment in the man. If you wish to prevent the man's committing a certain act which clearly is in his mind associated with the name, the simplest thing to do is to break down the connection between the name and the sentiment. That may be a shallow proceeding, and the deep, true, sound way may possibly be to change the sentiment. A profounder man than Talleyrand might have gone to Blücher and urged him to forgive his enemies, pointed out that the blowing up of the bridge would not be consonant with the Sermon on the Mount, that the existence of a *pont de Jéna* did not in the least injure Prussia, and a good deal more, supported by religion and common sense. Only, would that profounder man have been able to rebuild the bridge Blücher would certainly have blown up?

Talleyrand was largely responsible for persuading Louis to constitute the Upper Chamber as a House of Peers on the same principle of heredity as that prevailing in the English House of Lords. Louis had resolved to preserve a personal appointive power in the Upper Chamber, but Talleyrand persuaded him that an hereditary chamber would gain stability and permanence more useful to Louis than any personal influence he might obtain. Talleyrand was certainly not omniscient. This stable and permanent institution had a life of fifteen years.

The elections of 1816 produced the famous *Chambre Introuvable, plus royaliste que le roi.* So soon after Waterloo, with the Leftist elements in hiding, with the White Terror in full force in certain departments, with the royalists for once showing a certain ability at electioneering, a reactionary Chamber was inevitable. Louis could hardly do less than sacrifice to it the regicide Fouché and the revolutionary Talleyrand. Substantially, that is the reason for the fall of Talleyrand's ministry. Louis knew that he would have trouble managing the new Chamber, and that Talleyrand was not the man to make this task easier. In the *Memoirs,* Talleyrand would have us understand that what really bulked largest during his ministry was the negotiation of the second treaty of Paris, and that at bottom his resignation was due to his unwillingness to truckle to allied demands. Yet Talleyrand had stomached a good deal in his life, and had he had the King or a party behind him, one suspects that he would have signed the second treaty as he did the first, and that in the *Memoirs* we should have learned how it was the best possible treaty to be secured at the time.

Richelieu, who had spent his exile in the service of the Tsar and had built up Odessa as if he had been a French *intendant* of the old régime, signed the treaty of Paris, which, as we have already seen, took away a few bits of French territory, laid an indemnity upon France, and restored to their own countries the works of art Napoleon had centralized in the new Athens. Richelieu, and not Talleyrand, had the difficult task of managing the *Chambre Introuvable.* Louis XVIII had taken quick advantage of a complaining word from his Minister, and on September 24, 1815, sent him back to private life. Talleyrand for once had overreached himself. He was to pay for his mistake by fifteen years of exclusion from power. The philosopher might feel that to be shut out from the career of a minister of the Bourbon Restoration was on the whole a reward, not a punishment. Talleyrand in his *Memoirs* says a few conventional things about how he welcomes leisure and retirement. But politicians are not philosophers, and though the cares of office line his face, ruin his digestion, destroy his nerves, and drive him to a premature grave, a politician out of office is a politician baulked and unhappy. Whatever he may say, Talleyrand's loss of power was a disappointment to him, and when, as he neared his eightieth year, another miracle gave him another chance for power, he grasped at it with delight.

CHAPTER SIX

Orleanist

I

TALLEYRAND had already in 1814 received from a grateful sovereign the title of Prince de Talleyrand. For a time he remained also Prince de Bénévent, but the Hundred Days and the new settlement of Italy finished that title. As Prince de Talleyrand he has remained in history. The restored legitimate sovereign of Naples, Ferdinand, knew well what a good supporter Talleyrand had been against the usurper Murat, and to compensate him for the loss of an Italian principality wished to bestow upon him an Italian dukedom. Talleyrand had honors enough, at least of that sort, but was delighted to have Ferdinand pass the title on to his nephew Edmond de Périgord. Edmond became therefore Duc de Dino, and his wife, Talleyrand's favorite Dorothée, the Duchesse de Dino, a rank she found very convenient at Court. To finish with the Talleyrand titles: in 1817 Archambaud, father of Edmond, was made first Duc de Talleyrand-Périgord, as much in reward for the faithful service of his uncle, made Cardinal and Archbishop of Paris in the same year, as for the less faithful if more useful services of his brother, Charles-Maurice, once Bishop of Autun. Later a dukedom of Valençay was erected for the younger son of Edmond. Finally, from Dorothée's Baltic estate there came, through failure of the male line, the dukedom of Sagan. Four dukedoms is not bad for one family, even in republican France.

Talleyrand's last, and to many his most shocking, love affair was consecrated by his retirement. It is reasonably certain that Talleyrand's affection for Dorothée de Dino was not wholly avuncular. After all, Dorothée was in no sense a blood-relation, and to speak of incest here has no meaning. She was, indeed, nearly forty years his junior, and his nephew's wife. All the proprieties, and perhaps even good taste, would have the relation between the kindly uncle and the devoted niece what it then seemed to the less malicious part of the world to be. Unfortunately, Freud and the facts, for once in agreement, seem to be on the side of the more malicious.

The best evidence of the true nature of this relation lies in the birth to Madame de Dino in 1820 of a third child seven years after her second, and six years after her permanent separation from her husband. It is true that in 1820 Edmond re-appeared and began again very publicly to live with his wife, and that he was on hand when the child, Pauline, was born. It is also true that his considerable debts were mysteriously paid at the same time, and that after Pauline's birth he resumed separate residence. Old Madame de Souza, who as Madame de Flahaut had known Talleyrand very well indeed, was in no doubt as to this pregnancy. As Mr. Duff Cooper reports her, she wrote: "Madame Dorothea has become mystical. Poor Edmond is a pitiable spectacle of this pregnancy conferred by grace of God. He fears his uncle may force him to stay in bed when Dorothea is delivered. He sees their minds so inclined to miracles that for all he knows he may be asked to suckle the infant." Edmond pretty clearly was not Pauline's father. In view of the closeness of the relations between Dorothée and Talleyrand, in view also of the affection and care Talleyrand later bestowed on the child, it would seem almost certain that he was the father.

Madame de Dino was an intelligent, well-bred young woman with large dark eyes and an ambition to be indispensable to some great man. The French are incapable of lavishing logic or sentiment on the Rights of Women, but one of their dearly cherished illusions is that women really rule this world, since, by being inexpressibly feminine, they really rule men. This may not be an illusion. At any rate, Madame de Dino believed it, and after a bit of experimentation, decided to do her share of world-ruling through her uncle. At Vienna she gave proof of how much help she could be to him, and shortly after she came to live with him in the rue St. Florentin, and set up a household dissolved only by Talleyrand's death.

There is no need to infer that Madame de Dino was not very fond of her uncle, that she acted quite coldly and heartlessly to exploit his greatness. On the contrary, every detail we have of this by no means Victorian household would indicate that in it were to be found love, good taste, order and happiness. Madame de Dino was an admirable hostess and a consoling Egeria. As Talleyrand grew older, and as the bodily afflictions of old age came upon him, she became quite indispensable as a nurse. For some time, indeed, there had been traces of mild hypochondria in his behavior. He was mortally afraid of an attack of apoplexy during his sleep, and had his bed so hollowed in the middle that he slept in what was virtually a sitting position. Even then, he wore several thicknesses of night-caps to protect himself from concussion should he fall out of bed. He suffered from various rheumatic disorders of the sort that provide the clientèle for many European watering-places. He would eat but one meal, dinner at the end of the day, and never drank except with this meal. On rare occasions, he drank enough to be a bit loquacious. True to his eighteenth-century bringing up, he always preferred Madeira to other wines. Never a hearty eater or drinker, he was in his later years almost abstemious. The anecdotes never show him as a cantankerous old man, however, and we may assume that even when her uncle was in his eighties, Madame de Dino never regretted her strange choice of career.

The family continued to live in the *hôtel* in the rue St. Florentin, but with enough travel and change of residence to prevent undue boredom. Valençay, now freed of its Spanish guests, once more became one of Talleyrand's favorite residences. In 1826 he actually allowed himself to be elected mayor of the little town of Valençay, and after his term was out he continued to serve as *conseiller municipal.* There was something irresistibly Roman and English, a touch of Cincinnatus and Washington, about the old statesman returned to serve his little village, and one suspects that Talleyrand thoroughly enjoyed the picture he made. On the estate he planted and improved with all the enthusiasm of a Whig lord; many of his trees are flourishing yet. The people of Valençay were proud of their patriarch, and the municipality named a street after him which has survived the changes of Second Empire and Third Republic. Madame de Dino, a rich woman in her own right, bought in 1825 the château of Rochecotte, on the Loire near Langeais, and from that time Talleyrand had two country estates. Rochecotte was smaller and more peaceful and there the family went for complete rest and recreation.

Talleyrand was still faithful to his "cure" at Bourbon l'Archambault, though from time to time he varied this accustomed sojourn by wider travels. One year he watered at Aix-la-Chapelle in what was now Prussia, and had once, incredibly, been France. He and Madame de Dino took two trips in the Pyrenees, stopping at such well-known watering-places as Cauterets, and several others trips to Provençe and Languedoc. Talleyrand, as befitted a *grand seigneur,* traveled in state with his own coach, servants, and baggage train. We must assume that he enjoyed traveling, if only as an antidote to staying at home. He was no man, however, to waste his time transferring his enjoyment of scenery to paper, and from what has survived of his correspondence you can make no additions to the literature of travel. Talleyrand was again loyal to his eighteenth-century upbringing; wherever he went he focused his attention on men and women rather than on rocks and trees and sky.

Talleyrand was now reaping one of the rewards of longevity: he was surviving old friends and old enemies. Choiseul-Gouffier, the Duchesse de Courlande, Cambacérès, Louis XVIII, Alexander I, Napoleon—the list of deaths is interminable. What is much rarer with old men, he continued to make new friends. Two of these at least are worth mentioning for the light they throw on Talleyrand's character. In 1822 Royer-Collard, the upright and stern leader of the "doctrinaires," as the idealistic liberals of the Chamber were called, inherited through his wife the domain of Châteauvieux in Berry, only ten miles distant from Valençay. Talleyrand wrote to this newcomer among the landed gentry of Berry a letter of welcome which shows that he was as much a master of the art of distinguished flattery as when he wrote to young Bonaparte in Italy: "It is an excellent thing for us to have you take a liking for our Berry, and wish to return there when you are without business, or rather without duties, in Paris. That will bring celebrity to our region, and celebrity will perhaps help us get better roads. Celebrity is a good means of working on the authorities, and one which you have at hand; I suspect you of not having any others." Royer-Collard was a strict moralist, known for his political purity and devotion to principle. Yet he yielded completely to the charm of Talleyrand and his niece and remained all his life a firm friend of the wicked old diplomatist. Perhaps Royer-Collard, who was only a good Catholic, was not so rigidly virtuous as those anti-clericals who have written about Talleyrand, and who would have avoided him like a leper. Perhaps also Royer-Collard's principles, doctrinaire though they have been called, really shut him off less completely from the world than their ugly little principles did the anti-clericals.

The other new friend was a promising young Provençal named Thiers. Talleyrand, who was old enough to be his grandfather, had singled the young man out from the journalists of the Left who were attacking the government in the *Constitutionnel*. Adolphe Thiers was a bright young man obviously destined to succeed, and Talleyrand had the acumen to be sure of his importance long before he had begun to stand out from the other bright young men. Thiers was to Talleyrand a useful link with the politically active forces which were preparing the overthrow of Charles X, the tactless old Comte d'Artois who had succeeded to the throne on the death of his brother, Louis XVIII. Talleyrand was too old for conspiring, or even for the politics of the pressure-group. But he had to have his hand on the pulse, and Thiers served for that very nicely. Moreover, Thiers was a pushing plebeian, and he felt towards the old aristocrat that mixture of feelings—awe, respect, envy, discipleship—usual in such a relation. He was planning his history of the French Revolution, and Talleyrand had been a great man during the Revolution. All in all, it was a profitable friendship on both sides, if not a very deep one. On Talleyrand's side, it gave proof of his continuing open-mindedness, of the extent to which he was free from the less profitably romantic illusions of his caste. To most grandees of the old régime and the emigration, Monsieur Thiers was a very objectionable young man.

Talleyrand's retirement was by no means idleness. His social obligations alone were enough to have occupied a less active old man. In Paris his *salon* was always full. In the country, there were visits to be made and received as well as the routine work of the squire and the mayor of Valençay. Immediately after his retirement, he worked industriously for the better part of a year on his *Memoirs,* of which the first eight parts bring the story down through the Congress of Vienna. From time to time he appeared in the Chamber of Peers, and occasionally took part in the debates. He was never very far from the central interest of his life—politics.

Talleyrand was driven into opposition by the action of Louis XVIII in dismissing him. He might have expressed that opposition by going over to the ultra-royalist group around Artois, and indeed there are a few indications that he began to cast out feelers in this direction. He was too sensible a politician to pursue them very far, and certainly never proposed to commit himself to the extreme Right. Fouché had found himself cast off by the Faubourg St. Germain, and Talleyrand knew that he was personally hardly more acceptable to the ultras than had been the regicide. Moreover, he seems to have made up his mind that ultra-royalism was already in the 1820's a lost cause, and that something like a bourgeois monarchy must sooner or later come in France. Finally, all his sympathies were with the enterprising, industrious young liberals of the Left and not with the self-satisfied, rigidly Catholic and conservative, already self-pitying and oppressed young romantics of the Right.

His first year of retirement was marked by an incident from which he apparently learned a good deal—again, a remarkable achievement in an old man. He had been deeply wounded by his dismissal, and his resentment turned largely on Louis's new favorite, Decaze, who had been made Minister of Police. On his return to Paris from Valençay in 1816, his *salon* in the rue St. Florentin became a gathering-place for all sorts of people hostile to the government, and Talleyrand became a kind of extra-parliamentary leader of the Opposition. Encouraged by so many supporting voices, and, it is not unlikely, warmed by the wine he had taken with this, his only meal of the day, Talleyrand one evening after a dinner at the English Embassy broke out into public invective against the ministry, which culminated in a reference to Decaze as a pimp.[1] Now in well-run monarchies to call a minister of the King a pimp is to reflect on the dignity of the monarch himself. Talleyrand's outbreak was not diminished by rumor, and Louis was obliged to banish him from Court for a while. The episode may be explained as an attempt on Talleyrand's part to see how far he could go, or as a temporary loss of self-control, or as a mere lapse, an error in judgment. At any rate, he never again laid himself open to such censure. He was duly forgiven, and resumed his place at Court next season.

The Prince de Talleyrand had, of course, a seat in the House of Peers, and here he made several important speeches. In 1821 and again in 1822 he attacked the ministry for attempting to revive the censorship which had served the old régime so ill. These speeches, like all his political acts, are aimed at an immediate goal, at identifying himself with the liberal opposition. But they contain reflections on the rôle of free speech in a modern state which, if they had come from anyone but Talleyrand, would have been taken by everyone as examples of sound political thought. He spoke also, and equally in vain, against the proposed French

1 *maquereau.*

intervention in Spanish affairs. In 1820 the Spanish liberals had revolted and set up the radical constitution of 1812; in a Europe ruled by Legitimacy, this could not be permitted. Here Talleyrand had to take up a new abstraction. He brought forward the doctrine of non-intervention which Canning in England had espoused, and established a precedent to which he could appeal very effectively in 1830. The administration, however, was steadily moving in the direction opposite to that which seemed wise to Talleyrand. After the accession of Charles X in 1824, outright reaction set in. Censorship, church monopoly of education, indemnity to the *émigrés,* led up finally to the famous ordinances which really repealed the constitutional charter of 1814. Charles was taking Legitimacy too seriously. Talleyrand had never meant all that in his famous slogan. He had been noticeably silent about Divine Right. In the Revolution which broke out in July, 1820, on the publication of the ordinances, he was once more on the side of the angels.

The Restoration was, then, a quiet time for Talleyrand, one that hardly affords much scope for his evil-doing. Yet even here his enemies have managed to find major treason. A recent discovery, aired by Messrs. Bénédek and Ernst in the *Revue de Paris* for December 15, 1933, proves clearly enough that in 1817 he sold to Metternich twelve packets of letters written by Napoleon between 1799 and 1813 to himself, Champagny, and Maret, his successors at the Ministry of Foreign Affairs. Of these there are now left in all 832 pieces, 73 originals signed by Napoleon, the rest copies, none of very great interest or importance. For these Metternich paid 500,000 francs in gold. Lacour-Gayet is convinced that the original packets contained pieces compromising Austrian reputation, and that it was for them that Metternich paid so high a price. These compromising documents he would then have destroyed. It is possible; it is also possible that Talleyrand held up Metternich for more money than the letters were then worth. The whole transaction is not one of the sort an upright Christian gentleman would glory in; but it is something less than high treason. The documents certainly betrayed no secrets of state, gave enemies of France no hold on France. They are now, if only for the letters signed by Napoleon, worth at least what the Austrians paid for them. Lacour-Gayet's *vendidit hic auro patriam* for this mildly amusing little job is a grotesque bit of language.

II

IN the *Memoirs,* Talleyrand is very insistent on his complete passiveness in the Revolution of 1830. He was a mere spectator, looking on sadly at the destruction of the noble edifice he had worked so hard to build in 1814 and 1815. He had tried to warn Charles X and his advisers, but in vain. This was one revolution, however, for which he was not responsible. Once the revolution had gone through, once Louis Philippe had accepted the Crown, once faced with a new government, he made the best of it: "I accepted it, I clung to it as to a sheet anchor, and I served it energetically; for if this government fell, I saw nothing before us but another Republic, and the terrible consequences it would entail—anarchy, a revolutionary war, and all the other evils from which France had been rescued with so much difficulty in 1815." For the first part of this statement there is every evidence. Talleyrand hated to see the Bourbon Restoration fail, for it was partly his work. He had written pessimistic letters all through June and July, 1830, and had guessed so well the date of the crisis that he gave his broker orders for very heavy short selling the day before the first of the Three Glorious Days which made the July Revolution. *Jouez à la baisse, on le peut.*

That he is telling the truth when he says he had no part in the final decisions which made Louis Philippe King of the French is not so certain. There is the usual crop of anecdotes, which prove only what people thought of Talleyrand. One relates how on the first of the Three Glorious Days he noted the sounding of the tocsin: "Listen, there's the tocsin. We're winning." "*We?* Who, *mon prince?*" "Ah, not a word; I'll tell you who we are tomorrow." But there is fairly reliable evidence that Talleyrand at the critical moment sent a messenger to Louis Philippe's sister, Madame Adelaide, with whom he had the most friendly relations, and that his message helped decide Louis Philippe to put himself at the head of the revolutionary movement. Certainly Talleyrand's *hôtel* was during the Three Days a rendezvous for all sorts of liberals, and men like Thiers knew quite well the importance of the moral support given the cause by the old Prince. Louis Philippe, once in office, knew he could count on Talleyrand; and the European situation was one in which all the skill and experience of Talleyrand were needed.

Europe had broken out with a relatively mild rash of revolutions in 1820, chiefly in the Mediterranean lands where the common people, lacking the Nordic virtues, gave the liberals no real support. The idealistic, or merely adventurous, minorities who engineered these revolutions were easily suppressed by the armies which a Europe organized on the principle of Legitimacy quite logically sent against them. The suppression of these revolutions, and other less dramatic problems, made necessary some kind of formal coöperation between the powers signatory to the treaties of Vienna; hence the system known as the Congress system, in which representatives of the powers met at various places to settle specific problems—at Aix-la-Chapelle in 1818, at Troppau and Laibach in 1821, at Verona in

1822. Metternich, Alexander and the other authors of the settlement of 1815 were not going to let their work be destroyed.

The ejection of Charles X was a patent violation of the principle of Legitimacy, and of the underlying principles of European government which provided, very roughly, a kind of constitution for the Congress system. If revolution in Italy and in Spain in 1820 had been contrary to this constitution, then revolution in France in 1830 was clearly also contrary to this constitution. Organized Europe had sent armies into Italy and Spain to put down revolution and uphold the European constitution. The term "constitution" is here used advisedly, and for the purpose of clarifying the actual situation; Metternich and his followers would, of course, never have used it of their own position, for to them the term constitution had only the specific sense of a written document patterned on American and French precedents, and was a word as charged with emotion as the word "soviet" now is. France in 1830, by overthrowing her legitimate monarch, had clearly violated the constitution of Europe, and should be treated as Spain and Italy had been treated, by the armed intervention of the forces of Law and Order, the armies of Austria, Prussia, and Russia.

There were indeed obstacles to any such intervention. For one thing, the experience of several hundred years had made it clear that foreign armies could not as a rule expect to find traveling as easy in France as in Italy and Spain. Moreover, though the Three Glorious Days may have been the work of a minority at Paris, the French people had shown in the past that they were willing to identify themselves with revolutionary acts as the people of Spain and Italy had not. A new generation had grown up in France, not to be horrified by tales of the Terror, but ready to be electrified by tales of Napoleon, now become the true hero of the great French Revolution. Most important of all, one great European power had already virtually withdrawn from the Congress system. A good many Englishmen, moved by a sentimental and wholly explicable attachment to the revolutionary traditions of their own country—after all, they, too, had once cut off a king's head, and forced another king into exile—had distrusted the organization of Europe under the principle of Legitimacy. Perfume it as you might, Legitimacy smelled to Englishmen like Divine Right of Kings; and Englishmen did not like phrases of that sort. The realist, as well as the devotee of the economic interpretation of history, will point out that, especially in Spanish America, British trade followed non-intervention, but not Legitimacy. They will insist that an England already organized along lines determined by the Industrial Revolution could not have had interests in common with feudal Austria. The fact, at any rate, is evident; by 1830, England had ceased to coöperate with Metternich.

Now if Louis Philippe could secure and retain the support of the English government, danger of intervention by the Central and Eastern European powers would be over. Danger of direct intervention was perhaps slight; but danger of a general European war was, in the summer and autumn of 1830, considerable. For the July Revolution had given the signal for two other uprisings, each of which might well bring on a general war. The Congress of Vienna had "compensated" the House of Orange for its loss of colonies to Britain, and thus maintained the principle of Legitimacy, by uniting with Holland the former Austrian Netherlands, better known to us as Belgium. The Belgians, Catholics, and as far as their enterprising industrialist middle classes went, fundamentally French in culture, did not get on with the Protestant Dutch traders who now ruled them, and a revolution broke out in Brussels on August 25. The constitutional Kingdom of Poland had survived Alexander, but Nicholas was too much for it. Revolt broke out in Warsaw on November 29, the putting down of which occupied the Russian army for some months. Throughout Europe people of "liberal" affiliations were aroused to emotional participation on the side of the rebel Poles and Belgians; people of "conservative" affiliations were aroused to emotional participation against them. Ambitious young men, schemers, exhibitionists, fanatics took one side or another, and in a hundred cross-currents the kind of passion that takes itself out in war flowed through the consciousness of Europeans.

A firm Anglo-French alliance was the surest guarantee against war. A great many conditions in 1830 favored such an alliance; the two countries were both limited monarchies, with parliaments, free press, government by discussion; the recent Revolution in France had been so bloodless that it seemed rather like that Glorious Revolution of 1688 in England than like the indecent great French Revolution; both countries were more interested in the maintenance of European trade than in the maintenance of Hapsburg, Hohenzollern, or Romanov absolutism; the middle classes of both countries had, even before 1830, come to regard France and England, the "liberal" states, as standing together emotionally over against the "despotic" states, Austria, Prussia, and Russia. Sympathy for Poland was fashionable both in France and in England. The Belgian Revolution was, however, a real danger to Franco-British friendship, and hence to European peace. Some Frenchmen, and some Belgians too, wanted to take advantage of the uprising to bring the Belgian provinces back into France, as they had been under the Republic and the Empire. Others, afraid of so radical a step, wanted a French prince, preferably a son of Louis Philippe, to rule over an independent Belgium, which some hoped would eventually be absorbed in France. Few Frenchmen, even those condemned by their principles to disapprove revolutions, could bring themselves to regret very deeply that a French-speaking people had overthrown its boorish Dutch rulers. On the other hand, many English Tories wished to see the King of Holland restored to his rightful rule over the rebellious provinces, and many English Protestants were not happy to see a Protestant kingdom weakened. Moreover, English statesmen had blessed the union of Holland and Belgium because they wished a moderately strong power immediately north of France and opposite the mouth of the Thames. No Englishman with a proper feeling of patriotism and an understanding of the time-proven traditions—the logic-ridden French would call them invariable principles—of British foreign policy, could, of course, even contemplate the possibilities of French annexation of Belgium, or a Belgium ruled by a French prince.

To Talleyrand, as French Ambassador to the Court of St. James, Louis Philippe entrusted the task of preserving peace by solving in a way satisfactory to the rest of Europe the problems arising from the Belgian Revolution. Once more the aged diplomat was called on to help find a formula that would satisfy the warring prides, greeds, aspirations, and—at long last—interests, of half Europe. Once more, as in 1815, he succeeded, and the great powers of Europe enjoyed almost a whole generation of something like peace. Others besides Talleyrand wanted peace, or he could not have attained it. Here as elsewhere he achieved no miracle—unless, indeed, you are inclined to regard the triumph of common sense in this world as a miracle.

In spite of his seventy-six years, and his various bodily ailments, Talleyrand seems to have welcomed an opportunity to play once more an important rôle in world politics. He refused Louis Philippe's request at first, but allowed himself to be persuaded, and on September 25, 1830, arrived in London as Ambassador of the King of the French. Socially he was a great success from the start. Madame de Dino charmed English society as she had charmed Austrian and French society. Entertainments at the French Embassy acquired an excellent reputation for taste and splendor, which they well might, for Talleyrand was paid almost a million francs a year during his stay in England. Wellington was still in power on Talleyrand's arrival, and the two men were great friends. Talleyrand hated Napoleon well enough to love his conqueror, and Wellington was too good an Englishman not to be flattered by Talleyrand's admiration for English political wisdom. There is an anecdote which has the two conversing in London after the revolutions in France, Belgium, Germany, Poland and elsewhere and in the midst of the bitter English agitation over the Reform Bill. Talleyrand asked the Duke if he could suggest any place where an old man might retire in peace and security. The Duke thought seriously for some moments, and then replied in magnificent monosyllables: "No, Prince, by God I can't!"

With the man in the street the French Ambassador was at least as popular as with the ruling classes. Byron had made wickedness fashionable and admirable, and indeed your ordinary Englishman, for all Gladstone and Queen Victoria, has always admired a rake. Since Talleyrand was a Frenchman, and couldn't therefore ever have had a chance to be a real gentleman, one could admire his success without jeopardizing one's respectability. He represented a government which had paid England the appreciated compliment of imitating its institutions. Nodding, saluting from his coach, he was a fine figure of a man, a hearty old gentleman who might almost have been an English squire. He was prodigiously old, he had lived through countless revolutions, and here he was, alive, triumphant, wise. No wonder London crowds cheered him at his passing, shouted "Hurrah for Louis Philippe!" and welcomed for the first time that tri-color flag which the ragged armies of the First Republic had borne victoriously against them. It was heartwarming.

There is little heart-warming in Talleyrand's career. He was more used to the sometimes envenomed praise of Court and *salon* than to the innocent huzzas of the multitude. Even his enemies ought not to begrudge him this tardy, brief acclaim. Not for long would he be a Grand Old Man to anyone. Perhaps only an English crowd would ever be generous enough, undiscerning enough, to cheer a man so very human.

Talleyrand's first task was to allay English fears that the new French Revolution might after all be the old one in disguise, that the guillotine and the Terror—Carlyle and Dickens had not yet written, and we may therefore omit the knitting-women—might follow hard on the barricades. In conversations with the Tory Prime Minister Wellington and his Foreign Secretary Aberdeen he brought to bear his old friendships, his associations with the Congress of Vienna, his reputation for political conservatism, to the task of allaying these fears. He was too sensible to be apologetic. A passage from a letter of his to Molé, then French Foreign Minister, shows how cleverly he defended the respectability of the new government: "The Duke of Wellington's sentiments are quite favorable to the state of things which fortunately now exists in France. Nevertheless, as in the course of our conversation he made use of the word unfortunate in speaking of the Revolution, I thought I ought to take notice of this expression, and said that no doubt it had been suggested to him, by a very natural feeling of pity for those whom this Revolution had dethroned; but that he must feel that it was not a misfortune, either for France—saved by it from the terrible position in which the policy of the late government had placed it—or for the other States, with whom we are desirous of remaining on friendly terms, and from which we shall never deviate, if, as we have the right to demand, the dignity of France is always respected." The Duke withdrew the expression "unfortunate," and all was well. The continued conservatism of Louis Philippe's government, the closing of the popular societies which threatened to revive Jacobinism, the successful side-tracking of republicanism, made Talleyrand's task here easy enough. He himself was to the English a satisfactory guarantee that the government which sent him would not go beyond the bounds of political respectability.

Belgium made the real difficulty. Talleyrand was faced at the start with a problem which threatened to bar further progress. The Congress system had indeed broken down, but there was left in the institution of the ambassadors' Conference an instrument for European federative action which might still work. The obvious first step was to call such a Conference of the ambassadors of the great powers at some capital city. Molé and other important political leaders in France wanted the Conference held in Paris. The English wanted it held in London. Talleyrand cared no more about where the Conference was held than he had cared about the name of the *pont de Jéna.* Molé, and for a while Louis Philippe himself, worked their emotions up to the point where the honor, reputation, glory, and existence of the new French government were involved in holding the Conference in Paris. To say that for the English the honor, reputation, glory and existence of England were *not* involved in holding the Conference at London would perhaps be paying the English too great a compliment. But they did have more definite reasons to urge in favor of London: time was of utmost importance, and the ambassadors at London already had their credentials, and could get to work at once with full powers; in Paris this was not so. Reasons not adduced to Talleyrand, at least not officially were even more valid: Paris was a city still greatly distrusted by the envoys of the Central and Eastern European powers; it was still in the full aftermath of Revolution. Talleyrand was instructed to press for Paris, and in his official correspondence he insists almost too much that he lived up to the letter of his instructions. In private letters to Madame Adelaide, however, he wrote frankly that he agreed with the English, that Wellington was right, and that the Conference ought to be held in London. These letters were of course taken straight to Louis Philippe, and finally convinced him. Molé resigned, and the Conference was called to meet in London.

It was this London Conference which, after many sessions and many protocols, put in its first form the famous "scrap of paper" of 1914. The erection of a neutral, independent Belgium was a long and complicated process, and the final treaty was not signed until 1839, but the essential steps were taken in 1830 and 1831. Talleyrand was an important figure in all the work of this Conference. The Tories, who fell from power in the autumn of 1830, to make way for that Whig ministry under Lord Grey which finally put through the Reform Bill of 1832, pretended that he dominated the Conference. Lord Londonderry protested to the House of Lords on August 9, 1831, that "I see France overawing us all by the aid of her skillful and active politician here, and I fear that he has in his hands the power of decision, and exerts that, which I shall call a domineering influence, over such of the political arrangements of Europe as are carried on and decided upon in this country, which formerly were always directed by the wisdom and genius of England." His Lordship was no doubt carried away a bit by party feeling. But there can be no doubt that Talleyrand was at London, as sixteen years before at Vienna, one of the men who determined, as far as God and economics will let any man determine, the decisions of high diplomacy.

The assembled ambassadors succeeded in forcing an armistice on the Belgian and Dutch combatants, and, after numerous sessions, decided to proclaim Belgium an independent state. When on January 20, 1831, the five powers—England, France, Austria, Prussia, and Russia—signed a protocol declaring that the new state should be perpetually neutral, and that each of the five powers guaranteed that neutrality, as well as the integrity and inviolability of Belgian territory, the heaviest work of the Conference was done. The new state would clearly, in the prevailing political atmosphere, have to be monarchical in form. The best solution appeared to be to put on the throne the Prince of Orange, eldest son of the King of Holland, who had openly shown his sympathies with the rebels. The Belgian National Congress, however, voted that no prince of the House of Nassau might occupy the throne of Belgium. Next the Belgian Congress proceeded formally to choose as king the Duc de Nemours, son of Louis Philippe, and Louis Philippe formally refused to permit his son to accept. "The throne of Louis Philippe," wrote Talleyrand in delight to Madame Adelaide when this good news was confirmed, "is today as old as that of St. Louis; had war broken out, it would have been born but yesterday." Finally the right man was found in the person of Leopold of Saxe-Coburg-Gotha, a house destined in the nineteenth, and even in the twentieth, centuries to provide the best of constitutional monarchs in all corners of Europe where its luck at marriage carried it.

Here, as at Vienna, the study of Talleyrand's methods is instructive. His was the task of defending before the rest of Europe revolutionary governments in France and in Belgium. His old principle of Legitimacy would never do, for it was still the cherished possession of Metternich, Nicholas, even his friend Wellington. He had to have a new principle and this he found in non-intervention. Now non-intervention, like *laissez-faire,* may seem to certain temperaments a mere negation, a refusal to act. In reality, both imply a very definite and very positive pattern of values. Into the theories which men used to explain and justify their adoption of the principle of non-intervention we need not here adventure, any more than we did with the theories centering on Legitimacy. The sentiments which the principle of non-intervention satisfied are worth a word. They were, of course, sentiments chiefly important in the ruling classes of England and France, though they are found in the nineteenth century among "liberals" in most of Europe. Talleyrand, of course, was concerned in 1830 and 1831 first of all with the sentiments of the English politicians.

Now non-intervention suggested to an Englishman the happy fact that he inhabited an island. It reminded him of his long-cherished independence of continental messes—an independence hardly borne out by history, but certainly existing in English sentiments. That "Niggers begin at Calais" has long been an article of faith for all sorts of Englishmen. Non-intervention held out the promise that Englishmen would no longer have to bother about the petty quarrels of dirty foreigners. It had, in fact, the same magic value the word "neutrality" has for many Americans in

1936. Again, non-intervention sounded quite a bit like fair-play. You allow a people to settle its own fate, instead of tyrannically dictating to it from the outside. Self-help, self-government, that's what's good for the Belgians, as it's good for the British. Finally, non-intervention was the principle most completely anathema to Metternich and his black crew of the Holy Alliance. If you were liberal and forward-looking, you hated Metternich, and loved what Metternich hated.

That Metternich hated non-intervention was clear enough. In 1830 he wrote to the Austrian Ambassador in London: "The principle of non-intervention is very popular in England; false in its essence, it may be maintained by an island-state. New France has not failed to appropriate this principle and to proclaim it loudly. It is brigands who object to police, and incendiaries who complain about firemen. We can never admit a claim as subversive as this is of all social order; we recognize, however, that we always have the right to answer any appeal for help addressed to us by a legitimate authority, just as we recognize that we have the right of extinguishing the fire in a neighbor's house in order to prevent its catching our own." As against such reactionary nonsense, non-intervention was a fine modern thing. What if England *had* set up greater Holland partly to have a stronger power on the French frontier? What if you now set up two weaker countries instead of one stronger one? This is what the Belgians want, and, by the principle of non-intervention, what they want they ought to have. Besides, the new France of the July Monarchy is a peaceful, industrious, bourgeois nation, almost as enlightened as the English, and quite anxious to learn more from the English.

Legitimacy had not in 1815 unduly tied anyone's hands at Vienna: the simplification of the map of Germany, the union of Norway and Sweden, indeed, as far as that goes, the union of Belgium and Holland, had all been quite far from legitimate. So now in 1830 the principle of non-intervention did not prevent the Conference of London from intervening quite successfully in Belgian affairs, and dictating boundaries, choice of king, international status, and a good deal else. Only, the principle permitted Talleyrand and Earl Grey to intervene, and prevented Metternich and Nicholas from intervening. That is, of course, the mark of a good principle on this earth. One-way principles may lead to Heaven or the scaffold—perhaps to Heaven by way of the scaffold—but not to diplomatic victories.

III

THE Belgian problem and the resulting London Conference of ambassadors filled the most important place in Talleyrand's four-year embassy at London. His popularity in England grew rather than lessened. After Londonderry had attacked him in the Lords, Wellington and Holland both came to his defense and praised his character as well as his abilities. Talleyrand was deeply touched by this tribute from Wellington, who was, he said, "the only statesman in all the world who ever said a good thing about me." But no other major problems arose, and Talleyrand had now reached his eightieth year. In 1834 he resigned his position, and left London forever.

He returned to France and a life much like that he had led before the brilliant opportunities of the July Revolution: Paris, society talk, followed by quieter months at Valençay or at Rochecotte. He had been chosen member of the newly reconstituted Academy of Moral and Political Sciences, and before his colleagues and a large public he made in 1838 his last dramatic appearance before the world. At eighty-four, he read, without glasses and with a firm voice, a *Eulogy of M. le comte Reinhard.* Count Reinhard was a faithful if minor diplomatist, a member of the Academy, and recently deceased. The *Eulogy* comes very near to being a eulogy, or at least an apology, of the Prince de Talleyrand. Reinhard had studied Protestant theology at Tübingen; Talleyrand seized the opportunity to explain how useful a theological education might be to a diplomatist. As he followed Reinhard's career, he referred constantly to the standards of the ideal diplomatist; the speech is really a little essay on the diplomatist as a type, like those favorite Renaissance essays on the courtier, the gentleman, the statesman. It is polished, weighty, sensible. There is in it nothing of the doddering old man. The audience was greatly moved by the dramatic quality of the performance. In the mid-nineteenth, they were face to face with the century of Louis XV. *"C'est du Voltaire,"* exclaimed the modern, eclectic Victor Cousin in the audience, loudly enough and frequently enough to be noted by the newspapermen, *"C'est du meilleur Voltaire."*

Talleyrand's old age was a singularly happy and dignified one. Now, even in France, he was not unpopular with the anonymous many who somehow contrive to have opinions. He was lame and rheumatic, but he was also tactfully waited upon by servants, nurses, and the faithful Dorothée. His mind seems never even touched by senescence. The Princesse de Lieven, by no means a charitable lady, wrote of him in his last years in London: "You can hardly imagine how many good sane doctrines one finds in this disciple of all forms of government, in this political *roué,* in this personification of all the vices. He is a strange creature; there is much to learn from his experience, to gather from his intelligence; at eighty years, that intelligence is wholly fresh." He was still not forbidden some of the pleasures of the *gourmet,* and he could still talk with pleasure about food and drink. He could still drive in the lovely countryside of Touraine. He was, in spite of the painful death in 1834 of Princess Tyszkiewicz, one of the most beloved of the ladies who had attached themselves to him and his career, still watched over by women who loved him—Madame de Dino and Pauline, now an adolescent girl touched for the first time with the mysteries of Christianity. God had clearly decided not to punish Talleyrand on this earth.

Talleyrand's earthly relation to his God is the last problem offered to his biographer, and the chief interest of these last four years of his life. The marriage with Madame Grand had prevented his complete reconciliation with the Church. He had returned to private life, but he had not been admitted to lay communion. Were he to die suddenly, he would die unblest, an exile from the Church in which he had been brought up, an unrepentant sinner condemned to eternal punishment. One suspects that Talleyrand himself could bear the prospect, though in such matters no wise man will betray an indecent certainty. Neither Madame de Dino, nor Pauline, full of the youthful freshness of religious conviction, could bear the prospect without horror. The Prince must reconcile himself with his God.

Talleyrand's conversion has given rise to a whole pamphlet-literature. Detailed descriptions of what went on at his bedside have been given by witnesses, and by many who were not witnesses. To Catholics it was an edifying spectacle, to neutrals a comedy, and to anti-clericals a farce, a Jesuit plot, a final mockery on the part of a man who had never believed in anything—not even in anti-clericalism. At his death the newspapers praised or scoffed at this deathbed repentance, according to their party lights. To his biographer it leaves a final and quite insoluble problem of motivation.

Like many other famous deathbed conversions, it had

been long and carefully planned. The Princesse de Talleyrand had died in 1835, and the one insuperable obstacle to the reconciliation of the Prince with the Church had thus been removed. She died unregretted by her husband, with whom she had not lived for nearly thirty years. For years he had had the best of relations with certain clergymen, and for years too he had been in the habit of going to mass. Something extraordinarily like piety does seem to have come upon him with the years. He made of Thomas à Kempis's *Imitation of Christ* his favorite reading, and for this we have not only the word of the interested Madame de Dino, but that of the Princesse de Lieven also. He was kind and gentle with Pauline, and helped her take the first steps in religion. But he signed nothing, and confessed nothing.

As happens so often in works of piety, the women in Talleyrand's household took the first steps. Pauline had been greatly impressed with a young priest at the Church of the Madeleine, the Abbé Dupanloup, destined to a great career. Madame de Dino and Pauline both praised this young priest to Talleyrand and emphasized his clarity of word and thought. Talleyrand, perhaps not unaware of the subtle suggestion and loving pressure surrounding him, gave the word, and asked the Abbé to dinner. Dupanloup was astonished by this invitation; it was a trifle like getting a neatly engraved card from Satan himself. He was a simple priest, as yet wholly outside the world of fashion and politics. In some confusion, he refused the invitation. The ladies were not discouraged, and on a renewed invitation, Dupanloup, one imagines somewhat frightened, accepted. The dinner was delightful. Talleyrand could always charm those who knew him only by reputation, and he never lost that charm. He talked to Dupanloup about religious matters, about preaching standards when he was young, about the weaknesses of the Anglican religion and the strength of the Catholic, and so on. Dupanloup left convinced that common opinion maligned the Prince. "I kept thinking in spite of myself of that noble, high forehead, those expressive and imposing features, that penetrating, profound glance of the eye; I kept thinking above all of the respect, the attentions, the tenderness, I might almost say the cult which his family and his friends professed towards him, and behind which the private citizen seemed to rest from the agitations of the world, looking out from this peace with such perfect tranquillity upon the extraordinary violence of insults and injuries showered upon the public man. For one thing of which I had been ignorant, is that M. le Prince de Talleyrand was venerated and cherished by all who were close to him."

The Abbé Dupanloup was the link between Talleyrand and the ecclesiastical world he had left so long ago. The Prince was pleased with the young priest, and told the ladies so. The stage was now set; the dénouement was hastened by the onset of a serious illness. One last stroke of wit is reported. Talleyrand was told that his old enemy, the now outmoded poet and politician Chateaubriand, had grown deaf; "he thinks he's deaf now that he no longer hears himself talked about," remarked the Prince.

The old man was in no hurry to assume sackcloth and ashes. Dupanloup returned, and left several works of piety. The Prince talked daily with Madame de Dino or with Pauline about the faith, or death, or some detail of his long life. On the other end of this curious grouping of human wills, which has a startling resemblance to the grouping of wills in a diplomatic conference, the high authorities of the Church were stirred to take notice of the impending conversion. The Archbishop of Paris, Monseigneur de Quélen, was in constant touch with his plenipotentiary, Dupanloup.

To record the repentant return of one who had so ostensibly and successfully deserted it would be a victory not to be disdained by a Church struggling to maintain itself in a society fallen prey to that worst of heresies—*enrichissez-vous.* Wiser than the jealous cults of Reason, of *la Patrie,* or of Dialectical Materialism, the Church knows no treason as absolute as itself, no treason, therefore, proof against the miracle of repentance.

Even after he had been obliged to take to his bed, the dying Talleyrand maintained the highest standards of his art. A kind of protocol had been prepared, a compromise between a two-page statement originally drawn up by Talleyrand, and the amendments made to it by Monseigneur de Quélen. In it Talleyrand made a dignified but complete confession of his sins, and announced his repentance. But the old man would not sign. Did he wish to preserve to the end the high formality, the dramatic conventions, the ritual of diplomacy? Only a few years before he had compelled the Duke of Wellington to observe the forms, and retract his description of Talleyrand's latest revolutionary loyalty as "unfortunate." He must be the Prince de Talleyrand even in negotiations with God's representatives on earth. Did he, perhaps, think he might survive even this illness, and wish to protect himself from the railings of the anticlericals, certain to follow upon his conversion? He must by now be used to the most venomous of attacks. Yet hitherto he had always been the triumphant villain, and even in the scorn of his enemies there had been no laughter. Now, were he to sign and survive, he might for the first time appear to some people ridiculous. Was this his final act wholly insincere, or was it, as his family and his friends maintained, the culmination of long and patient return upon himself and his past, a genuine conversion to the Church into which he had been baptized? This last question we cannot answer.

As Talleyrand's strength failed, he listened once more to Dupanloup's recapitulation of the situation, and on May 16 announced firmly that he wished to die as "a true and faithful child of the Catholic Church." That evening like a good diplomatist, he promised to sign the necessary documents between five and six o'clock the next morning. At the promised hour, in the presence of Dupanloup, the Duchesse de Dino, Pauline, the Duç de Valençay, his friend and literary executor Bacourt, the doctor in attendance, and a *valet de chambre,* he signed a rather vague document recapitulating his life, and concluding: "I have never ceased to consider myself as a child of the Church. I deplore again those acts of my life which have saddened the Church, and my last wishes are for it and for its supreme head." He also signed a personal letter to Pope Gregory XVI, in which vague and diplomatic generalities cloud his repentance sufficiently to maintain his dignity. It was done. Talleyrand was once more a Christian. To avoid any possible accusation that he had not been in sound mind, he had the documents antedated as of March 10, at an epoch when he had just delivered his eulogy of Reinhard at the Academy, and when all the world could testify to his soundness of mind. "Done the 10th of March, 1838. Signed at Paris the 17th of May, 1838." A precaution like this certainly proves that his was no ecstatic surrender. And yet one hesitates to conclude that it proves Talleyrand insincere to the last. After all, there are many sentiments more unchristian than *il est avec le ciel des accomodements.*

Later in the day the dying man received the visit of the King of the French and Madame Adelaide. He was still the Prince de Talleyrand, and he made formal presentations to the King of the persons in the room. After the King's departure he fell into a coma, and on awakening was given the last rites of the Church by the Abbé Dupanloup. At the proper point in the ceremony he extended his hands closed, as must a bishop. "Do not forget, M. l'abbé, that I am a bishop." Shortly afterwards he died.

After formal funeral services at Paris, attended by the dignitaries of court and society, he was buried, as he had wished, in the private chapel of St. Maurice in the convent of the Sisters of Charity at Valençay. No funeral monument calls the attention of the visitor to the burial place of the Prince de Talleyrand. Only within the vault, and inaccessible to the public, does a simple plaque mark his coffin. Nor are there any monuments to him in Paris, or elsewhere. The Prince de Talleyrand is not among those whom modern France delights to honor.

CHAPTER SEVEN

Politique et Moraliste

I

THE impossibility of literal translation could hardly be better illustrated than by the two words which head this chapter. "Moralist" in twentieth-century American English is at least as far from reproducing the second as is "politician" from reproducing the first. For a moralist today in America, and even in England, is a preaching, puritanical, repressive person occupied largely with matters of sex. The French are truer to the Latin origins of the word. A *moraliste* in the French tradition is anyone occupied with the objective observation of certain uniformities of behavior to be noted in human beings. He may also approve or disapprove of what he observes; he does commonly consider himself in a sense the custodian of some of these uniformities, or *mores,* but the *moraliste* is not necessarily a judge, and certainly is not necessarily a prude. Men like La Rochefoucauld, La Bruyère, Molière—and Talleyrand—are *moralistes.* As for the *politique,* he is not indeed the academic political theorist or political philosopher, though he is nearer to that than to the ward politician. The *politique* is the man whose interest in the political behavior of his fellow beings is both theoretical and practical. He is the engineer, whereas the American "politician" is either the contractor or the gang foreman, or both. Here unfortunately the comparison must stop: the political theorist does not yet hold the same relation to the *politique* that the "pure" scientist holds to the engineer.

Now Talleyrand is a *politique* and a *moraliste*, and as such deserves more critical treatment than he has received. Sainte-Beuve, in spite of his hatred of Talleyrand the man, has written well on some aspects of the statesman and diplomat. Dr. Hermann Wendorf in an essay on "Prince Talleyrand's System of Ideas" [1] has said some very sensible things about the materials for judging Talleyrand's ideas; but he will have Talleyrand a philosopher, and he endows the Prince with a much too imposing *Weltanschauung*. Talleyrand's true philosophical antecedents are not to be found in Descartes, nor even in Voltaire, but in Montaigne. They are indeed not philosophical at all in the sense the word has for most Germans. There is not much sense in assimilating his thought to philosophical thought in the formal sense. He knew that certain generalizations could be made about human behavior in the European world of the late eighteenth and early nineteenth centuries. Why those generalizations were true, what God or eternal principle had so arranged things, were questions that never seem to have troubled him. He was not, it must be repeated, inclined to metaphysics. But he was certainly a thinker, a *politique et moraliste*, and as such his thought is well worth attention.

One difficulty must, however, be disposed of. Talleyrand, it may be claimed by those who accept the cruder form of his legend, had in life one simple aim: get to the top of the heap and stay there. He was, *according to this view*, willing to say or write or do anything at all as long as he thought his ambition could be furthered thereby. He was the complete opportunist, and you cannot make sense out of the whole body of his expressed opinions, for they run the whole gamut of possible opinions; they are a complete

[1] *Die Ideenwelt des Fürsten Talleyrand.*

chaos. You cannot write on the political ideas of Talleyrand, because in the sense that faith and habit are essential to having, to possessing, he *had* no political ideas.

The full implications of the problem suggested by the foregoing commonplace objection to Talleyrand as a serious *politique et moraliste* reach to the very heart of this study, and must be partly postponed to the final chapter. As a matter of fact, the point of view described in the previous paragraph confuses *theories* and *uniformities*. Here it may be noted, first, that the legend exaggerates greatly Talleyrand's range of adaptability, that his stock of principles was by no means as miscellaneous as the above view implies. This will come out clearly in any fair appraisal of what he has left behind him—*Memoirs*, reports, speeches, letters. Second, and much more important, even were Talleyrand's career explicable in so simple a formula as "always keeping office," the record of what he said and did would still be an invaluable part of a well-rounded political theory. For staying in office, it may humbly be pointed out, is the first condition of political achievement. Political theory ought to deal with politics. Even if you wished only for a theoretical knowledge of the game of tennis, you would not go exclusively to treatises on ballistics; you would, if you were wise, also watch Tilden play—and play yourself. The comparison, if to the pure intellectual undignified, is all the sounder. In one sense, the word consistent may be applied to Talleyrand as to Tilden; they were both consistent winners.

The success of men like Talleyrand is not due to their not thinking, but to their thinking in a certain way, and to their avoidance of thinking in certain other ways. To be more specific: Talleyrand uses abstractions not as dogmas, but as hypotheses, as does a physicist. Though to influence other men he may talk of a "principle of Legitimacy," he never really thinks of "Legitimacy" *except in relation to courses of action which he can conveniently describe as legitimate.* It is not that any or all courses of action are to him a matter of indifference; it is not even that the *words* attached to courses of action are to him a matter of indifference. But he is quite incapable of divorcing words—even such nice abstract words as Justice—from courses of action. He is thoroughly modern, or something more than modern, in his refusal to set up such dichotomies as *noumena* and *phenomena,* ideal and real, theory and practice, thought and sentiment.

Now most men do think in terms of such dichotomies, which they feel to be true descriptions of "reality." They have in recent years commonly seen the process of historical change as a simple causal relation: either the horse Idea draws along the cart Matter, or the horse Matter draws along the cart Idea. The greater and more subtle thinkers in each set make so many concessions to the position of those in the other set that they end up . . . well, great and subtle thinkers. But some men never, after a certain stage of development, think in these horse-and-cart terms at all. They are almost, but not quite, unaware of the tragic contrast which is eating out the heart of poet and philosopher—the contrast between what men are and what men want to be; or if you prefer a touch of cynicism, the contrast between what they have and what they would like to have. Almost, but not quite. For if they were wholly unaware of this contrast, of this gap between what is and what may yet be, they would indeed not be men at all. But for them the gap is so small that they can go busily and not unhappily to work trying to fill it in. They are not tempted to stand on one side of the gap, contemplating wistfully or indignantly the other side, or sometimes refusing to contemplate it at all. They are not Titans. They do not live in ecstasy. They are not poets or philosophers. They do not move heaven and earth.

They do get things done. They are the practical men about whom so much has been written in praise and in scorn. All men lead some of their lives at this level, for not the most sensitive of men can always be aware of the contrast between the dinner before him and the dinner that might be before him. Bread is, fortunately perhaps, commonly indistinguishable from ambrosia. The practical man may take occasional leaps into the intense inane—usually not in the best Shelleyan style—and he may hold doggedly to a lot of rather abstract and extreme generalizations, usually outside the field in which he works and earns a living. Doggedly, but not dogmatically. For these men do not build the great systems which, hardened into dogma, defy and deny all change. They are not even as a rule articulate, and the record they leave behind them is not as easily read as is the record of writing and talking men.

For words have always invited some men to build them into systems, or to play with them as symbols, or to use them to obscure the gap between human awareness and human purpose. That true poets have achieved something more than these tricks with words is beside the point. One thing is pretty clear. The vast majority of writings and sayings on what is now known as the "social sciences" belong to the kind of thinking and feeling we have above described as system-building, as at bottom convinced of some dualistic interpretation of the universe, as, therefore, tending to put all questions in the simple cart-and-horse formula. Most men recorded on the subject of man as a political animal have used words more or less completely separated out by a process of abstraction from the contexts in which they are related to other parts of experience. To use a phrase blunt enough to exercise the ghost of outraged epistemology:

they have all lived somewhere in Utopia, even though they daily commute to offices on this earth.

Now a great many men have concerned themselves in quite other ways with man as a political animal. Men have dealt with other men in politics without building political systems, without abstracting words from their context in experience, without taking out citizenship in Utopia. Such men have not often recorded themselves, at least not in the imposing terms of the political philosopher. They have been known by many names, usually dyslogistic ones—"tyrant," politician, opportunist, boss, intriguer, factionalist and many more. They have been highly praised by only one conspicuous abstract thinker, Machiavelli, who showed by his own career that on the whole he was not himself one of these "practical" men. They are men who have the gift of working in the medium of men as painters in the medium of color and drawing, or musicians in the medium of sound. And this gift escapes complete formulation in words.

To try and describe a few rough uniformities in the manifestations of this gift may, however, well be very worth while. Since these men exist, they ought to be fitted into any attempted understanding of political problems. To say that they are mere wretches who prevent moral progress, or narrow creatures who lack the long view, or simply unintellectual men, is to dismiss them far too cheaply. Now Talleyrand is one of the most successful of these men, and one who has left, for an intriguer and man of action, a good deal of written work. He is a man who had a lively curiosity, indeed an intellectual curiosity, about a world he did not wish, or did not believe it possible, to change very much—certainly not by declaring that since all men *are* equal, they *ought* to be equal, or by any similar use of abstractions.

All this, you say, is battering down open doors? In this

modern world of ours few men will defend old-fashioned philosophy, and our admiration is all for the hard-headed and the hard-boiled, for the Machiavellian politician, for success in the sense of mere prevailing. Perhaps so. But in the social sciences the more vocal thinkers are still on the side of the angels of light and abstraction. Rousseau and Bentham are still political thinkers, Talleyrand and Canning political managers. No, the door is still shut, and worth opening, if only in a crack.

II

UPON Talleyrand is usually cast, with intent to damn, the epithet Machiavellian. Many of the overtones suggested by the epithet do not really apply to him at all accurately. Its essentials clearly do apply. These essentials may be stated as follows: that the ethical systems current among men have set standards well above the capacities of the mass of mankind; that this mass will continue to *act* in accordance with its capacities—that is, it will continue to lie, to steal, to commit adultery, to be jealous, self-assertive, cruel and cowardly, as well as, occasionally, honest, humble, and even quiet; that, however, the mass of mankind admires immensely, and in one sense wishes to attain, high moral standards; that, therefore, one who wishes to have influence among men will try and adapt himself to their acts while seeming to adapt himself to their aspirations; that he will consciously use the moral absolutes men admire, and the imperfect worldly appetites they share, to attain power over them.

Yet—and this is very important—it is only because of his actions, and an occasional epigram not meant for the great public, that Talleyrand can be judged to accept this Machiavellian point of view. In his speeches of the revolutionary period, in his *Memoirs,* even in his private correspondence, he appeals constantly to principles, to abstract moral ideas. He is never on the side of evil, never even counsels a bald pragmatism. In his correspondence with Louis XVIII during the Congress of Vienna, there is nothing on the surface of his letters to show that he did not believe in Legitimacy as completely and as metaphysically as Robespierre believed in the Republic of Virtue, or as Bentham believed in Utility, or Herbert Spencer in Evolution. Occasionally one suspects beneath the surface an irony so veiled as hardly to exist, an irony which might suit communication between two gentlemen of the old régime; but even here we may read too much between the lines. The *Memoirs* are strewn with what in another might seem moral platitudes: "Man is composed of a soul and a body, and it is the first which rules the second"; Locke, Montesquieu, and the first generation of *philosophes* "have constantly repeated and often strengthened the eternal basis on which repose the morals of the human race."

How then do we know that Talleyrand did not believe at least as much as most men the abstractions he employed, the ideals he asserted? We know partly because of the skeptical flavor of much of what he said and wrote more privately, because of the whole pattern of his values, to which we shall recur. But we know also, just as did his more acute contemporaries, from the rapidity and skill with which he shifted ideals and principles. In short, we know from what he did. To "believe in" ideals and principles means that the sentiments of the believer are in correspondence with his ideas and principles. *And human beings simply cannot change their sentiments as rapidly and as completely as Talleyrand changed his principles.* It does not of course follow that Talleyrand had no sentiments; they were simply not attached to the more abstract principles to which he gave utterance. Though the preachers will never believe it, some men do divorce their sentiments from words of high abstraction.

A list of abstractions in which it is fairly evident that Talleyrand did not believe would be easy to make. In a speech before the National Assembly on July 7, 1789, he defended by an ingenious and fashionable appeal to the General Will of Rousseau the cancellation of the so-called *mandats impératifs,* definite instructions given by their constituents to deputies to the Estates General to vote in a certain way on certain questions. On October 10 he showed that the property of the clergy was not like other property, and could therefore be confiscated without contradicting the Declaration of the Rights of Man and the Citizen, which had declared the right to property to be "natural and imprescriptible." In another speech of February 11, 1790, he has a phrase which sums up one of the ideals of the Revolution, "substitute for the self-love of the province the true love of the fatherland." [1] One might add to that one of his later *pensées,* "I am blasé about success: *The fatherland is saved* does not mean anything to me any more." [2] Better yet: the National Assembly has had reason to believe "that the Supreme Being, in endowing man with Perfectibility, the especial characteristic of his nature, has not forbidden him to apply it to the Social Order, now become the most universal of his interests and the first of his needs."

There is not much use in repeating this process for other faiths and other systems Talleyrand defended. Suffice it to remark that a similar collection could be made in defense of Napoleonic Order, Bourbon Legitimacy, and Or-

[1] *Substituer à l'amour propre de province l'amour véritable de la patrie.*

[2] *Je suis blasé sur le succès: 'La patrie est sauvée' ne me fait plus rien.*

leanist *laissez-faire*. It is much more important to realize that Talleyrand did have sentiments, did make judgments of value, did indeed have principles, if you like to call them such. To say that he was guided solely by ambition is, like saying that he valued only success, to confine one's self to abstractions not particularly illuminating. Neither ambition nor success operate in a vacuum; even in the pseudo-scientific popular formulation of "the survival of the fittest" one is driven back to consider the whole context of a given act of a given person. Talleyrand was willing to achieve success by talking about human perfectibility as though he believed in it. He was not willing, or not able, to achieve success by wearing a red liberty cap and inscribing cemeteries with "death is an eternal sleep"—which his colleague Fouché did very well. He was willing to write to the First Consul as to a God-given leader, and be to him for years as servant to master. But he was not willing, or not able, to follow the Emperor in his earth-rending, and self-rending, expeditions to Eternity by way of Madrid and Moscow. It is not important here to consider whether these limitations, which like all limitations mark off positively as well as negatively, came from within him or from without. They are at least there. They serve to define the pattern of existence within which his ambition had to be satisfied, within which success was possible.

Talleyrand was far from immune to the common human desire to appear consistent, to appear to have retained over long periods the same tastes and opinions. With him, the task may seem offhand so difficult that one wonders he attempted it. But it must be remembered that, especially at the time he wrote the most important part of the *Memoirs,* in 1816, he had not among most of his contemporaries the extraordinary reputation for complete lack of permanent tastes, opinions, and especially principles which the later nineteenth century gave him. Some of the passages in the *Memoirs* insisting on his consistency were no doubt dictated by his constant desire to appear puzzling, and therefore interesting to other men. Yet even in such famous assertions as that he had never betrayed a government which had not already betrayed itself, or, to use his own words in the *Memoirs,* "I have never conspired in my life, except at those times when I had the majority of France for an accomplice, and when I sought with it the salvation of the country"—even in these assertions there is not lacking a certain correspondence with fact. Talleyrand was consistent throughout his life in respect to certain tastes, certain judgments of value, certain mental attitudes, which, though complex, superficially shifting, and never purely abstract, do still form the kind of unity discernible in the life of a man, or in a work of art.

Returning from America Talleyrand found in Hamburg the former mistress of the Duc d'Orléans, Madame de Genlis—of whom he wrote the famous phrase, "in order to avoid the scandal of coquetry, Madame de Genlis always yielded easily"—and, remarking that she appeared to be the same woman he had known before in prosperity in France, in exile in England, he concluded: "The unchangeableness of compound natures proceeds from their suppleness."[1] He might well have written that sentence about himself.

Talleyrand, as Dr. Wendorf has pointed out, belonged all his life to the eighteenth-century world of the Enlightenment. This was not the Enlightenment of nineteenth-century text-books, the age of abstract, purely deductive thought, of the predominance of cold Reason over warm Feeling, the age of "botanizing on his grandmother's grave" —an age which never existed, and whose characteristics ap-

[1] *La fixité dans les natures composées tient à leur souplesse.*

pear nearest to existing only in the works of second- and third-rate men like Holbach and Godwin. It was the Enlightenment of Locke, Molière, Voltaire, Montesquieu, of Addison, Pope, Boileau, yes, and of Robert Walpole, Fleury, Chesterfield, and Frederick the Great. We cannot here attempt another essay on the intellectual history of the eighteenth century. It will be better to go direct to Talleyrand's own words and acts, and attempt to fit them together into a pattern. The essential is, however, to forget the textbook pattern, the pattern of shallow, optimistic, mechanical "Reason."

Through all Talleyrand's life there runs a strand of pessimism. This is never romantic pessimism, never the moaning of a lost soul; it is simply a recognition of the fact that most men want what they cannot get. When the old man reflects that "the century has the character of an octogenarian; it seems to me the image of old age—impotence and self-love" or "As to what will become of the world, I know nothing.—What I do see, is that nothing is replaced; what does end, ends entirely. One sees clearly only what one has lost," these may be simply the disillusions—or illusions—of old age. But, like other great French moralists, La Rochefoucauld, La Bruyère, Sainte-Beuve himself, he does not close his eyes to the imperfections of ordinary human nature. Talleyrand felt, and felt deeply, something like that uneasiness which has possessed the prophets. As he was not a prophet, but an eighteenth-century gentleman, that uneasiness does not turn into high poetry, but into maxims: "that disposition which leads us to discover what is above all essential—to do, to be, like everybody else"; "Great ease of access on the part of sovereigns inspires love rather than respect, and at the first difficulties love passes"; [1] "Envy, the

[1] *Au premier embarras l'amour passe.*

great principle of the French Revolution, has assumed the mask of a derisive Equality; it sweeps its insulting level over everyone's head, to destroy those innocent superiorities established by social distinctions"; "the spirit of the multitude, accustomed to take the successes of bad faith for skill"; "In politics as elsewhere one must not love too much; it confuses; it lessens the clarity of one's view—and it is not always counted to one's credit."

This list, too, could be greatly extended. What is common to all these maxims is a sense of inadequacy in human beings, of their inability to live up to their advertised aims. In Talleyrand and his generation it is partly no doubt a Christian inheritance, a reflection of the doctrine of Original Sin, a doctrine *felt* as well as *conceived.* Indeed, the common basis of the pessimism as regards human nature to be found in Stoicism, Christianity, the earlier part of Enlightenment and in Messrs. Adler and Jung and Freud is most striking, however differently these faiths attempt to overcome this pessimism. It is not, in sane men, an obsession. In Talleyrand it is simply a part of his gift for seeing himself and others with complete objectivity, for seeing human hopes, fears, passions, sentiments, words and deeds as *given,* like the weather, and as unmixed with ethics. He could regard human failings with a technician's interest, as a good doctor regards human diseases. Pessimism is almost too strong a word to describe this attitude, which is rather a complete absence of faith in the reforming power of abstract ethical ideals. Yet, since there is no better word available, we shall continue to use it in this sense to describe one phase of Talleyrand's attitude towards his fellows.

Now the roots of this feeling of human inadequacy go very deep into experience. We must assume that all men are aware of a contrast between the situation in which they find themselves at a given moment and other situations in which they might find themselves. The point is hard to make except in metaphysical terms, and metaphysics is a highly specialized art which the layman quite rightly hesitates to practice. In particular, words like "Reality," "Nature," or even "external world," are traps. The appeal to common sense cannot be used in the twentieth century as successfully as it could in the eighteenth. But—to take the plunge—the contrast might be put as that between the real and the ideal, between what is and what ought to be, between the present and the past-present-future. On a less metaphysical plane, some such contrast is the root of tragedy and comedy alike. Man's *awkwardness* can be either tragic or comic; and man is awkward because of the contrast, plain to the spectator at least, between what he is doing and what he is trying to do, between what he is and what he evidently thinks he is. This contrast is inescapable; all the great monisms are really dualisms.

One doubts whether this contrast is of great importance to the lower animals. Certainly in man it is sharpened rather by his capacity for symbolic thinking than by what we commonly call his will. Even if you are so fond of pseudo-scientific monism that you find it helpful to regard thought as simply one way in which the human organism responds to environment, even then you do not escape awareness of the contrast between what is and what may be. For thought modifies the environment in a way no other organic response does, by creating an infinite number of potential environments, some of which even sensible men regard as "possible."

But thanks to their capacity for abstract thought and abstract feeling—the phrase is deliberately provocative, and will be nonsense to many; *capacity to attach abstractions to feel-*

ings, followed by capacity to attach feelings to abstractions may be better—thanks to these capacities, men may lighten this contrast between the real and the ideal by exaggerating it. At the metaphysical extremes the truth of this paradox is evident. If you can, in an access of mysticism, extinguish all awareness of this world of sense-experience in Nirvana, *theoria,* or the body of Christ, you have obviously lifted yourself above these awkward contrasts; if you can, with what seems to be more mystic effort, convince yourself that the bashing about of a lot of tiny particles of "matter" watches over you as over the fall of a sparrow, you have just as obviously made yourself comfortable in a world not disturbed by these contrasts. Few men are capable of these extremes. Most men are capable of attaining some consolation by traveling part way along the road to one or the other.

Some men, however, attempt to lighten the contrast by minimizing it; that is, by planning and carrying out useful actions known to be at least sometimes possible because previously observed. They are constantly endeavoring to adapt themselves to the situation in which they find themselves. They will not have too great a gap between the real and the ideal. They are men commonly qualified as stable, sensible, moderate, practical. They like equilibrium, balance, peace on earth. They distrust enthusiasm, violence, storming of the heavens, the peace of the mystic. *But they are not necessarily unfeeling men,* as the romantic nineteenth century affected to think them. In particular, they may feel quite as strongly as other men the fundamental tragic nature of man's plight. They may indeed well feel it more strongly, since they cannot explain it away to their own satisfaction, as can their more exalted brothers. Pope's lines are surely in deeper and more universal concord with human experience than anything Keats ever wrote:

Chaos of Thought and Passion, all confused;
Still by himself abused, or disabused;
Great lord of all things, yet a prey to all;
Sole judge of Truth, in endless Error hurled;
The glory, jest, and riddle of the world!

The men of the early and middle eighteenth century, the men who, rather than Rousseau or the late *philosophes,* made Talleyrand's intellectual and emotional education, were in some ways more deeply moved by the tragic contrast between life as it is and life as it might, or ought to be, than their predecessors or their successors. They lived at a time when the great achievements of seventeenth-century science had become the heritage of all educated men. The kind of thinking that had produced the work of Newton had proved itself in its results. Men had now perfected a tool that hardly any of their ancestors had possessed in anything like the same perfection. Most of these fine gentlemen were in no sense laboratory scientists, even if they did occasionally dabble about with experimentation in "natural philosophy." But they had learned from science to distrust both immediate sense-experience and the traditional theoretical explanations of such experience—explanations theological in origin, or like pre-Copernican astronomy, encased in a theological covering. They had a glimpse of boundless possibilities contained in this new way of thinking. But the glimpse had not yet become for them, as it became for so many of their grandchildren, a vision distracting them from what lay about them. Reason as used by Newton, and even by Descartes and Locke, provided less a pattern of a better world than a very tentative map of this one. Yet even for these moderate men, reason helped to heighten the contrast between the confused world of the senses—and of common sense—and the clear world of science.

At the same time one of the great refuges of the human

spirit in distress was closed to them. Christianity as represented in the formally organized churches had lost what reason had gained. A Newton might retain his faith, and even his orthodoxy. But by the middle of the eighteenth century most upper-class Frenchmen and Englishmen had been so brought up that traditional Christianity had no way of getting at them. Christianity had become an unfashionable superstition, useful for the masses of mankind—though even for them a nice providential Deity would be better than the vengeful old Hebrew Jehovah—but distinctly not up to a gentleman's standards.

Even these gentlemen required a refuge from the distresses they stoically and brightly refused to admit they felt. One of their refuges is irony, the clearest indication that these sensible people were not also shallow people. For irony, like prayer, is a cry of distress. Prayer may spring from humility and irony from pride, and both may become matters of habit. But both are proofs of an awareness of man's insufficiencies, and both are signs of feeling for one's fellows. Irony may sometimes be close to exhibitionism. It may be an instrument to wound others or one's self. But it is also, and perhaps chiefly, a way of keeping up one's courage, of facing a world which obstinately refuses to fit into any of the formulas in which one would like to wrap it up. One of Talleyrand's maxims is a perfect illustration of the way in which irony is founded upon an imaginative awareness of man's predicament as he faces the contrast between the real and the ideal: "The happiness of a man in love is extreme, because it is founded on a reality placed in the domain of the imagination." We need not here point out how much a master of irony Talleyrand proved all his life to be. You cannot read for long anything he has left behind without coming across touches like, "To get on it isn't intelligence which you must have, it is delicacy which you mustn't have"; [1] or, "There are so many charms in affection that there is even a sort of pleasure in becoming aware that one is just a bit taken in by the sentiments which it inspires"; [2] or the malicious "Marriage is so beautiful a thing that one ought to think about it all one's life." [3]

This irony is never, like Byron's or Heine's in a later generation, the "pageant of a bleeding heart." What prevented it from degenerating into self-pity or a kind of cosmic belly-ache was the fact that the gentlemen who employed it had other refuges from reality. To describe the cult of stability in which so many of the aspirations of the early eighteenth century were summed up as a refuge from reality is perhaps in the nature of a *boutade* inspired by dislike for the short and easy way in which our grandfathers dismissed the "Age of Prose and Reason." To begin with, reality is a very dangerous word. But the stability at which the eighteenth century aimed, if not an ideal in the sense of the word so dear to the nineteenth century, was clearly a pattern which men strove to impose on disorder, on chaos. It was by no means an effortless surrender to existing conditions. The famous line, "Whatever is, is right," if taken literally is a libel on the age, and to judge the eighteenth century by it is as silly as to judge the Middle Ages by such stupid Renaissance jokes as the debate over the number of angels who could dance on the point of a needle. Voltaire's *Candide* is, of course, the final answer to the accusation. Complacent the age was not, and even its nineteenth-century enemies rarely brought that word out of their arsenal for use against it.

Stability, then, implied struggle. As a pattern of exist-

[1] *Pour faire fortune, ce n'est pas de l'esprit qu'il faut, c'est la délicatesse qu'il ne faut pas.*

[2] *Il y a tant de charmes dans l'affection qu'il y a même une sorte de plaisir à s'apercevoir qu'on est un peu dupe des sentiments qu'elle inspire.*

[3] *C'est une si belle chose que le mariage qu'il faut y songer toute sa vie.*

ence, it was clearly in the tradition of the Greeks: a well-rounded life in which the senses were requited but not indulged, in which the intellect was free to range widely within the limits of common propriety, in which the manifold tasks of manipulating the finite kept men from anything more than an ironic glance at the infinite. Just as in fifth-century Athens, this was an aristocratic pattern of life, and one that proved impossible of imposition upon the masses, and even upon many of the ruling classes. Against this stability, working to destroy it, was the hunger and filth and disease which it never touched. There is no way of starving in moderation. Men starved in Hogarth's London. Even more important, against this stability was the ambitious and ill-educated middle class, more and more "naturally selected" for their ability as innovators, open to all the winds of doctrine, undisciplined as yet by experience in the use of power, and willing to feed their appetites upon abstractions which promised them eternity. Finally, against this stability was its very success. For as the efforts of thousands of moderate and intelligent men in eighteenth-century Europe and America to lessen violence, to obtain orderly government, to encourage industry and trade, to bring science to bear on life through mechanical invention, as all these efforts bore fruit in a society on the whole more abundantly supplied with this world's goods than any human society had ever been, it was natural for the educated upper classes to feel that there were no limits to this process and to attempt in the nineteenth century to achieve by excess what they had achieved in the eighteenth by moderation.

The nineteenth century proved them, in a sense, right. When it does succeed, nothing succeeds like excess. But the great civilization our Victorian fathers built up seems now to some of us socially about as unstable as society can well be. The efforts of each individual to pursue as far as possible his appetites, and those most human modifications of his appetites, his ideals, had produced a society astonishingly rich in novelties, eccentricities, faiths. You can find almost everything in the nineteenth century, except general agreement on anything.

We cannot, however, in the fourth decade of the twentieth century afford to be too scornful of safety, stability, moderation, harmony, realism, conformity, even conventional good manners and other unromantic ways of adapting ourselves to one another's habits and limitations. Only at rare moments can society afford such luxuries as a general pursuit of happiness, especially when, as in the last century, happiness is understood to combine simultaneously the delights of satiety and ecstasy. For John Jones has against the toxic properties of the idea of perfection neither the protection of the ironic spirit nor that of preoccupation with keeping other men out of mischief; that is, he is likely to be an irresponsible person. John Jones, if told often enough that he can have the moon, is likely to believe what he is told, and to be very disappointed, to say the least, when he fails to get it. The nineteenth century got great things out of him by giving him a promissory note for the moon. We have hitherto not been able to redeem that note, though in countries like Germany and Russia John is trying very hard to collect it. We shall, indeed, be very lucky if we can get back to the world of values of the early eighteenth century, when the moon was not worth crying for.

The defense of this pattern of stability meant for the privileged group in power in the early eighteenth century devoting themselves to the business of government. They had no very high ideals as to what could be done in politics. They did, however, hold that the best of success in politics, as in other arts, is to come as close as possible to doing what you set out to do. They had the obvious, if to some natures contemptible, advantage of knowing what they wanted to do: keep peace in Europe, satisfy as many people as possible at home, improve economic conditions, keep discontented elements as quiet as possible, play off interests and appetites one against another so as to secure a maximum of satisfaction all around, and hence a maximum of stability. Most of them thought that the general level of creature comforts could be lifted for most of the population. But—and this is very important—they did not think they could measurably push human beings much nearer actual life according to the Sermon on the Mount. They have made themselves legendary figures as masters of the art of politics, a legend neatly and provocatively put forth in F. S. Oliver's *The Endless Adventure.* Perhaps they came to love their art for art's sake, and so lost some of their effectiveness in this world. Perhaps they turned their backs not only on metaphysics, but also on all kinds of theory, and hence lost the ability to learn, even to learn new tricks. Perhaps they over-estimated the extent to which human beings are guided by their appetites and their sentiments rather than by their ideas; or better, they clearly failed to realize that in times of collective madness, like the great French Revolution, ordinary men are susceptible to a kind of mass hysteria under the influence of which they may, very briefly, act in ways no one who had limited his observation to their ordinary conduct could surely predict. But they were unquestionably very great artists, whose example one hopes has not been altogether lost on the world.

Finally, these men had a certain restrained and tempered faith that the kind of life they lived was not only interesting, but significant. They displayed towards the concepts of Reason and Progress, not the unmeasured surrender of the generation which followed them, but at least a mild conviction of their usefulness, and of their possible place in a stable society that yet would avoid stagnation. They by no means cherished the intellectualist fallacy that sustained a man like Condorcet, who, outlawed by the cruel fanatics of the Republic of Virtue, yet maintained to the end that men would shortly attain the perfection of which they were so evidently capable. They were not at all convinced that ordinary men were capable of learning from the Enlightenment. With Voltaire, they went no further than a hope that enlightened despots might contrive to lead the blind herd a little less blindly. Nor were they influenced by Rousseau's doctrine of the natural goodness of man. Their attitude towards their fellows was very near that of current anti-intellectualism. They were very far from denying the value of the instrument of thought; they had a high opinion of its usefulness, and made it a constant tool. But they never thought of it as a key to unlock the gates of an earthly paradise. It was simply—though they probably didn't realize this—an instrument for ordering experience.

Talleyrand, though he was born at a time when the second generation of the *philosophes* were preparing the education of the shock-troops of the Revolution, belonged by temper and by education to the earlier generation. He was one of the last great Frenchmen to have grown up in this guild of practical, "unscrupulous" politicians. From them, and from experience, he learned the art of politics, which is the art and adventure of getting men to do what you want them to do. What you want them to do depends on your knowledge of what they can do, and on what you think desirable for them to do. Talleyrand's knowledge of the first he acquired from his masters and from first-hand experience; his standard for the second grew from the by no means unexacting cult of stability in which he had been brought up. That cult may not have been heroic, but it was not the dull acceptance of uninspired routine later generations held it to have been. Dullness, self-sufficiency, lack of imagination, unwillingness to adventure, to expand—all these stock pseudo-romantic reproaches against the Age of Prose and Reason fall flat against the complexities and depths of Talleyrand. "Always to admire moderately," he wrote, "is the mark of mediocre intelligence." And where better will you find expressed the necessity for the *esprit de finesse* in practical life, the inadequacy of the fixed, abstract workings of the *esprit de géometrie* than in Talleyrand's phrases: "The habit of judging gives to men of the world a superiority, a skill in tact, which rarely leads them astray; they draw from things indifferent in appearance important consequences. The gesture, the bearing, everything that can reveal the man, is noticed by them. Their observation is not reasoned, it derives from instinct." "I do not believe either in the intelligence or in the learning of people who do not recognize approximations and equivalents, and who are always defining; what they know they know only through their memory, and therefore they know badly." And, describing the society of Louis XVI, already among its fashionable intellectuals won to revolutionary doctrines: "The emotions were replaced by philosophical ideas; the passions, by the analysis of the human heart; the desire to please, by opinions; amusements, by plans, projects, etc." Finally, a passage of pretty extreme anti-intellectualism, with Tory implications suitable to 1816: "The use of analysis, useful when it is applied to the physical sciences, incomplete, when it is applied to the moral sciences, dangerous, when it is applied to the social order."

Talleyrand, even in the romantic reaction of the Bourbon restoration, after Chateaubriand had made the Catholic faith a thing of mediæval beauty, and a hundred poets had raked over the coals of their emotions, never wholly forgot the reasonable world of his childhood. "It is a reflection which I make with sorrow, but everything indicates that in man the power of hatred is a sentiment stronger than that of humane kindness in general, and even than that of personal interest. The idea of greatness and prosperity, without jealousy and without rivalry, is an idea too abstract, and of which the ordinary thought of man has not the measure." Or again, a remarkable passage which marks well his reluctance to accept the nineteenth century's repudiation of the Enlightenment. "*They (prejudices) are tied to men by roots too deep for the process of changing them suddenly not to be dangerous. I struggled long to keep myself from admitting this truth, but since the* philosophes *of the eighteenth century, with all the means, good and bad, which they used, failed in their enterprise of enlightenment, I surrender to those of the nineteenth who are of quite another sort, and with them cease to concern myself with the matter.*"

III

WE must not expect from Talleyrand any systematic writings on the state, or on political science, or on forms of government in general. He was too good a representative of his age and class not to agree with Pope's

For forms of government let fools contest
Whate'er is best administered is best.

He damns democracy with few reservations, and he has a number of pages—not very original ones—in praise of "mixed" monarchy, of which England always seemed to him a pattern. This too marks him as belonging to the first generation of *philosophes.* For just about 1760 the opinions of the fashionably intelligent in France turned from admiration for England and English government to distrust of, and even contempt for, the incompletely free islanders of George III, and Lord North, of the Unreformed Parliament, Test Act, debtors' prisons, and Middlesex elections. Lacour-Gayet, in the fourth volume of his *Talleyrand,* has unearthed a few pages on political theory omitted from the *Memoirs.* These are highly abstract, not to say philosophical, and may have so bewildered the worldly and intellectually limited Bacourt, who edited the *Memoirs,* that he simply omitted them. They are an interesting proof of Talleyrand's ability to employ dialectical reasoning, and show that he might have been a political philosopher in the traditional sense had he judged it worth while. These four pages attempt to refute the fashionable doctrines of popular sovereignty and of political and social equality by an appeal to the analogy between society and an organism. Here again Talleyrand gives evidence of his alertness, for the organic analogy, raised to the dignity of the organic theory of the state, was to become one of the stock bits of nineteenth-century political philosophy.

In general, one must piece together Talleyrand's ideas about politics from specific statements about concrete problems or from generalizations thrown off in the midst of other occupations. If one is not too exacting about grand systematic structures, one can certainly find a very great deal of political thinking in his work.

Talleyrand's methods were not those of the hit-or-miss opportunist, the experimenter in a void. The opening pages of his *Memoir concerning the Commercial Relations of the United States with England,* read at the Institute in 1797, and published in English in Boston in 1809 as part of the Federalist war against Jefferson, are excellent examples of sound empiricism.

"There is no science more dependent on facts than political economy. Indeed, the art of collecting, arranging, and drawing conclusions from them, constitutes almost the whole of the science. . . . Yet we must guard against the folly that would in all cases recur to first experiments; and which arrogates to itself the right of being ignorant of everything, in order that it may take nothing upon credit. Nor should we be less anxious to discard that temerity which, disdaining everything positive, finds it convenient rather to guess than to examine. . . . We should guard ourselves against first conclusions, the axioms of idleness and ignorance; and we should have the greatest distrust of those generalising principles, which would embrace everything; or rather, correcting the meaning of a word which has been so much abused, should give the name of *principle* to that idea only, which is first in the order of our reasoning, and not to the more general idea."

Those who draw their conclusions from their hopes will in France, continues Talleyrand, conclude that for a number of reasons—hatred of the English, gratitude for French aid, republican sympathy for republican France, dislike for English titled nobility—the Americans will transfer their trade and their affections from England to France.

"Observation, close observation alone, can prevent these false conclusions. Whoever has well observed America cannot doubt that she still remains altogether English in the greater part of her habits; that her ancient commerce with England has increased, rather than declined in activity, since the epoch of the independence of the United States; and that consequently, that independence, far from being of disadvantage to England, has benefited her in many respects."

First and foremost, then, are the facts—facts observed by a trained, intelligent person. But Talleyrand certainly never thought that facts can take care of themselves. He does not disdain theories; he has great respect for theories that correspond with the facts, and with theories that are proved by experience to be socially useful.

At the basis of any theory of man as a political animal must be an opinion of man as man. In other words, all political theorists, Plato as well as Hobbes and Rousseau, take their start in political psychology. Talleyrand is a pessimist in politics as in morals. He does not think that man is naturally good or naturally reasonable, or both. He does not, on the other hand, break out into Swiftian misanthropy. Your misanthrope is an over-sensitive lover of his fellow-men, or at any rate of himself. Talleyrand is willing to take men as he observes them to be, a very varied lot, with varied notions of good and evil, and even more varied ways of living. In general, he may be said to agree with Machiavelli that men are more prone to admire virtue than to practice it. What is more important, he does not believe that any efforts of church, state, or individuals can greatly alter the private lives of ordinary men—that, in other words, men will continue for a long time in any given society to practice approximately the same amount of lying, cheating, whoring, and similar actions commonly listed as vices.

Talleyrand would probably, then, have agreed with a person at first sight poles apart from him as *politique* and *moraliste,* John Stuart Mill, that "ordinary human nature is such poor stuff." There are signs that Talleyrand disliked moralists and reformers who try by preaching and lawmaking to make the world over more or less rapidly, though he has not left behind him any such outbreaks against the "Vertuistes" as distinguish the work of Pareto. Indeed, Talleyrand got along admirably with Royer-Collard, a most pious and improving man, quite without the lighter touch. Yet of Royer-Collard and the other doctrinaires Talleyrand in private made the unfriendly remark that "they are people who stay between courtyard and garden: they never see as far as the street." As for men like Lafayette, whose desire to improve the world is rather naïvely mixed with exhibitionism and sheer love of great symbolic words, he showed all his life an amused contempt. He did not mind Virtue if it were the product of an old-fashioned education in the French classics, a genuine devotion to the Catholic Church, a seriousness lightened by a love of familiar things; and even, in such instances, he preferred these virtues in women rather than in men. His male friends, Choiseul-Gouffier, Montrond, Jaucourt and the rest, were all gay blades. We need not infer, however, that he thought highly of their social utility.

Talleyrand's "lack of moral idealism" may then be traced both to his own detached observations of the way men behaved, and to his own very positive tastes. He was, however, fully aware of the difference between better and worse. That difference was to him, as to most men of his kind, rather a political than a moral one. Given your human animals with fairly consistent appetites, you will none the less find that at certain periods a given group of these animals politically organized is more prosperous than at other periods. This prosperity, again, does not necessarily mean that men are morally greatly improved under it; it does mean that they do not in such great numbers starve, or die of disease, in battle, or by the guillotine, that they are not robbed or assaulted in the streets, that they have peace and a chance to enjoy the fruits of their labor. Man is potentially, in civil society at least, an animal not subject to the bloodier extremes of which he is, as a mere animal, capable.

Talleyrand has a full appreciation of the extent to which custom, habit, tradition, prejudice, all help to tie the individual to a given society, and make him a peaceful citizen. Again we must note that aloofness and objectivity which make his character so distasteful to the romantically inclined. Just as his pessimism never turns into misanthropy, so his appreciation of the rôle of tradition and all that it implies never makes him a sentimental conservative. Unlike Burke, he was wholly unable to sigh over the past, or to boil with wrath at the sight of men trying to deny the past. He was pretty sure that the past would crop up again, not too damaged. "The more it changes, the more it's the same thing,"[1] is perhaps the best known of all the aphorisms attributed to him. This mental stand outside conservatism and radicalism on one of the points where there can usually be made a certain rough separation of human beings into sheep and goats—that is, into those who like old things, and those who like new things—is one of Talleyrand's most striking traits. It is of course easy, if you think anything is ever explained by such brusque dismissals, to say that Talleyrand was utterly indifferent to such questions, utterly unmoved by what he never felt. It is more likely that he represents a rare balance of positive traits, not a mere negative indifference. His pessimism, his sense of the limitations of men, his clear perception that laws and institutions are necessarily buttressed by habit and prejudice, all made him feel hesitant about political innovation. The experience of the French Revolution hammered all this home. Yet, as his great success in financial speculation showed, he was by temperament daring, experimental, innovating. Talleyrand certainly enjoyed his liberty, in the plain meaning of the term, too well to turn into a rigid authoritarian conservative. Moreover, his lack of moral idealism saved him from certain conservative excesses; he could not believe that if freedom failed to make men perfect, regimentation would do so either.

Society, then, rests at bottom on tradition. Talleyrand

[1] *Plus ça change, plus c'est la même chose.*

never, even in the early days of the Revolution, could talk in terms of "We are beginning anew the history of mankind." Even his most optimistically revolutionary document, the Report on Education, by no means assumes that it is either possible or desirable to start French education on an entirely new basis. Later he wrote that the Revolution had had no real leaders, no guides, that it had, however, been prepared by men of letters "who, wishing to attack prejudices, overthrew religious and social principles." Talleyrand had, indeed, what some may regard as a telltale fondness for that word "principle." As for all that tradition does to adorn life, for that side of tradition that is so evident to the person of taste, of subtlety, of emotional appreciation for ritual as salvation from devouring change, Talleyrand had full appreciation. "For there is a heritage of sentiments," he wrote, "which grows from generation to generation. New fortunes, new eminences cannot for a long time know the delights of such a heritage."

More important, in view of the common notion that Talleyrand had no standards whatever in politics, is the fact that he held law and custom to be important checks on the ambition of leaders and the delusions of the crowd. In a purely metaphysical sense, Talleyrand would probably not make the distinction between Law and Will. He certainly was incapable either of the emotion or the logic behind such statements as, "Let Justice be done though the heavens fall"—or its contemporary equivalent, the remark, "Let the colonies perish, rather than a principle!", falsely but not unfairly attributed to Robespierre. But he was far too wise in the ways of the world to think that Pragmatism, Force or Destiny or any other apparently hardboiled absolute came any nearer to corresponding with the infinite variety of concrete situations. At the very least, one can say that he was far too good a Machiavellian to believe in pure force in politics. Hence when he writes of Napoleon, "the emperor, who held as real only difficulties which could not be surmounted by force," he means just what he says, that this was a weakness in Napoleon's political equipment. Nor did he hold the melodramatic belief, common to many who think they are political realists, that all is intrigue. Indeed, he wrote scornfully of the Court Party in 1789 and its attempts to halt the Revolution that "after several attempts at force, abandoned almost as soon as conceived, they trusted solely to intrigue to destroy a power which they had allowed to grow too strong to be restrained, or even directed, by so feeble a means as intrigue."

Talleyrand believed then that law and tradition enter into the political situation which confronts, and in a sense restrains, us all. He did not think that either force or intrigue is in itself able to alter permanently that situation. Change, which in some respects is real and obvious enough, he thought would come about above all through economic freedom. Like most men of the Revolution, he defended the doctrine of *laissez-faire* as a real gain to humanity. He had, indeed, too little faith in the equipment of the common man to believe that complete Free Trade was possible in a nationalist Europe, or that if it came it would be the prelude to Utopia. But he did hold that the skill and daring of the entrepreneur class had brought Western civilization to a degree of economic prosperity not hitherto attained, and that continuation of such steps as abolition of guilds, freedom of internal trade, tariff agreements and the like were necessary to maintain these gains. Talleyrand was no man to be made acutely uncomfortable by the plight of the factory operative, and on the whole he seems relatively unaware of the profounder influences of the Industrial Revolution on the hopes and fears of the many. His economics are taken pretty immediately from the Physiocrats and Adam

Smith. They may lack depth and prescience, but they were eminently fitted to his time, and they make him seem almost liberal in contrast to the ultra-royalists and the clericals.

For Talleyrand was far from hostile to experimentation and novelty in various fields of human effort. Too much of an aristocrat, and too certain of human limitations, he could hardly sympathize with the radicals of the post-war world of his time, with Utopian Socialists, Christian Socialists, Republicans, Youth Leaguers, and the rest. Nor, though he patronized both Lamartine and Delacroix, was he very appreciative of Romanticism. Yet, even when he grew very old, there is in him almost no trace of genuine neophobia. His habits never quite got the better of him. At seventy-five, he made friends with the leading young radical politician of France, Thiers, destined to be a president of the Third Republic. Throughout his writings you will find passages like this, which indicate a belief in freedom, if not a passion for it: "It has often occurred to me that the celibacy of priests has essentially contributed to prevent the spirit of caste from establishing itself in Europe; and one need but open history to observe that this spirit of caste tends in general to arrest the progress of civilization." Or again, take an arresting passage from his Report on Education, where he speaks of "the contrast, or rather, the absolute opposition, which existed in the old régime *between what the child was obliged to learn,* and *what the man was expected to do.*" It is true that the rest of his speech is perhaps a bit optimistic. But in its insistence on the value of science, on the need of providing different courses of study for different children, in its tentativeness and freedom from dogmatism—even positivistic dogmatism—it is in the best liberal tradition. "Several sciences have yet to be born; others no longer exist; methods are not fixed; the principles of the various sciences cannot be fixed, opinions about them still less; and, in none of these respects, does it become us to impose laws upon posterity."

Finally, Talleyrand was, if not a nationalist, at least a patriot. He loved France, as he loved other good things of life, too sincerely and too well to sacrifice her to a metaphysics, or to any other kind of self-assertion. Talleyrand was no Barrès, nor even a Clemenceau. For Talleyrand's patriotism was perfectly consistent with a loyalty to the civilization of the European world. It was not the wordy, brutal, aggressive, romantic patriotism of the Jacobins and their successors, but the steady, sober love of country of d'Aguesseau's famed oration for Louis XIV. Here again, Talleyrand is a true child of the early eighteenth century.

Talleyrand's contributions to the understanding of politics are by no means negligible. If such contributions are measured by the invention and circulation of sweeping abstractions, surely the man who made of Legitimacy the catch-word of a generation deserves to rank with the fathers of the General Will and the Rights of Man? The Rights of Man seem nowadays only a trifle less metaphysically abiding than Legitimacy.

If, however, the test of a man's contribution to the understanding of politics is something more than the extent of his production of catch-words, then Talleyrand appears as a still greater political thinker. We may sum up his contribution under two heads—his elaboration in practice of the Machiavellian technique, and his use of moderation as a norm of political action.

Of Talleyrand's skillful use of his knowledge of what men want in order to get them to do what he wanted we have given numerous illustrations in this study. The Congress of Vienna is the *locus classicus* for his use of abstract ideas to activate inactive sentiments in men, and thereby quiet active ones. The speeches in defense of the confiscation of the property of the clergy in 1789 are the best examples of his skill at the analogous, but to us more familiar, art of parliamentary sophistry, an art admirably analyzed in "Single-speech" Hamilton's *Parliamentary Logic.* The crowded months of February, March, and April, 1814, when Napoleon's hold on France was collapsing, give the best instances of his skill at planning ahead, *but not too far ahead*—like the successful speculator on the Stock Exchange—three or four possible courses of action, and of his extraordinary gift for timing his final action. His career is full of illustrations of minor skills—of his ability to win over hostile men and women, of his rich resources at flattery, of his success at getting subordinates to work for him, of his ability to feel his way through the details of financial or diplomatic problems to a solution capable of simple, convincing statement. These are not little things. In particular, his life-long exhibition of an ability to distinguish between men's acts and what men say about their acts, between men's desires and what men say about their desires, is of utmost value to the student of politics. Talleyrand never over-simplified. He was convinced, and acted very successfully on the conviction, that most men do not live up to their expressed moral code. But he certainly did not think all men wicked, even under Christian standards. He knew that certain men make sincere and not wholly unsuccessful efforts to live up to very high moral notions. Himself as nearly lacking as is possible to human beings in that quality that makes the reformer, the meliorist, he never took refuge in cynicism. Even his irony has a placid touch. He refused to fit men into air-tight compartments, but saw them as a varied, changeable lot, to be approached with tact, caution, and willingness to experiment.

How all Talleyrand's gifts could be directed towards achieving a given end is best shown at Vienna. Here a comparison suggests itself, not with Brockdorff-Rantzau at Versailles, for such a comparison must be in terms of the "ifs" of history, but with Woodrow Wilson, whose achievements are not wholly in the conditional. Talleyrand wanted the best possible terms for France, and at least a breathing-spell of peace for Europe. By using "Legitimacy," not as an abstract ideal, but as means of handling men, he obtained his end. Woodrow Wilson seems to have wanted to organize the world into peace-loving nation-states, democratically organized and joined together into a League of Nations. His great abstraction was "Self-determination." There is no evidence that he had thought out the actual effect on human beings, on human sentiments, of this grand, meaningless word. For it *is* meaningless, as those who tried to reorganize Europe in terms of Self-determination soon found out. Indeed, as any modern physicist can see, there is no *unique operation.* No one could learn experimentally where Self-determination began and where it ended, what administrative areas, what races, what religious, social, cultural or economic groups did or did not come under its magic power. A very clever diplomatist might perhaps have used the abstract principle of Self-determination to promote the peace of the world; but the task would have been difficult. Self-determination was certainly a popular catch-word, as Legitimacy had been in 1815. But Wilson's abstraction had much greater obscurities and many more inconvenient overtones than had Talleyrand's; and Wilson had neither the subtlety nor the pliancy necessary to shape his beloved abstraction to the hard facts he faced. Surely one reason for his failure was that to him—but not to others—the abstraction was even harder than the facts. One may, of course, insist that Wilson's failure is a nobler achievement than Talleyrand's success, that truth is great, and will prevail, that *real* statesmen succeed in the future, not in the present. There is no reply possible to this sort of objection; but one may reflect privately that the future is not in all respects one of man's happiest inventions.

Talleyrand's detachment, which comes surprisingly close to the detachment of science and learning, saved him from the great error of his master, Napoleon. The Emperor, too, was in a sense a Machiavellian. He prided himself on always asking himself how the *gros paysan* would feel about a proposed measure. We have already noticed his reply to someone who referred to the Legion of Honor as a mere *hochet* (toy, bauble): *C'est avec des hochets qu'on gouverne les hommes.* But the Emperor in the end over-simplified as his minister never did. Certain processes in society are limited in velocity and duration, like chemical reactions. The Emperor was apparently unaware that men, if they are selfish animals easily led on to glory and to booty, are also fairly lazy animals, and that neither for glory nor for booty will they march forever. He never understood, as did Talleyrand, how complex and varied in different men is the interplay between ideas and interests. He thought of all men at bottom as little Napoleons, but lacking his energy, his intelligence, and his luck. Talleyrand never came near making the mistake of thinking the world filled with potential Talleyrands.

In fact, he managed to think about men in society very much as the scientist thinks about his subject. Misguided and usually somewhat optimistic thinkers have, especially since the eighteenth century, written and talked much about making politics a science, about applying the methods so successful in the natural sciences to the study of man in society. Almost all of these men have been intellectuals, and almost all have thought that, by superimposing statistics, documentary evidence, and technical jargon on a lust to improve mankind along lines marked out by various abstract ethical ideas, they were being "scientific." Now only an obscurantist will deny the value of statistics, evidence, patient research, and even of technical jargon, in scientific work. But, if we may be permitted to deal simply with an extremely complicated subject, the essential condition of all scientific work is that the worker must not, *while he is working as a scientist,* have any ethical ideas or emotions at all. This very simple statement will be incomprehensible to some people, which does not alter the fact that it is true.

Now, without using any elaborate formal research methods, without benefits of graphs, correlations or other statistical devices, Talleyrand approached the scientific study of politics infinitely closer than any Comte, any Spencer, any American college professor of government. He was able to do this partly, no doubt, because he had an excellent and well-trained mind, and partly because he had had a wide experience of men in politics, and had observed their behavior carefully. Neither intelligence nor experience would, however, have enabled him to approximate the achievements of science had he not had the ability, excessively rare among students of politics—and in the nineteenth century rare even among politicians—to think about men in such a way that his thinking was not distorted by what he, Talleyrand, wanted in this world, not by his greed, not by his vanity, not by his ambition, not by his hopes and fears, not—and this is the miracle, for this is the most fatal and most common distortion—not by his ethical standards. So when we say that Talleyrand was a pessimist, an ironist, even when we say he was a skeptic, we are in a sense far from his greatest gift, are to no small extent coloring falsely his singularly clear mind. He could study his fellows without confusing his conclusions with his desires, which, contrary to the legend, were the desires of a kindly, civilized, moral person.

This kind of thinking is not the kind connoted by the word "academic"; it is not the kind which the romantic attempts to describe as the inhuman, dry-as-dust assembling of a jig-saw puzzle. It employs to the full the faculties somewhat loosely described as imagination. In one sense, it has a superficial resemblance to the effort of the sincerely religious person to achieve self-annihilation. What used to be the Calvinist conscience is nowadays frequently exercised in the effort to use words wholly unstained by the purposes, moral or æsthetic, of the user. But on the whole, the analogy is misleading, for the modern scientist is not haunted by any dualism of soul and body. Scientific thinking is a difficult task, but it is not a duel with the devil. With Talleyrand, the ability to think about men in society approximately as the scientist thinks about problems in physics or biology was no doubt a gift. He worked hard to cultivate the gift, as a born tennis player has to work hard to cultivate his gift. But he never had to make a struggle in the Christian sense of a moral struggle. Perhaps this is one reason why so many earnest people have disliked him. He never fought when he was not obliged to; and he never felt any inner compulsion to fight phantoms.

His life-long moderation in all things has doubtless firm roots in his physical being and in his early education. But it can appear as a guiding principle, as an idea. For one thing, Talleyrand sought the middle path because in the actual complexity of men and motives that seemed to him to be the path that best took account of the complexity and left open the widest range of possibilities in the future. For another thing, moderation seemed to him best to assure that stability in European society, of which he wrote the revealing maxim: "Stability frequently adds something to perfection and perfection itself cannot add anything to stability."[1]

This is not a heroic sentiment. To many it will even be a disgusting sentiment. The nineteenth century, though it admired and envied a British greatness commonly attributed to an aptitude for certain sorts of compromise, was on the whole hostile to compromise, balance, moderation, stability, and other Augustan virtues. The nineteenth century was all for scaling the heights and sounding the depths. Now Talleyrand was a thoroughly Augustan figure, and if he is compared with Plato, Dante, Shakespeare, Luther, or Napoleon he no doubt seems shallow, superficial, insensitive to the full range of human experience. One is rarely conscious in Talleyrand of that intense desire to use words to go beyond words, to express the inadequacy of all forms of communication between human beings, to suggest an infinite, inexhaustible, incomprehensible appetite, which is so evident in romantic art, and which has just been unconsciously caricatured by Mr. Thomas Wolfe. Talleyrand probably does lack depth. Shakespeare saw and felt things Talleyrand could not see and feel. Talleyrand's was no rich Renaissance nature. But one has at times an uneasy feeling that rich Renaissance natures are at their best—for themselves and for the rest of us—in art and letters. They are wasted on politics, a pursuit more fitting for shallow sensible Augustan natures.

And yet shallow is not quite the last word one would wish, even ironically, to write of Talleyrand *politique et moraliste*. Since man has won the gift of literary speech, he has built more firmly than ever his other worlds against this world. He has built him monuments more enduring than bronze in material quite proof against the second law

[1] *La stabilité supplée souvent à la perfection et la perfection elle-même ne saurait suppléer à la stabilité.*

of thermodynamics. Words are in this world pitiful things, and they fill no bellies and sate no passions; but even in this world they may prove immortal. And men of words have this final revenge over men of deeds, that since the word, and not the deed, is immortal, we remember men of deeds only through what men of words have said about them. Talleyrand was not inarticulate, but he was not a man of words. He enjoyed life too well to love words for their own sake, or for his. As immortality goes in our Western society, men like Kant and Rousseau and Goethe seem far more likely than Talleyrand to survive. Yet—to take the comparison at its most exacting—why should we call Goethe profound and Talleyrand shallow? Goethe did not, and Talleyrand probably did, understand himself very well. And have not those founders of our modern world, the Greeks, decreed that "know thyself" is the beginning of wisdom? Depth and wisdom in human beings are, however, in no metaphorical sense unfathomable. Metaphysics, art, religion, poetry, have their own fathoms. But human life itself is no more to be measured than to be judged. Talleyrand lived richly, adventurously, wisely, humorously, and long. One wonders whether Plato himself did more.

CHAPTER EIGHT

—plus c'est la même chose

I

IT is a cheering reflection for those who like to think of the kindlier qualities as uppermost in human beings that so many biographers are well disposed towards their subjects. True, the choice of a subject may well have been determined in advance by sympathy, or liking, or by heir-apparency. The biographer may come to identify himself with his subject, or at least to feel that, if his subject is not virtuous and important, he himself may not be. If familiarity does breed contempt, it is not by parthenogenesis. There are, of course, exceptions. Some biographers are sustained by hate. The simpler followers of Lytton Strachey have sometimes thought of themselves as moved by scorn, or amused contempt, as well as by love of truth. The de-bunkers are commercial artists, and as such are able to simulate hatred, if hatred seems profitable. Other biographers, incapable of so lyrical and intense an emotion as hate, and usually also incapable of conciseness, drone along at a dead level of dislike for their subjects. This is one of the reasons why Lacour-Gayet's *Talleyrand* is such a dull book, and such a long book. Hatred would have had a quicker way. Yet the majority of biographers are kindly. If we may use the product of several thousand years of biographical writing with faith in its statistical soundness, Heaven must be far more densely populated than Hell.

One thing, then, you may be sure the biographer will do; as a good servant of Clio, he will give his opinion as to whether his subject was a good man or a bad one. It may be an opinion arrived at only after balancing many considerations, an undogmatic opinion; or it may be a verdict of swashbuckling simplicity and firmness. But the biographer rarely abstains from giving it. Now the techniques of historical investigation, as well as those of such other sciences essential to the study of the individual, as biology, psychology and sociology, though in varying stages of perfection, have nevertheless reached a point where it is perfectly possible to write a good deal about many historical personages without judging them at all. Indeed, common sense, which has always been able to do some of the things science can do, makes it possible to come pretty close to objective biography. If you do not try to make judgments of value, you can present an extraordinary amount of knowledge about all sorts of things quite objectively—that is, in such a way that all sane men will accept your presentation as corresponding with their own experience.

But no one wants to read objective biographies. The human being is an evaluating animal. He wants to know whether your subject is one of the Ten Greatest in his field. Would he have won the Nobel Prize, had there been one in his day? Men are not interested in an account of what Cézanne has done unless they also learn whether or not Cézanne is a good painter. They already know that Rembrandt is a good painter, but they need help with Cézanne. Moreover, the objective biographer would have to give up all the little tricks dear to the craft—the nice bits of motivation, the rhetorical turns, the irony and compassion. He would have to vacate the most comfortable bit of furniture ever designed, the judgment seat. And in reward for all this self-denial, no one would read him! The present study of Talleyrand's life aspires to nothing beyond the conventional, and makes no pretense to objectivity, save in its main theme: the "goodness" of Talleyrand.

Now so much has been written, so many facts accumulated, so many judgments passed on important historical personages that any man can have his own Lincoln, his own Goethe, his own Napoleon. Most men, it is true, find it easier to take the conventional figure folk-wisdom and the schools offer them at any given moment. But there are various levels of judgment at which modifications of an historical personage appear, and a possibility of choice lies before anyone seeking to make his mind up about that personage. For the heartening commonplace that the great never die means that the great are no safer from change than the rest of us. The history of a reputation like that of Cromwell, may, as Mr. W. C. Abbott has shown us, be even more interesting and varied than the history of the man himself during his brief stay on earth. Simply for convenience, we may distinguish three of the levels of judgment, very differently subject to change.

First there is the level at which the subject appears as a man, as a private citizen, as husband, father, as astride his hobbyhorse. There are, even at this level, degrees of intimacy between subject and reader. One may look at a man, as the French say, *en pantoufles;* or one may never get beyond the frock-coat. Here the human disposition to stab desperately at some fragment of the chaos of the concrete and stick to it has full play. The strangest and most insignificant concrete detail may turn a man from villain to hero. The logic of "I-do-not-like-thee-Dr.-Fell,-the-reason-why-I-cannot-tell" applies to relations between the living and the dead as well as among the living. In this category fall such common biographical tricks as the admission that the subject was not a great statesman, but was a loving husband and a kindly father. This trick infuriates many who find the opposite combination—the great pianist and wife-beater—irresistibly attractive. Such are the variety and unpredictability of human sentiments involved that the advocate-biographer of Talleyrand had better suppress such testimonials of the serenity and Christian happiness of life in the rue St. Florentin as those offered by the Abbé Dupanloup. They will do him no good with the kind-hearted, and they will injure him with the moderns, the realists, the sophisticates.

Obviously at this level a man's reputation is at the mercy of all sorts of accidents. At the next level there is a good deal more stability. This is the level of common judgment of a man and his work held by a given generation. The elements that go into this sort of judgment are usually sorted out into preliminary generalizations, which are in turn more or less completely integrated with the tastes and fashions of the age. Here the man appears more a pattern of principles and aspirations and less a creature of whimsy than at the level of private life. He may, however, and indeed at this level almost always does, appear very differently to different generations, and even to different groups within the same generation. Joan of Arc, once a witch, is now a saint, having been also patriot, peasant girl, charlatan, madwoman and *das ewig Weibliche*. In the arts the total judgment made of the artist varies with the judgment made of his works, and therefore the reputations even of men like Shakespeare are by no means wholly fixed in content.

At a third level reputations are as stable, as fixed in content, as anything on this planet. This is the level of pure symbolism, where the individual has come to stand for some of the more abiding abstractions. Some part of the reputation of all very great men is of course at this level. Shakespeare as "the poet" has now been raised by Anglo-Saxon successes in quite other fields than poetry to the point where even for Frenchmen he is a symbol of something ultimate. What he will be to a Mongol in 2300 is not safely predictable, but he has very good chances of being quite simply "the poet." Usually these symbolic figures are very good or very bad—Washington or Nero. The more completely they enshrine abstract principles, the less likely they are to suffer change. Thus Washington, in spite of de-bunkers and new historians, remains to the average American as bloodlessly real as the Statue of Liberty, while Lincoln, just as much a hero and just as much revered, has a possible private life, an existence *en pantoufles,* and is much more adjustable to one's purposes and moods.

Now Talleyrand, though he is by no means a universally known figure like Shakespeare or Washington or Cæsar, nevertheless for those who have heard of him at all is at this third most abstract and most immutable level. He belongs to a special class within that level, the class of the Machiavellians. Why the label Machiavellian should have become a universal term of reproach suggests interesting vistas into psychological and sociological questions we cannot here consider. As Lord Acton's most learned essay on Machiavelli shows, this dyslogistic use has a very long history. Even in that most Machiavellian of periods, the early eighteenth century, and in that most Machiavellian of classes, the Augustan ruling class in western Central Europe, the word was still a reproach. The fury—occasionally disguised as contempt and even as ignorance—which has descended in our times on Pareto is explicable partly at least by the fact that he has frankly allied himself with Machiavelli.

Our attempt to make Talleyrand into a good man starts then under difficulties which almost condemn it to failure in advance. He is in the firmest and most unyielding of categories of bad men, the unprincipled schemers whose schemes are not even unconscious tributes to God and morality. As a private citizen, he does not come out badly. But to stand any chance at all of rehabilitating him, we must at least remove him from this category of symbolic evil. This is precisely what we cannot do, for on the whole he belongs there. We must attempt the more difficult task of defending, or at least examining without horror or delight, the position loosely termed Machiavellian. It would be more tactful perhaps not to use that term, but to attempt merely to show that in the balance of Talleyrand's political career more emerges that now seems good and desirable to us than seems bad and undesirable. Indeed, such a procedure might be defended on other grounds than tact or expediency. The word "Machiavellian" has become a scarecrow, and to try to use it for purposes of persuasion is as futile as trying to use a scarecrow as a bird decoy. Let us then, without labeling Talleyrand's political attitude, see what implications it may have for us today.

II

IT is well—and since Bacon, especially fashionable—to go from the particular to the general. Suppose we make a start with a problem general enough in its implications, but also very concrete—the problem of war and peace in a world of organized, sovereign, and civilized states, in a world like ours and Talleyrand's. Let us assume that other things being equal, peace is desirable and war undesirable. This is, of course, an assumption. There are people who, to take them at their word, start from the opposite assumption, that war is desirable. But you must make a start, and the desire for peace is a desire observably shared by many men.

Now the next step is to garner in facts from observation. Here history, anthropology, sociology, psychology may all be drawn on for contributions. It will easily be evident that for thousands of years men have, at longer or shorter intervals, taken part in those conflicts between organized groups we call wars. To go on from this simple and verifiable statement of fact to talk about a "natural belligerency" in man as an individual is to take the kind of step that marks the decline from the methods of the natural sciences to those of the social sciences. Some such *hypothesis* may be a useful lead in social psychology; actually a concept like "natural belligerency" tends to become in the mouths of journalists, army officers, social Darwinists, and other such gospel-mongers a phrase to fling before the appetites and emotions of their listeners.

All we need say here is simply that war is a phenomenon which, thanks to the fact that human beings leave records behind them, we may state is "observable" in most human societies. We must, then, say that unless the conditions under which the phenomenon has appeared in the past change, the phenomenon will almost certainly appear in the future. The historian—still carefully avoiding such dangerous terms as "natural belligerency"—can readily assemble and list a great number of the conditions which have been present at the outbreak of wars in the past. We can then observe similar conditions about us at present. A given war is the product of a number of mutually dependent variables. These variables we see in existence about us at this moment. Just when their mutual variations will reach the combination that actually *is* war we cannot accurately predict, anymore than the meteorologist can accurately predict the weather. But the meteorologist can predict, for instance, that for a long time in the future, there will be hurricanes in the Caribbean and snowstorms in Quebec. (Analogy is the curse and the temptation of this kind of thinking; it loses much of its danger if it is taken simply as an expository device, and not as part of the argument.) The social scientist can safely predict that there will be wars in the future.

This is neither fatalism nor determinism. Within the wide and adventurous limits of the variations of our variables, a great deal of range exists even for the optimist. A war may be postponed; the number of belligerent nations may be diminished; the horrors of war may be lessened by medicine and even by codes of war; a war may be abbreviated by skillful diplomacy. War may be avoided for comparatively long years. The possibilities are very great. But they do not extend, at the moment, to the total abolition of war. One may perhaps jump legitimately at this point from the observation and coördination of facts to the making of a moral aphorism: You may not on this earth completely close the gap between any code of morals and human behavior, and you will do better not to try. For some time yet there will probably be wars, drunkenness, whoring, gambling, thieving and a good deal else that many excellent people would like not to be. The experience of the Eighteenth Amendment is not very hopeful for pacifists.

Yet it is at just this point that many will refuse to accompany us any longer. There are men who, though they are forced to give in to the evidence, and admit that the past has been full of wars, none the less maintain that there will be no more wars. The abolition of war is in their programs variously dependent on certain specific steps. They vary greatly in optimism and fervor. We shall call them, loosely and without scorn, pacifists. Now, though pacifists range from simple maniacs to quite useful citizens, and though their programs and methods show almost as great a range, it can be said broadly, first, that they commonly isolate one single variable from the situations out of which wars arise, and insist that that variable alone "causes" wars and therefore its elimination will eliminate wars; second, that they commonly hope to eliminate that one villainous variable by talking, preaching, or otherwise exorcising it from men's souls. Kings were once supposed to make wars, peoples to suffer them. Many nineteenth-century liberals thought wars were made by the scheming few, and that the common man, once he was duly enlightened, and given power, would prove pacifist in action. The obvious thing to do then was to preach to him. The Marxians have their pet variables: war is the inevitable result of capitalist enterprise. In the classless society, there will be no war. There is the old and nearly forgotten Christian explanation: war is a consequence of the Fall, the mark of the devil in man; through Christ's sacrifice we are cleansed of this stain, and a Christian world will be a world without war. There is the very quaint theory that wars are made by munition makers, and that if the state as we now know it—the governments as we now know them—had a monopoly on munitions making we should be well on the way to world peace.

Few of the proponents of these theories have done more than preach them. If to the limited and shallow realist they seem sometimes to be crying peace where there is no peace, they do no harm, and they often add to the lyrical content of this life. To cry peace is to make folly not unlovely. Those who more prosaically announce peace—as did the late Woodrow Wilson—are perhaps more dangerous. A crusader who fancies himself as a horse-trader is likely, circumstances aiding, to upset any social equilibrium.

To continue our analysis: We have reached the point where, after agreeing that wars have been and are now, the pacifists, maintaining that wars ought not to be, and therefore will not be, have left us. Some pacifists, who do not really think they can abolish war, but who feel that to talk as if they did may at least postpone and diminish war, are in a sense still with us. These are the people who insist that you must set up moral absolutes or you will have moral chaos. You must have, or at least preach, chastity and the monogamous Christian marriage, or you have complete sexual promiscuity. The relation between the ideas and the sentiments of such people is an interesting problem, but one we cannot linger over. With most of them their assertion that you must set up the whole-hog ideal in order to obtain a bit of the bacon is probably a form of self-delusion. Often it is a delusion useful to them and to society. Sometimes, however, it is a delusion dangerous to society. In this matter of postponing and diminishing the horrors of war, to preach pure pacifism is rather likely to work against your intentions. For such preaching unnecessarily angers a great many people, from professional militarists to simple conservative patriots. Few subjects, indeed, illustrate more perfectly than this of pacifism how much democratic political discussion is really a cock-fight of the emotions. As our cartoonists have discovered, the militant fury of the convinced pacifist at debate with a good, red-faced army colonel commonly exceeds that of the colonel himself.

We shall, if we really wish to do something to help peace, come pretty close to trying to do what Talleyrand did all his life in his efforts to diminish the evil of war. We shall very definitely avoid going to the root of the evil, simply because there is no root. We shall not be made uncomfortable by bad medical analogies which accuse us of prescribing for the symptoms and neglecting the disease. We shall not concentrate our attention on any one single variable in the complex international system. We shall, instead, try and analyze the situation as objectively as possible. This analysis will include, not merely a description of the military, economic, and political distribution of power in and among the nations, but a description of the way important groups—and, in spite of the cruder Marxians —*important individuals* in each state *feel* about such matters. We shall obviously have here materials for equations more complicated than any the mathematician can handle, but which a genius like Talleyrand can, with the aid of both the *esprit de finesse* and the *esprit de géométrie,* contrive to solve after a fashion. The slightest change in one of the myriad elements of the situation—the death of a king, a bank failure, an accidental explosion on a battleship, the publication of a book—may alter a whole equation in a way and to an extent bewildering to the mind which works at the level of plain moral truths. To attempt to guide one's self by any yet formulated moral code in such a situation would be like attempting to solve a most complex problem in calculus on the basis of the first proposition of Euclid.

What certain people say they believe about Justice, Right, Expediency and the rest will for us be a very important series of elements in the equation, along with what they do and with other indications of the nature and intensity of their sentiments. But after all, what are we trying to do? Don't we need *some* guiding principle? Well, for the moment we are trying to keep the peace. We might, of course, be trying to engineer a war, or make France great, or keep in office—but it is clearly unwise to try and do too many things that are mutually contradictory. This, in a given situation, is an activity which can be tested by failure or success as much as tight-rope walking or mountain-climbing. If you must still have a teleological explanation, the philosophers' closets are full of them. But peace in this sense, even more than the peace of the doctrinaire pacifist, is peace at any price? Quite so. That may be, indeed, the only price at which you can get anything on this earth.

III

IT should be clear that the foregoing discussion of the differences in method between the professional pacifists and the Talleyrands—who might be called the professional peace-makers, a very different thing—is an illustration of the differences between men's attitudes towards the gap, discussed in the preceding chapter, between their awareness of their immediate sensations, self, and surroundings and their awareness of another world opened to them by thought, a world of words and symbols. The pacifist is one who, able to think and talk about peace, comes in the long run to widen immeasurably the gap between the two worlds. He may be lucky enough to be able to live wholly in the world of thinking and talking. Completely doctrinaire belief centered on some one social "plan" or gadget is astonishingly immune to the touch of this world, and many a single taxer, pacifist, or prohibitionist exhibits a self-insulation from this world parallel in mystic strength, if not in serenity, to the achievements of the religious anchorite. Only the exceptional individual can thus insulate himself. The world is finally with most of us. Few generations can have been more unhappy than the liberal, optimistic, pacifist young men and women who stepped from the pages of *Joan and Peter*—into the Four Years' War.

Your Talleyrands, on the other hand, are men whose awareness of the gap is just sufficient to incite them to the artistic manipulation of the world about them, just sufficient to enable them to work out guides for their animal instincts rather than be wholly guided by them. Words are to them the scouts, never the whole body of the army; they would not dream of engaging a major battle relying solely on their scouts to bear the brunt of the fighting. They know very well the use of words—in their place. To return to our earlier metaphor: they never confuse the two worlds, never show themselves able to live in the world of words, ideas, aspirations as if they were living in the world of immediate sensations, self, and surroundings. Whether for themselves they thereby widen or diminish the gap between the two worlds is not to be answered as confidently as the early nineteenth century would have answered it. They do not seem now quite such dull, unimaginative and contented fellows as they seemed a hundred years ago. Wordsworth may have expressed the inexpressible better than Pope. He certainly never knew his Westmoreland neighbors as Pope knew his own London circle. Your thoroughgoing idealist is sometimes a consecrated snob. To transcend, to escape, to dodge —an interesting descending stairway of synonyms. If you dislike them enough you may find pleasure in calling the Transcendentalists dodgers.

Ordinary men—and who are not ordinary men?—are not torn between the claims of the Ideal and the demands of the Real. Ordinary men are not painfully or cheerfully aware of the gap we have talked so much about. Yet, if one were to look for some concrete and verifiable indications of the existence of our metaphorical gap, one could hardly do better than look at the daily round of ordinary men. Let us take an ordinary Protestant Christian, taught to go straight to his Bible. He must hold his Saviour as a pattern for himself. From the New Testament account he learns that his Saviour was a pacifist, that He would not permit rich men to enter His kingdom, that He was, as regards certain laws accepted by His countrymen, an anarchist. We need hardly point out that all this does not prevent our ordinary Protestant Christian from fighting, from making money, from obeying the most pharisaical of laws and customs. The point has been made again and again, usually by anti-Christians misnamed skeptics. The anti-Christian is here, of course, like the doctrinaire pacifist, a man who looks in a rather heroic and uncomfortable, and very inhuman, way at the gap between the world of words and what the Christian himself calls *this* world. The Roman Catholic Church, which has always been nearer Talleyrand's position than to that of, say William Lloyd Garrison, has managed to get along very well in spite of the obvious *logical* inconsistency between certain words and deeds of its Founder and the practices of its members; but the Roman Catholic Church has not sent the faithful to the naked Bible.

For what closes—and even heals—our metaphorical gap for the common man is the almost automatic control over his aspirations exercised by adequate ritualistic practices and routines. What is commonly known as his religion may well be the most important of such practices, but it should be obvious that for many modern Western men patriotism, socialism or another "Cause" may bulk larger in his life than his church. Nor must the phrase "ritualistic practices" be understood too narrowly. Ritual is any device whereby men regularly and habitually acquire, keep active, and even intensify sentiments that reconcile their aspirations with their lot. One may—indeed, one commonly does—make a ritual of breakfast. In this very wide sense, the word ritual may be used to cover the external forms taken by that whole nexus of custom, law, and doctrine which the tradition of Burke exalts as the earthly salvation of man. And Burke was no doubt right, if a bit over-excited. Men have never, in large numbers and over long periods, attempted to cut through this nexus, and in spite of frightened conservatives, are not likely to do so. If men really were commonly unsatisfied until they attained *direct,* rather than ritualistic or vicarious, satisfaction of their aspirations, then the William Lloyd Garrisons would long ago have brought us into earthly bliss, or sent us back to join the dinosaurs. If men commonly were capable of living up to their ideals, if with them word and deed were in logical, or even evangelical, correspondence, then indeed the Talleyrands would be not so much wicked men as blind and stupid men.

Now a society in which all men's wants were satisfied, either directly or by ritual, would be by definition a completely stable society. Not even Tennyson's Cathay was ever such a society. The stablest of human societies have not attained more than a rough and temporary equilibrium. This study, which has already trespassed over much on the aspiring social sciences, cannot attempt a solution of one of the central problems of sociology. From the Chinese metaphysicians who made the alternation of Yin and Yang the key to human destiny down to Pareto, who, in spite of his hatred for metaphysics, has his alternation of the lions and the foxes, thinkers have sought to translate into words human experience of alternate periods of rest and of unrest. We have dozens of expressions for the antithesis. In these days of triumph for the natural sciences, "static" and "dynamic" are easily understood. Like all such dualisms, this conception fades into monism if you think metaphysically, into pluralism or worse if you go to work testing it out on concrete data of sense-experience. To apply it grandly to all human society is probably to run unavoidably into metaphysics. Even moderately applied, it must offend the precise and literal-minded.

The imperfect equilibrium, or "static" phase, of any given society is menaced obviously by "dynamic" elements in the physical environment of that society. A new Ice Age would discourage even the Scots. The Marxians are clearly right—though their weighting of the sub-factors is faulty—

in reckoning the factory system as an important environmental factor in maintaining modern Western society in a pretty constant state of disequilibrium. Indeed, all kinds of institutions—political, religious, social, economic—have varying effects on the equilibrium of society. Institutions are clearly not independent of human action, and so we come to the problem of the effect on the equilibrium of a society of the various dispositions of the people who make it up. One may use an antithesis between the "environmental" and the "human" factor, but only for convenience in sorting out the mutually dependent variables. The whole problem must never be seen in the cart-and-horse framework—i.e., as a question whether Man or Nature is responsible for breaking up the imperfect equilibrium. With this caution, let us consider the relation of certain human factors to the social equilibrium.

Several sorts of men, not of course capable of being divided into mutually exclusive groups, seem by temperament likely to disturb a given social equilibrium. First, there are the clever, energetic, ambitious men anxious above all to attain power and wealth, men not in any conventional sense moral idealists. A good many problems of equilibrium are involved in the status of such able members of inferior castes or classes. A society which permits such men to rise freely to the highest classes would no doubt save itself from the rebellion of suppressed ability and ambition. On the other hand, such a society would be deprived of certain caste or class distinctions which have in the past proved a very useful means of maintaining stability. For mediocrity is often as ambitious as ability, and it is very difficult to maintain the career open to talents without opening a scramble in which the beaten are prey to painful, and socially dangerous personal maladjustments. In a world where men starve, the difficulty may seem trivial, and our Marxist friends will not be impressed with it. But the kind of suffering experienced by the ambitious young American Jewish lad who fails to make Phi Beta Kappa, or by the English County Scholar worsted in scholarship and in accent by his public school rivals, has no parallel in a rigidly organized caste-society. The ramifications of this problem, which Pareto calls that of the "circulation of the élite," are fascinating.

A second class of disturbers is that of the moral idealists, from prophets to revolutionists. The question as to whether such moral idealism is "pure" or debased with ambition, envy and the like is one which may interest the moralist, but which we may here pass over. In practice, it is easy enough to tell a Robespierre from a Bonaparte. The moral idealist acquires—and the sources for such acquisition are innumerable in civilization—a moral absolute, or series of such absolutes. To choose a relatively recent one, let us take Liberty, Equality, Fraternity. To a man like Danton, who is a splendid example of the clever, unscrupulous and ambitious man of low birth, these were mere words. To Robespierre, the moral idealist, they stood for the Republic of Virtue, for a state where every man was honest, upright, a good father and a good husband, neither rich nor poor, envious of none, and wholly untouched by the normal vices. To Robespierre, men *had* to become what he, aided by generations of moralists, thought they ought to become. If this meant facing Terror and guillotine, he was ready to face them.

The Robespierres are few. In quiet times, they usually attain, not the guillotine, but the less dramatic martyrdom of the common man's contempt. They go to make up the lunatic fringe, the professional rebels, the pacifists (who, like Robespierre, sometimes make good killers), the vegetarians, the free-lovers, the nudists. These are the eccentrics we Westerners still mostly tolerate but whom not even John Mill has persuaded us to admire as exemplars of the beneficent workings of the principle of Liberty. For your common man is usually a prop of social equilibrium. That environmental changes can drive the common man into rebellion your hardest realist is willing—the Marxians are too willing—to admit. There is also the possibility that, along with environmental changes, something like moral idealism can very briefly infect quite large masses of men, and drive them abroad in quest of the Grail, or to realize the Republic of Virtue, or to add little red patches to the map of the British Empire, or to achieve the classless society. But these eruptions are usually brief, and the search for the Grail, for those who survive it, commonly ends in the cultivation of one's garden.

With a natural environment subject to all sorts of changes, and with so many unappeased human beings, it would seem that any social equilibrium must be very imperfect indeed. And yet one of the greatest difficulties in this whole problem is to arrive at any kind of objective measure of equilibrium. Your speedometer, as well as your senses, will tell you whether your motor car is in a static or in a dynamic state. The properly equipped scientist can tell whether a given physico-chemical system is or is not in equilibrium, can even tell under what conditions a new equilibrium will follow certain given or observed changes. But, to take an example at the heart of our discussion, can we state objectively that Western society was in 1736 in a more perfect, or less imperfect, equilibrium than in 1836—let alone in 1936? Obviously the mathematical analysis that permits the physicist to use a term like equilibrium with exactness is here lacking, and we are speaking in analogies, which is dangerously near to speaking in parables, an old and useful trick of the moralist. A clever man might well make a convincing case that Western society was more stable, nearer an equilibrium in 1836 than in 1736. We cannot here attempt to enter a subject which would demand a book in itself. Expert opinion is in general pretty well agreed that Augustan society was stabler than early Victorian society. The historian really is in certain matters an expert, and, though the best of the practitioners would shy away from such terms as "social stability" and "social equilibrium," they would concur pretty well on the facts that do after all underlie even sociological generalizations. At any rate, we shall assert modestly the hypothesis that the society in the last days of which Talleyrand was born was a stabler society than the one in which he died.

Early eighteenth-century society did indeed make a cult of stability. It was a stability, however, in which a good deal of intellectual daring and economic enterprise was balanced by habits and institutions of long standing, and by the political realism and skill of a small ruling class. To isolate this ruling class, and treat it as the single variable which determined the whole social equilibrium, would of course be a great mistake. The nineteenth century did not differ from the eighteenth because men like Gladstone, Guizot and William II took the place of men like Walpole, Chesterfield, Fleury, and Talleyrand. Rather, this difference in the kind of men politically important, in their political ideas and methods, is a measure of a change brought about by an infinite variety of concurring changes. And yet the existence of this Augustan ruling class is in itself an active element in the precarious equilibrium of a society in which men starved, fought, colonized, explored, speculated, experimented and, in convulsions, saw God. Had all men been Addisons or Boileaus, or even Samuel Johnsons, eighteenth-century society might well have been as stuffy and conservative as our Victorian grandfathers liked to think it. Actually the eighteenth century—it must be remembered that we are considering only Western society and its colonial offshoots—gives an almost unique example of a society actively, indeed dramatically, changing, and yet preserving in its art, its manners, its tastes, its standards of appraising human beings, the moderation, the respect for self-restraint, for forms, the willingness to accept the authority of one's superiors, characteristic of relatively unchanging societies. With the American, French, and Industrial Revolutions this precarious balance was destroyed, and Western society began its heroic attempt to make this planet safe for Democracy, Humanity, Liberty, Equality, and at least very uncomfortable for common sense.

At this point—so much are even the most sociologically inclined of us still in the tradition of the historian as judge over human beings—we are disturbed by questioning. If after all this ruling class in the eighteenth century was so able, so completely up to the requirements of its job, if it is to be regarded as a model of political realism, why was it swept away in France by revolutionary catastrophes, why did it in England give way to the evangelical virtues of the great middle class? If these were Supermen, how do you explain their defeat by ordinary men, men for the most part excluded from the benefits of training in this most rigorous art of governing? This questioning is a typically moralistic one. You do not blame a dam for bursting; you do not even blame its engineers and builders, if they have built the dam according to specifications determined by previous experience with similar dams. Determinism and Free Will have always been happy co-tenants of man's mind, whatever the logician may have to say of their incompatibility, and modern scientific determinism gets along just as well with Free Will as did the God of Augustine and

Calvin. Hence we are pleased to understand that the Revolutions of the eighteenth century were the inevitable result of forces beyond men's control, and at the same time delighted to realize that they were produced by the moral delinquency of George III, and Lord North, of Marie Antoinette and hundreds of dukes and marquises who had peasants beat their frog ponds to silence the frogs, and who habitually enjoyed the *ius primae noctis* at every peasant wedding.

It seems more sober to conclude that the ruling classes of the eighteenth-century Western world were overthrown by a change in society, brought about by changes in the infinitely numerous variables that compose any modern society—a change which, since the combinations that produced it were so complex, may be regarded as unpredictable, or as undetermined, or, if you like, as miraculous. For nothing is clearer than that, if God or any other Absolute has arranged everything, He or It has not yet wholly confided these arrangements even to a Karl Marx or a Herbert Spencer. The ruling classes of the eighteenth century were not short-sighted, not narrow and incompetent because they failed to foresee and forestall the changes of the late eighteenth century. Many of them, like the Marquis d'Argenson, foresaw these changes very clearly; many of them, like Turgot, actually helped hasten them by trying to forestall them. They were faced with the challenge of a situation in the full sense of the word *new;* had they wholly succeeded in adapting themselves to it they would have been, not men, but Gods.

Isolated and extremely able individuals like Talleyrand did, even though they held very high position, succeed in adapting themselves to the new situation—or rather, series of new situations. The group as a whole failed, and were replaced by other groups, groups which did not have the same sort of political skill as that possessed by the displaced group when it was at its best. What we have called, without making intentionally too barefaced a use of eulogistic terms, political realism did not depart this earth in 1789, nor even with Talleyrand's death in 1839. A very great deal of it is to be found in Disraeli, in Bismarck, in Thiers, not to speak of Tammany Hall or the *cartel des gauches*. Yet it is surely not now the social heritage of any class in the modern world. We have had able and talented bureaucracies, notably a German bureaucracy which until 1933 was able to weather after a fashion, at least, an extraordinary variety of political insanities in people and rulers. But a bureaucracy is by very definition not a ruling class, is not capable of those subtle and half-instinctive adjustments the politician must make.

The truth is that since the Revolutions of the eighteenth century the Western world, where it has not been ruled by routine, has been ruled by abstractions; where it has not been ruled by bureaucrats, it has been ruled by moral idealists. Let there be no exclusively pious and Wilsonian connotation to this last phrase; for our purposes Napoleon III, William II, Theodore Roosevelt, and Clemenceau may be labelled moral idealists. Routine is indeed the salvation of poor moon-struck man, who without its consoling demands might be quite overwhelmed by the power of thought. The infinite forms of routine suffered no general decline in the nineteenth century. But in a fairly stable society, like that of the Middle Ages or that of the eighteenth century, abstractions become, as ritual, part of routine. That too happened in the last century to such abstractions as Liberty, Equality, Fraternity and the rest, but only very incompletely and ineffectively. An extraordinary number of men—poets, politicians, and business leaders—were in the nineteenth century apparently mastered by the desire to be true to some principle. The famed division of labor was extended to the pursuit of the ideal. Poets were almost exclusively poetical. In fact, the slight but distinct overtones of dispraise in the word poetical date from the nineteenth century—a fact not wholly to be blamed on the philistines. Politicians not only talked about equal rights, national honor, manifest destiny, even-handed justice, fair play for all, but a great many of them also believed what they were talking about. Business men sought, not merely to grow rich, but to become Napoleons of Industry. Waterloos, under various names such as crash, crisis, panic, depression became appropriately endemic in the careers of these Napoleonic industrial leaders, following hard on the Austerlitzes of booms and prosperity.

There is no doubt that in a good many senses this nineteenth-century society was successful. Its successes hardly need recounting here. We are all living on them, traveling in them, wearing them, and not infrequently cursing them. Even such pious windbags as Gladstone seem not to have wrecked the states they governed with such an extraordinary open disregard for what generations of politicians had regarded as the facts of human nature. Moral idealism kept many a nineteenth-century man industrious, sober, and law-abiding, and made largely possible the tremendous scientific and industrial achievement of the age. That achievement depended also on individual initiative, on a willingness to experiment, to gamble, on fighting qualities not always sober and law-abiding, and not ordinarily inspired by moral idealism. In one sense, a Gladstone served the Victorians where a Walpole never could. The combats, the tensions, the movements of the variables which compose any society were in Victorian society so extreme that common sense could never have mediated among them, and they could only be kept in a tentative working agreement by an illogical, and apparently hypocritical, agreement on very abstract principles, such as those commonly called moral principles. Virtue in the nineteenth century was a constitutional monarch who reigned, but did not govern. Respect for virtue, like respect for the British Crown, bound together groups that otherwise had no common rule.

This constitutional rule of virtue is still sometimes called liberalism. Now liberalism at its height in the second half of the nineteenth century was almost, if not quite, a new equilibrium. In theory, liberals believed that ordinary human beings were intelligent enough, and well-disposed enough, so that if they were free to act as they wanted to act, life on earth would on the whole be pleasanter for everyone. That is, the theoretical basis of nineteenth-century liberalism is a philosophical anarchism with its immediate roots in the optimistic late eighteenth-century belief in the natural goodness and natural reasonableness, and perfectibility of man. But a glance at John Mill's essay *On Liberty*—to say nothing of the acts of liberal governments—will show that liberalism thoroughly distrusts the common man, that it is haunted by the fear that the common man will be responsible for the tyranny of the majority, for the rule of a dead-level mediocrity, for plebiscite-chosen dictators. Liberalism values most highly those qualities which past experience seems to show are developed only among privileged groups—self-control, toleration of the peculiar ways of other people, willingness to experiment, an ability to compromise. Most liberals had by the late nineteenth century become uneasily aware that John Smith and John Jones were not even potentially John Stuart Mills.

Liberalism was, however, committed by its respect for principle to a system of politics which really meant suicide for it. Other factors concurring, the suicide has been accomplished in most of our Western world. Liberals really did not trust the common man; but true to nineteenth-century love of abstractions, they followed their principles and gave him the vote. They provided him with opportunities for education, but true to their principles they abstained from educating him; or rather, they saw to it that he was properly exposed to their principles, and left to others the real process of educating him. They allowed and encouraged the career open to talents, but true to their principles they did nothing to prevent their cherished equality from translating itself into plutocracy. In simplest terms: nineteenth-century liberalism pursued the abstractions to which it was devoted to a point where the gap thus made between the ideal and the real, theory and practice, aspiration and performance became too great to be closed even by ritual.

The Four Years' War revealed the full extent of the gap. For while liberals had been hoping and planning, things on the this-worldly side of the gap had been changing with unusual rapidity. It has now become a commonplace to assert that the post-war world is moving away from liberalism, away from the precarious equilibrium of a society based on *laissez-faire,* towards collectivism, order, stability, a new equilibrium, even to a society static rather than dynamic.

IV

TO men brought up in the long Western tradition which dates at least from the Renaissance, and in a sense from the Greeks, such a prospect is unpleasant. Time by no means makes more attractive to such men the kind of society that is growing up under the great dictatorships, and that is sprouting clearly even in the so-called constitutional democracies of the West. Some consciousness of this change, and of its significance in bringing to a close that freedom of thought which has flowered in Western science, inspired the anti-intellectualism of men so different in other ways as Sorel and Pareto. The latter, indeed, hated though he is by the remnant of our liberals, is really a liberal embittered by the knowledge that the liberal way of life is increasingly impossible here on earth. The anti-intellectuals are not enemies of Reason; they are the last worshippers of Reason in a mad world.

Things are perhaps not quite as black as that. Even if communism or fascism or some other form of the authoritarian state masters the Western world, old habits, old commonplaces, old trivialities will assert themselves. Not even the totalitarian state can live up to its name. Life, which has been too much for liberal principles, will perhaps prove, as it always has, too much for other principles.

Perhaps, too, some fragments of the liberal way of life may yet be preserved in the West. And here is where the example of Talleyrand is important. Talleyrand on the whole, as we have tried very hard to show in this study, furthered a liberal, if not heroic, way of life, helped make it possible for a changing France to avoid the extremes of disintegration. Yet Talleyrand was not strait-jacketed by liberal, or any other, principles. Talleyrand had neither the nineteenth century's desire for the moon nor its willingness to be satisfied with a cardboard moon on a stage horizon. Talleyrand did not love virtue. Talleyrand was not, measured by the abstract principles accepted in the last century, a good man. Surely he would be a good man now?

One of the strongest of liberal principles is that the statesman must not lie, that the people must not be deluded, that in politics as in private life truth is great, and will prevail —that, in short, the good man and the good citizen are identical. For those who really believe this, argument and demonstration are futile, and facts make their usual surrender to faith. Yet it is interesting to speculate on what might be accomplished by a corps of able and unprincipled political leaders in defense of the liberal way of life, the way of life in which most living Westerners born before 1900 have been formed. You may argue that men like the present Mr. Roosevelt—to say nothing of Theodore Roosevelt—exhibit an extraordinary skill at Machiavellian politics. Yet they are not quite the kind of men Talleyrand was. The "New Deal" is in its way as happy a phrase as was "Legitimacy." But Mr. Roosevelt seems to believe in the New Deal in a way Talleyrand never believed in Legitimacy; and he certainly has a belief in experiment guided by abstractions or by mere rule of thumb which Talleyrand never displayed. Talleyrand's criterion of success was never the crudely pragmatic one of survival, but the survival of things he valued—France, Europe (for Talleyrand was a good European), peace, toleration, opportunity for growth and experiment. Moreover, your Talleyrands are chary of "plans"; they prefer the play of the artist's intelligence, the subordination of abstract intelligence, not to instinct or to mere hand-to-mouth living, but to the skill, the gift, the foresight of intelligence bound down, and yet emancipated, by constant contact with this dull and obstinate world we live and move about in.

Are such men inevitably enlisted, in our contemporary world, on the side of the dictatorship? Is it impossible for England, France, and America to develop a ruling class as skilled as that of the early eighteenth century, and yet devoted to maintaining the decencies and varying illusions of our grandfathers? Surely no firm answer in the affirmative is possible. It is not that good, idealistic men are always unwilling to attempt mildly Machiavellian tactics. On the contrary, the Machiavellianism of the virtuous presents a very interesting subject for investigation. But they do it awkwardly. The will is there, but not the way. One raised to the very pinnacle of devotion to abstract virtue once speculated as follows:

"How then may we devise one of those needful falsehoods of which we lately spoke—just one Great Lie which may deceive the rulers, if that be possible, and at any rate the rest of the city?

"What sort of lie? he said.

"Nothing new, I replied; only an old Phoenician tale of what has often occurred before now in other places (as the poets say, or have made the world believe) though not in our time, and I do not know whether such an event could ever happen again, or would be believed, if it did.

"How your words seem to hesitate on your lips!

"You will not wonder, I replied, at my hesitation when you have heard.

"Speak, he said, and fear not.

"Well then, I will speak, although I really know not how to look you in the face, or in what words to utter the audacious fiction, which I propose to communicate gradually, first to the rulers, then to the soldiers, and lastly to the people. They are to be informed that their youth was a dream, and the education and training which they received from us an appearance only. [*Then follows the famous story of the three kinds of men—brass and iron men, silver men, and golden men, with the brass and iron men utterly excluded from political power.*] Such is the tale. Is there any possibility of making our citizens believe it?

"Not in the present generation, he replied; I do not see any way of accomplishing this; but their sons may be made to believe, and their son's sons, and posterity after them.

"I see the difficulty, I replied; yet the fostering of such a belief will make them care more for the city and for one another."

Plato, however, did not believe his Great Lie. He belonged to the fairly numerous group of men who have to believe that their actions conform to patterns laid up in eternity, and who therefore make all lies a matter of cosmic concern. He is ill at ease and apologetic in his handling of this quaint and partial anticipation of certain modern race theories. He is more than half persuaded that it is true, or that it is at least a graceful parable tempering the truth to the limitations of ordinary men. But can truth be limited? Plato, like most Western idealists, could never quite keep himself from dabbling in the affairs of the unhappy prisoners in the cave of this world; nor could he quite get over the feeling that the prisoners ought somehow to behave like free men. So when he apologetically admits that it may be wise to lie to men in order to get them to behave as you would like to have them, he is still not much better off than the well-meaning bachelor uncle lying improvingly to his little nephews and nieces. The children are likely to be a lot wiser, in some respects, than the condescending adult.

That the virtuously inclined should be such awkward liars is unfortunate. Nowadays it is particularly unfortunate, as the number and strength of politically important lies would appear to be growing. Plato had his doubts about his golden men; Hitler would appear to have none about his Nordic men. Any theory not in accordance with the facts is in a sense a lie; and practically no fashionable theories in the social sciences are in accordance with the facts. In a society as obviously out of balance as that of the post-war world, conflicting groups and ambitious individuals will, as they always have done in similar situations, seize upon any theories that promise them satisfaction. The theories—or Great Lies—of Marx, Lenin, Gobineau, Hitler and their like are mostly inspired by a great deal of moral earnestness, are indeed commonly developed without even the avuncular insincerity of Plato in dealing with his iron, silver, and golden men. In the long run, if our nineteenth-century prophets of social Darwinism were right, the truth or falsity of any such theories will not greatly matter, for the *successful groups will fit their action to facts and not to theories.* But we all live in the short run, and we may find that the process by which facts take their revenge on bad theorists and unskillful liars is, for any given individual, a rather uncomfortable one.

There is, of course, not much any one of us can do about the fate of liberalism. A dignified pessimism seems now the fashionable cast of the liberal spirit. Liberalism is a Great Lie that even its makers are beginning to doubt. Perhaps the greater builders of civilization have been given the energy necessary for their achievements by an immediate share in "the substance of things hoped for, the evidence of things not seen." Metaphysics may be as necessary to human beings as oxygen, and illusion may be the foundation of empire. If indeed liberalism is no stronger than its metaphysics, it is already a corpse. Yet liberalism may not depend entirely on its metaphysics. There is always the possibility that the kind of sentiments upon which liberalism depends may be at least no more incompatible with the facts of life than are the kind of sentiments fostered by the totalitarian states. In the form with which we of the Western world are familiar with it, liberalism perhaps expected too much, as it certainly promised too much, right here on earth. It would storm Heaven; or worse, pretend that *this* was Heaven anyway. Now, under the stress of attacks from so many quarters, remaining liberals are regrettably, but naturally, prone to stiffen their backs, which in practice means to stiffen their idealistic intransigeance. To many good liberals, our whole defense of Talleyrand has no doubt been an outrage, a treason. Yet we must insist that Talleyrand was no Nietzsche in satin breeches and silk stockings, and we have tried not to depict him as such. About things that really matter he made the kind of judgments of value that liberals make; his whole career showed that he possessed the ability to translate his judgments of value into a way of life.

There are two great issues which emerge from this study of Talleyrand, on neither of which can the doctrinaire liberal be expected to yield. They are essentially, in the form in which the doctrinaire liberal insists they be answered, metaphysical issues, and therefore unanswerable. But we cannot agree that liberalism is necessarily a metaphysical system, and we shall therefore at least sketch, not answers, but ways around, the issues.

The first is the issue of moral absolutes. The doctrinaire liberal will assert that the moral law is absolute, eternal, and that men in all their activities are bound to obey it. The good man and the good citizen are identical. Talleyrand stole as a man and lied as a citizen. Stealing and lying are immoral. Talleyrand was therefore an immoral man and not a liberal. Much of this is of course a reversal of the earlier Christian doctrine, in which though sin was condemned, the sinner was loved and forgiven. Nowadays we condone, or at least turn the apparatus of modern psychology upon, the sin, and denounce the sinner himself as unsocial or unintegrated, as somehow much worse than sinful. Our modern Protestant and positivist abstractions are simply not ripe enough, not pliable enough, and anyone who, like Talleyrand, tries to manipulate them into proper human pliancy seems to us shockingly wicked. It may be pointed out that Talleyrand did not seem to his own Church to be quite lost in sin.

In few human activities other than those of the professional moralist do we find such simplicities, such rigor, such unwillingness to face the challenges of experience as we find in the simpler and more evangelical moral codes. We should all starve if the farmer went about his farming as the Methodist or the Jacobin thinks he goes about the moral life. No artist, no scientist, could for a moment pursue his calling with a neat little set of rules and a good deal of energy as his sole stock in trade. Yet living well is probably at least as complicated an art as painting well, or thinking well. One of the great bogeys of the age is the notion that science and technology have outgrown morals, and one of the most fashionable of proposed remedies is to convert scientists, technologists, and ordinary men to good old moral truths. Hardly anyone has suggested that our moral outlook be raised to the level of scientific effort, that the good old truths might be brightened up a bit.

The suggestion would, of course, be nonsense, at least if it be taken to involve masses of men. Our moral code is, in the form of sentiments, thoroughly embedded in the minds and feelings of ordinary men—where, indeed, it ceases to resemble very greatly the same code as it appears to the doctrinaire liberal. There it is, and certainly no revolution will immediately remove it. But this fact brings us to the second issue with which we are immediately concerned—the issue of leadership.

Liberals have always had some trouble reconciling their dogma of equality with the fact of leadership, but on the whole, when opportunity offered, they have been not unwilling to assume positions as leaders. In the more violently democratic ideals of government, rulers and ruled are not classes, but groups determined by election or by lot, and subject to complete rotation. Actually, the rulers and the ruled even in the nineteenth century were pretty well mutually exclusive classes; and liberals have been known, especially in England, to speak without blushing of the existence of a "ruling class." But they have insisted that both rulers and ruled must at bottom think and feel alike about the processes of government, that the rulers must deal with the ruled as the most progressive schools—and parents—deal with children, as rational creatures, never to be hoodwinked, always to be reasoned with. The rulers are the shepherds, but somehow they too are the sheep. Hence, if there is one proposition more offensive to the doctrinaire liberal than that the good man should not be considered identical with the good citizen, it is the proposition that members of the ruling class should lie to the ruled, should be conscious hypocrites, should guide them by myth, fable, fairy-story and parliamentary logic. Yet there is every evidence that if a ruling class does not do just this, if it attempts to rule by enlightenment and good intentions, it will not long remain a ruling class. That again we can learn from the life of Talleyrand and from the contrasting lives of men like Lafayette. Rulers have hitherto always ruled with the aid of custom, habit, law and a good deal else—by a varying mixture of ruse and force. As ruse diminishes, or is used less effectively, force must be increased. Liberalism is committed to a minimum use of force; it must therefore use ruse, and use it skillfully. Talleyrand is at least a precedent for the skillful use of ruse by a liberal.

The problems involved in these last few pages are of a scope far beyond a simple essay on Talleyrand, and in this study we can do no more than to sketch them in outline. We have here tried to suggest first, that in politics a statesman need not be "moral" in the conventional Christian sense, and that the conduct of politics requires certain gifts, above all the ability to learn from experience, not likely to be found in a given individual along with doctrinaire adhesion to a set of moral absolutes; and second, that successful rulers will lie to the ruled, will govern partly, at least, by ruse. It would seem that the record of past events, as we now possess it, confirms these statements. It would also seem that that sort of confirmation is unconvincing to many excellent people, even to many intelligent people. Such people will continue to know that Truth will ultimately triumph over facts and will feel refreshed in spirit by the knowledge—

> "Right forever on the scaffold, wrong forever on
> the throne."

Such people are happy, and not to be converted. Their objections to our arguments are unanswerable. There is, however, one important objection which does rest on facts. It is this: that a liberalism based on the methods advocated by Machiavelli and practised by Talleyrand would have to be put into effect by a ruling class which would repeat, for the benefit of the ruled, the basic ritual of liberalism—Liberty, Equality, Fraternity, and so on—without, of course, believing it; that, in actual fact such a class would contain a large number of skeptics as regards conventional religious and moral standards; that, indeed, it might be called, not too imprecisely, a skeptical class; that, historically, when ruling classes have become thoroughly skeptical about certain fundamental conventions, they have always been near the end of their tenure of power, holding on by an excess of ruse, sure to go under at the least pressure from below; that, therefore, a skeptical ruling class is, save for a short period of time, an impossibility.

This is an interesting point, and one which, if space permitted, might be developed at greater length. It is not without validity. Two qualifications, however, suggest themselves. First, that a well-balanced and effective ruling class attempting to preserve something of the nineteenth-century ways of life, something of "liberalism," would obviously not be entirely composed of Talleyrands and not entirely deprived of Gladstones. Most of the class would probably be more like Gladstone than like Talleyrand. But there would be an adequate mixture of Talleyrands; and above all, the rank-and-file of the class would have to have some sort of realistic education, some training in the manipulation of men and things. Second, that, unless we are to throw over entirely nineteenth-century notions of possible growth and evolution, we cannot make *absolute* conclusions on the basis of history seen as a mere record. It may be that some men are capable of acquiring the kind of cumulative knowledge about the behavior of men in society which the scientists have for several centuries been acquiring in their fields of study. It may be that there will prove to be a sufficient number of such men to influence society. In other words, the social sciences may some day have something like the same uses for the statesman that the physical sciences have had for the engineer, or the biological sciences for the practising physician. Admittedly this seems unlikely at the present moment. Any such influence in the near future will probably hardly be more than that of a slight leaven. But we ought not to shut our minds to any possibility. There is, of course, no guarantee that scientific knowledge, if it should prove possible in the so-called social sciences, will be used to further the liberal way of life. But, to give scientists their due, they probably average out a shade more sensible than your Napoleons and your Hitlers; at least, their discipline does bring a number of facts to their attention.

Certainly Oxenstierna's famous aphorism—with how little wisdom the world is governed—is at first sight more consoling to the intellectual in retreat than useful to the statesman. Yet one cannot refrain from displaying one's own humanity by giving expression, as a summing-up, to what is no doubt a thought fathered by a number of wishes: may not disillusioned, sobered, skillful men somewhere on this planet develop into a ruling class capable of preserving society from a too ardent pursuit of the totalitarian state, or the classless society, or whatever form the Beautiful and the Good may take for John Jones? May not liberal and skeptical become synonyms instead of antonyms? Then indeed Sainte-Beuve's verdict would be reversed, and Talleyrand would seem again a great and even, in a slightly ironic sense, a good man. Perhaps our own times are not wholly unprepared for some rehabilitation of Talleyrand. To a generation which has seen a hundred abstract ideas run to ground, his serene superiority to abstractions should be very welcome. To a generation which is not unaware of the harm done in politics by conventionally good men, star-fixed leaders from Lafayette and Robespierre to Wilson and Ramsay Macdonald, Talleyrand's vices should seem virtues, his weakness, strength. To those exhausted by our Western effort to prove that hyperbole is not a figure of speech, Talleyrand's mastery of the art of living should afford a suggestive pattern for imitation. To a world tired of fighting, the peacemaker Talleyrand should seem a greater man than the brawler Bonaparte.

An unlovely Utopia? Alas! all Utopias are unlovely—which is doubtless one reason for the peculiar fascination they hold over the human mind. It is, perhaps, even more unlikely than unlovely. Talleyrand will remain a villain, and Lafayette a hero, and little Pippa will pass and re-pass before millions of mute, inglorious Brownings. Talleyrand himself would probably not have had it otherwise. Had his career made of him for posterity a great and good man, he would seem to have been mistaken about his fellows. The Machiavellians have always the supreme joy of their rejection. They have, perhaps, found an answer for our Lord's rhetorical question: What shall a man give in exchange for his soul?

Bibliography

I. TALLEYRAND'S OWN WRITINGS

Mémoires du prince de Talleyrand, publiés par le duc le Broglie. (Paris, 1891–1892) English translation by R. Ledos de Beaufort and Mrs. Angus Hall. (London, 1891–1892.)

This is the basis for any study of Talleyrand. Bacourt, who edited the manuscript before the Duc de Broglie was entrusted with it, may have re-touched the work here and there, but on the whole Talleyrand's mark is clear. Volume I and part of Volume II form a narrative, with many omissions, up to 1814. The other three volumes are almost wholly official correspondence, especially detailed for the Congress of Vienna and for the London Conference. For discussion of the authenticity and accuracy of the *Memoirs* see: Lacour-Gayet, *Talleyrand,* IV, 301–321; P. Bertrand, "M. de Bacourt et les mémoires de Talleyrand," *Revue d'histoire diplomatique,* VII, 75–123; H. Welschinger, *Communication relative au texte des Mémoires de Monsieur de Talleyrand* (Paris, 1895); J. Flammermont, "Le manuscrit des Mémoires de Talleyrand," *Revue historique,* XLVIII, 72–80.

Rapport sur l'instruction publique. Imprimé par ordre de l'Assembleé nationale. (Paris, 1791.) Reprinted in the *Archives parlementaires,* Ire série, XXX, 447–511.

Eclaircissements donnés par le citoyen Talleyrand à ses compatriotes. (Paris, an VII.)

Essai sur les avantages à tirer de colonies nouvelles, etc. Mémoires de l'Institut national des sciences et arts. Sciences morales et politiques (fructidor, an VII.)

Mémoire sur les relations commerciales des Etats-Unis avec l'Angleterre. (Londres, 1805.) English translation as *Memoir concerning the commercial relations of the United States with England.* By Citizen Talleyrand. (Boston, 1809.)

Eloge de M. le comte Reinhard. Institut royal de France. (Paris, 1838.)

There are many speeches, motions and reports made by Talleyrand in the National Assembly, and separately reprinted. These are best studied in the *Archives parlementaires* or the *Moniteur,* where they are indexed under Talleyrand's name.

Correspondance inédite du prince de Talleyrand et du roi Louis XVIII. (Paris, 1888.)

La mission de Talleyrand à Londres. (Paris, 1889.)

Le ministère de Talleyrand sous le directoire. (Paris, 1891.)

L'ambassade de Talleyrand à Londres, 1830–1834. (Paris, 1891.)

These volumes, edited by G. Pallain, anticipated much in Talleyrand's *Memoirs.* The text of the letters as established by Pallain is, however, probably more authentic than those of the *Memoirs.*

Lettres inédites de Talleyrand à Napoléon. Edited by P. Bertrand. (Paris, 1889.)

"Lettres de Talleyrand a Madame de Staël," *Revue d'histoire diplomatique,* IV, 79, 209.

Le prince de Talleyrand et la maison d'Orleans. Lettres du roi Louis Philippe, de Madame Adelaide, et du prince de Talleyrand. Edited by the Comtesse de Mirabeau. (Paris, 1890.)

Talleyrand intime d'après sa correspondance inédite avec la duchesse de Courlande. (Paris, 1891.)

"Correspondance de Talleyrand avec le Premier Consul pendant la campagne de Marengo." Edited by Count Boulay de la Meurthe, *Revue d'histoire diplomatique,* VI, 182.

Correspondance du Comte de Jaucourt avec le Prince de Talleyrand. (Paris, 1905.)

"Lettres de Talleyrand à Caulaincourt." Edited by J. Hanoteau, *Revue des Deux Mondes* (1935), 8th period, XXIX, 782: XXX, 142.

These new letters are interesting, though they add nothing important to our knowledge of Talleyrand. Throughout 1807–1813, Talleyrand insists to Caulaincourt that he is still attached to the Emperor. This is quite enough to start M. Jean Hanoteau, who edits these letters, reflecting on the diabolically clever treason of Talleyrand.

Lacour-Gayet's *Talleyrand* includes, especially in Volume IV, many hitherto unpublished letters and excerpts from letters. It is strange, however, that no collection has been made of Talleyrand's correspondence, especially in an age when any second-rate man of letters can have his correspondence assembled in imposing volumes. The task of editing such a collection of Talleyrand's letters would be enormous, for the letters are scattered about all over the world. The various works listed above do, however, contain all the really important correspondence yet unearthed, and form a body of material of great help in judging the man.

II. CONTEMPORARY LIVES, LIBELS, ANECDOTES

(Chronologically arranged)

Memoirs of C. M. Talleyrand de Périgord. (London, 1805.)

This libellous piece of war propaganda was once attributed to the anti-Napoleonic hack Lewis Goldsmith. It is now attributed to a certain Stewarton. Its subtitle is amusing: *One of Bonaparte's Principle Secretaries of State, his Grand Chamberlain, and Grand Officer of the Legion of Honour, Ex-Bishop of Autun, Ex-Abbé of Celles and St. Dennis, etc., containing the particulars of his Private and Public Life, of his Intrigues in Boudoirs as well as in Cabinets, by the author of the Revolutionary Plutarch:*

When men through infamy to grandeur soar
They light a torch to shew their shame the more.

C . . . P . . . , *Le masque tombé ou Talleyrand-Périgord, ce qu'il est, ce qu'il fut, ce qu'il sera toujours.* (n.d. 1815?.)

There is an immense pamphlet-literature of attack against Talleyrand, of which the above is given as a sample. No systematic bibliographical work has been done on this literature, not even by Lacour-Gayet.

Monsieur de Talleyrand. (Paris, 1834–1835.)

This anonymous life can pretty safely be attributed to C. M. de Villemarest, a dismissed employee of the Foreign Office under Talleyrand. It is hostile, but a much more solid piece of work than anything that had appeared before it.

A. Sallé *Vie politique de Charles-Maurice, Prince de Talleyrand.* (Berlin, 1834.)

Bitterly hostile and uninformed.

Le prince de Talleyrand, sa vie et ses confessions. (Paris, 1838.)

An amusing anti-clerical attack on his death-bed repentance.

Mémoires du Prince de Talleyrand par Madame la Comtesse O . . . du C . . . (Paris, 1838.)

An unimportant pastiche and probably a fake.

Baron de Barante, *Eloge de M. le Prince, Duc de Talleyrand.* (Paris, 1838); reprinted in his *Etudes historiques.* (Paris, 1857.)

L. Bastide, *Vie religieuse et politique de Talleyrand-Périgord, Prince de Bénévent.* (Paris, 1838.)

C. Place et J. Florens, *Mémoire sur Monsieur de Talleyrand, sa vie politique et sa vie intime.* (Paris, 1838.)

Riesco Le Grand, *Vida de Talleyrand-Périgord, Principe soberano de Benevento.* (Madrid, 1839.)

A sympathetic catholic life written in Spanish.

S . . . D . . . , *Histoire de la vie et de la mort de Monsieur de Talleyrand-Périgord.* (Paris, n.d. about 1839–1840?.)

By a certain Sosthène Dufour de la Thuilerie. Sympathetic.

M. Colmache, *Reminiscences of Prince Talleyrand.* (London, 1848.)

By a private secretary to Talleyrand in his later years. Not reliable, but certainly not mere hack-work.

Le retour de Talleyrand à la religion; Lettre de Madame la Duchesse de Talleyrand à M. l'Abbé Dupanloup. (Paris, 1908.)

La conversion et la mort de Monsieur de Talleyrand: Récit de l'un des cinq témoins. (Paris, 1910.)

The above are contemporary accounts of the death-bed conversion, only recently put in print.

Anecdotes about Talleyrand are innumerable. The following contain most of them:

A. Pichot, *Souvenirs Intimes sur Monsieur de Talleyrand.* (Paris, 1870.)

Baron de X . . . , *Les femmes de M. de Talleyrand.* (Paris, 1891.)

The author is Baron V. de Vars.

Mary Summer, *Les belles amies de M. de Talleyrand.* (Paris, 1893.)

A novelized account of Talleyrand's love affairs during the Directory. The author's real name is Madame C. F. Foucaux.

L. Thomas, *L'esprit de Talleyrand.* (Paris, 1909.)

F. Loliée, *Talleyrand et la société française.* (Paris, 1910.)

III. BIOGRAPHICAL AND CRITICAL WRITING ABOUT TALLEYRAND

There is already an immense Talleyrand literature. The following list includes the more important books and a selection of articles of especial significance.

Lord Acton, "Talleyrand's Memoirs," in *Historical Essays.* (London, 1906.)

F. Baldensperger, "Le séjour de Talleyrand aux Etats-Unis," *Revue de Paris,* 15 Novembre, 1924, 364.

C. Bénédek and Dr. O. Ernst, "Talleyrand et les archives de Vienne," *Revue de Paris,* 15 December, 1933, 766.

Lady Blennerhasset, *Talleyrand; Eine Studie.* (Berlin, 1894.) English translation. (London, 1894.)

The most careful of the earlier books on Talleyrand, and very fair-minded.

H. E. Blinn, "New Light on Talleyrand at the Congress of Vienna," *Pacific Historical Review,* IV, 143.

Lord Brougham, "Talleyrand," in *Historical Sketches of Statesmen.* (London, 1839.)

J. Cambon, *Le diplomate.* (Paris, 1926.)

Duff Cooper, *Talleyrand.* (London, 1932.)

The best available life of Talleyrand, written from the comfortable position of English conservatism, undisturbed by French political hatreds.

E. Dard, *Napoléon et Talleyrand.* (Paris, 1935.)

Scholarly, sensible, and for a Frenchman not unconnected with the bureaucracy of official learning, very fair-minded. In notable contrast to Lacour-Gayet, M. Dard grants Talleyrand quite a good deal of independence of Napoleon. Talleyrand is still, of course, a "traitor."

Ch. Dupuis, *Le ministère de Talleyrand en 1814.* (Paris, 1919–1920.)

The kind of exhaustive monograph the French now do even better than the Germans.

Anna B. Dodd, *Talleyrand, the Training of a Statesman.* (New York, 1927.)

Paul D. Evans, "Deux émigrés en Amérique. Talleyrand et Beaumez." *La Révolution française,* Jan. 1926, LXXIX, 51.

J. Gorsas, *Talleyrand.* (Paris, 1891.)

J. Grand-Carteret, "Portraits et caricatures de Talleyrand," *Revue bleue* (1891), XLVII, 451.

A. M. P. Ingold, *Bénévent sous la domination de Talleyrand.* (Paris, 1916.)

B. de Lacombe, *Talleyrand Evêque d'Autun.* (Paris, 1703); *La vie privée de Talleyrand.* (Paris, 1910.)

Perhaps the best straightforward biographical writing on Talleyrand.

G. Lacour-Gayet, *Talleyrand.* (Paris, 1934.)

This is the most thorough and complete life, the "definitive" life. As far as facts go, Lacour-Gayet has the honesty of his professional training. He is utterly lacking in insight, and altogether at loss in the field of general ideas, political, sociological, or psychological. He is a worshipper of Napoleon.

C. L. Lokke, "Pourquoi Talleyrand ne fut pas envoyé à Constantinople," *Annales historiques de la Révolution française* (1933), X, 153.

A. Loth, "Talleyrand et l'Eglise constitutionelle de France," *Revue anglo-romaine,* 17 Oct., 1896.

Sir H. Lytton Bulwer, *Historical Characters.* (London, 1858.)

L. Madelin, "Talleyrand" in *Les hommes de la Révolution.* (Paris, 1928.)

A. Marcade, *Talleyrand prêtre et évêque.* (Paris, 1883.)

J. McCabe, *Talleyrand, A Biographical Sketch.* (London, 1906.)

C. K. McHarg, *Life of Prince Talleyrand.* (New York, 1857.)

L. G. Michaud, *Histoire politique et privée de Charles-Maurice de Talleyrand.* (Paris, 1853.)

Hostile, but rather colorless. One of the first of the hostile biographies after Talleyrand's death.

F. Mignet, *Notice historique sur la vie et les travaux de M. le Prince de Talleyrand.* (Paris, 1839.)

P. Montarlot, "L'episcopat de Talleyrand," *Mémoires de la société éduenne* (1894), XXII, 83.

M. Paléologue, *Romantisme et diplomatie: Talleyrand, Metternich, Chateaubriand.* (Paris, 1924.)

C. A. Sainte-Beuve, *Monsieur de Talleyrand.* (Paris, 1869.)

Later printed in Vol. XII of the *Nouveaux Lundis.* This is the essay which fixed Talleyrand's evil reputation in the minds of cultivated people. Sainte-Beuve grants Talleyrand great gifts as a diplomatist, but thinks him fundamentally corrupted, shameful.

J. Sindral, *Talleyrand.* (Paris, 1926.)

A clever book, rather willfully disparaging Talleyrand. There is just a touch of the tired liberal in the author.

A. Sorel, "Talleyrand et ses Memoires" in *Lectures historiques.* (Paris, 1894.)

H. Wendorf, "Die Ideenwelt des Fürsten Talleyrand," *Historische Vierteljahrschrift* (1933), XXVIII, 335.

Rightly integrates Talleyrand's ideas with certain phases of the Enlightenment. Perhaps exaggerates the underlying consistency of his tasks and ideas.

IV. MEMOIRS AND SIMILAR WRITINGS TOUCHING ON TALLEYRAND

The period of Talleyrand's life is extraordinarily rich in memoirs, many of which are essential to understanding his rôle in politics. The following list is by no means exhaustive. It is confined, with few exceptions, to contemporary writings. Even a selective list of secondary historical work on the period would outrun the limits of this bibliography. The reader who wishes the latest bibliographical information, with some critical winnowing, will find it in the appropriate volumes of two series now in course of publication: *The Rise of Modern Europe,* edited by W. L. Langer (New York, 1934–) and *Peuples et Civilisations,* edited by Halphen and Sagnac (Paris, 1930–).

Abrantès, *Memoirs of Madame Junot, Duchesse d'Abrantès.* (Paris and Boston, 1895.)

Apponyi, *Vingt-cinq ans à Paris, 1826–1850. Journal du comte R. Apponyi.* (Paris, 1913–1926.)

Arnault, *Souvenirs d'un sexagénaire, par A. V. Arnault,* Nouvelle édition. (Paris, 1908.)

Barante, *Souvenirs du baron de Barante, 1782–1866, publiés par C. de Barante.* (Paris, 1890–1901.)

Barère, *Memoirs of B. Barère.* Translated by De V. Payen-Payne. (London, 1896.)

Barras, *Memoirs of Barras, member of the Directory.* Translated by E. E. Roche. (New York, 1895–1896.)

Beugnot, *Mémoires du comte Beugnot, ancien ministre, publiés par le comte A. Beugnot.* (Paris, 1868.)

Blanc, *Histoire de dix ans, 1830–1840.* Par Louis Blanc. (Brussels, 1846.)

Bourienne, *Memoirs of Napoleon Bonaparte*. By L. A. F. de Bourienne. (Paris and Boston, 1895.)

Brifaut, *Charles Brifaut, Souvenirs d'un académicien sur la révolution, le premier empire et la restauration*. (Paris, 1921.)

Broglie, *Personal recollections of the late Duc de Broglie*. Translated by R. Ledos de Beaufort. (London, 1887.)

Castellane, *Journal du maréchal de Castellane, 1804–1862*. (Paris, 1895–1897.)

Caulaincourt, *Mémoires du Général de Caulaincourt, Duc de Vicence*. Edited by Jean Hanoteau. (Paris, 1933.) Abridged English translation. (New York, 1935.)

Chastenay, *Mémoires de Madame de Chastenay, publiés par A. Roserot*. (Paris, 1896–1897.)

Chateaubriand, *Mémoires d'outre-tombe*. Many French editions. Translated as *The Memoirs of François-René, Vicomte de Chateaubriand*. (London, 1902.)

Coigny, *Mémoires de Aimée de Coigny*. (Paris, 1902.)

Dino, *Notice sur Valençay, par Madame la Duchesse de Dino*. (Paris, 1848.)

Souvenirs de la Duchesse de Dino, publiés par la comtesse Jean de Castellane. (Paris, 1908.)

Chronique de 1831 à 1862, par Madame la Duchesse de Dino. (Paris, 1909–1910.)

Duquesnoy, *Journal sur l'assembleé constituante, par Adrien Duquesnoy*. (Paris, 1894.)

Genlis, *Memoirs of the Countess of Genlis illustrative of the history of the Eighteenth and Nineteenth centuries*. (London, 1825–1826.)

Girardin, *Discours et opinions, journal de Stanislas Girardin*. (Paris, 1828.)

Goldsmith, *The secret history of the cabinet of Bonaparte*. [By Lewis Goldsmith.] (London, 1810.)

Greville, *Leaves from the Diary of Henry Greville*. Edited by the Viscountess Enfield. (London, 1883–1905.)

Guizot, *Memoirs to illustrate the history of my time*. By F. Guizot. (London, 1858–1861.)

Hauterive, *Histoire de la vie et des travaux politiques du comte d'Hauterive*. Par Artaud de Montor. (Paris, 1839.)

Holland, *Foreign Reminiscences*. By Henry Richard, Lord Holland. 2nd edition. (London, 1851.)

Queen Hortense, *Mémoires de la reine Hortense, publiés par le prince Napoléon.* (Paris, 1927.)

Hyde de Neuville, *Mémoires et souvenirs du baron Hyde de Neuville.* (Paris, 1888–1892.)

Kielmansegge, *Memoiren der Gräfin Kielmansegge über Napoleon I.* (Dresden, 1927.) French translation by J. Delage. (Paris, 1928.)

De La Garde-Chambonas, *Fêtes et souvenirs du Congrès de Vienne.* Par A de la Garde-Chambonas. (Paris, 1843.)

Lamartine, *Cours familier de littérature.* Par A. de Lamartine. (Paris, 1856–1869.)

Mémoires politiques. In *Oeuvres Complètes.* (Paris, 1860–1866.) Vols. XXXVII–XL.

Las Cases, *Mémorial de Ste. Hélène.* Par E. A. D. de Las Cases. (Paris, 1823.)

De La Tour du Pin, *Journal d'une femme de cinquante ans.* Par Madame la Marquise de La Tour du Pin Gouvernet. (Paris, 1907–1911.)

Lauzun, *Correspondance intime du Duc de Lauzun.* Edited by Comte de Lort de Sérignan. (Paris, 1906.)

Lezay-Marnesia, *Mes Souvenirs.* Par M. le conte Adrien Lezay-Marnésia. (Paris, 1854.)

Macdonald, *Recollections of Marshal Macdonald, Duke of Tarentum.* Translated by S. L. Simeon. New edition. (New York, 1893.)

Malouet, *Mémoires de Malouet, publiés par son petit fils, le baron Malouet.* (Paris, 1868.)

Méneval, *Memoirs illustrating the History of Napoleon I.* By Baron C. F. Méneval. (New York, 1894.)

Metternich, *Memoirs of Prince Metternich.* Edited by Prince Richard Metternich.

Miot de Melito, *Memoirs of Count Miot de Melito.* Edited by General Fleischmann. (New York, 1881.)

Mirabeau, *Recollections of Mirabeau and of the two first legislative assemblies of France.* By Etienne Dumont. (Philadelphia, 1833.)

Molé, *The Life and Memoirs of Count Molé.* Edited by the Marquis de Noailles. (London, 1923–1925.)

Montrond, *Le beau Montrond.* Par H. Malo. (Paris, 1926.)

"L'Ami de Talleyrand." H. Welschinger, in *Revue de Paris,* 1 Feb. 1895.

Moreau, *Mes souvenirs.* Par Jacob-Nicholas Moreau. (Paris, 1898–1901.)

Moreau de St. Méry, *Voyage aux Etats-Unis d'Amérique, 1793–1798.* Edited by S. L. Mims. (New Haven, Conn., 1913.)

Morris, *The Diary and Letters of Gouverneur Morris.* (New York, 1888.)

Napoleon I, *Correspondance de Napoléon I publiée par ordre de l'empereur Napoléon III.* (Paris, 1858–1870.)

Nesselrode, *Lettres et papiers du chancelier Comte de Nesselrode.* (Paris, 1904–1912.)

O'Meara, *Napoleon in Exile; or, a Voice from St. Helena.* By B. E. O'Meara. (New York, 1853.)

Ouvrard, *Mémoires de G.-J. Ouvrard sur sa vie et ses diverses opérations financières.* (Paris, 1826–1827.)

Pasquier, *Mémoires du chancelier Pasquier.* Nouvelle edition. (Paris, 1934.)

Potocka, *Memoirs of the Countess Potocka.* Edited by C. Stryienski; translated by Lytton Strachey. (New York, 1900.)

Raikes, *A Portion of the journal kept by Robert Raikes, Esq., 1831–1847.* (London, 1856–1858.)

Rémusat, *Memoirs of Madame de Rémusat.* (New York, 1880.)

A Selection from the letters of Madame de Rémusat to her husband and son. (London, 1881.)

Roederer, *Autour de Bonaparte: Journal du Comte P.-L. Roederer.* (Paris, 1909.)

Rovigo, *Memoirs of the Duke of Rovigo (M. Savary), written by himself.* (London, 1828.)

Salaberry, *Souvenirs politiques du comte de Salaberry sur la restauration.* (Paris, 1900.)

Ségur, *Histoire et mémoires.* Par le général comte de Ségur. (Paris, 1873–1877.)

Semallé, *Souvenirs du comte de Semallé.* (Paris, 1898.)

Shelley, *The Diary of Lady Frances Shelley.* Edited by R. Edgcumbe. (London, 1912–1913.)

Souza, *Madame de Souza et sa famille.* Par M. le baron de Maricourt. (Paris, 1907.)

Thibaudeau, *Mémoires sur le consulat par un ancien conseiller d'état.* (Paris, 1827.)

Mémoires sur la convention et le directoire par A.-C. Thibaudeau. (Paris, 1824.)

Thiébault, *Mémoires du baron Paul Thiébault.* (Paris, 1893–1895.)

Villèle, *Mémoires et correspondance du comte de Villèle.* (Paris, 1888–1890.)

Vitrolles, *Mémoires et relations politiques du baron de Vitrolles.* (Paris, 1884.)

NOTE ON TALLEYRAND LETTERS IN THE PRINCETON LIBRARY

THE following unpublished letters from Talleyrand are in the Beauharnais Archives now in the library of Princeton University:

A. Letter of courtesy to Eugene Beauharnais of 20 June, 1805, acknowledging receipt of congratulations.

B. Announcement of victory of Austerlitz dated 12 frimaire, an 14.

C. Description of the battle of Austerlitz, dated 14 frimaire, an 14.

D. Letter of 21 June, 1806, on Eugene's success in Dalmatia, and discussing the situation in Bosnia and vicinity, welcoming the rise of a new pasha unfriendly to Russia, announcing the appointment of two new consuls in the Adriatic district. Encloses copy of a letter from the French consul-general at Salonika on the new pasha, to be forwarded to General Lauriston.

E. Letter of 13 April, 1807, with news of the English repulse at the Dardanelles, of the coöperation of the Turks in the continental blockade, of Turkish successes in the Balkans against Russia.

F. Letter of 30 April, 1807, announcing the excellent condition of the Grand Army, the siege of Danzig, the siege of Glotz in Silesia, the losses of the Swedes in their sortie from Stralsund in Pomerania which resulted in the withdrawal of the Swedes from the war.

G. Letter of 10 July, 1807, with news of the treaty of Tilsit.

H. Letter of 10 July, 1807, with notice of the mission to Italy of General Ferrier who has a letter of instruction with regard to harmonious relations with Russia.

I. Note of 22 July, 1807, accompanying enclosed letter for Alquier.

J. Acknowledgment of letter, dated 20 Sept., 1806.

Index

IN THE NORTON LIBRARY

Aron, Raymond. *On War.* N107

Aron, Raymond. *The Opium of the Intellectuals.* N106

Bemis, Samuel Flagg. *The Latin American Policy of the United States.* N412

Billington, Ray Allen (editor) *The Reinterpretation of Early American History.* N446

Blair, Peter Hunter. *Roman Britain and Early England 55 B.C.–A.D. 871* N361

Bloch, Marc. *Strange Defeat: A Statement of Evidence Written in 1940.* N371

Bober, M. M. *Karl Marx's Interpretation of History.* N270

Brandt, Conrad. *Stalin's Failure in China.* N352

Brinton, Crane. *The Lives of Talleyrand.* N188

Brodie, Fawn. *Thaddeus Stevens.* N331

Brooke, Christopher. *From Alfred to Henry III, 871–1272* N362

Brown, Robert E. *Charles Beard and the Constitution.* N296

Burn, W. L. *The Age of Equipoise.* N319

Burnett, Edmund Cody. *The Continental Congress.* N278

Bury, J. B. *The Invasion of Europe by the Barbarians.* N388

Butterfield, Herbert. *The Whig Interpretation of History.* N318

Calleo, David P. *Europe's Future.* N406

Collis, Maurice. *Foreign Mud: The Opium Imbroglio at Canton in the 1830's and the Anglo-Chinese War.* N462

Cornish, Dudley Taylor. *The Sable Arm: Negro Troops in the Union Army, 1861-1865.* N334

Davies, John Paton, Jr. *Foreign and Other Affairs.* N330

Dehio, Ludwig. *Germany and World Politics in the Twentieth Century.* N391

De Roover, Raymond. *The Rise and Decline of The Medici Bank.* N350

Duckett, Eleanor. *The Wandering Saints of the Early Middle Ages.* N266

Dumond, Dwight Lowell. *Antislavery.* N370

East, W. Gordon. *The Geography Behind History.* N419

Erikson, Erik H. *Young Man Luther.* N170

Eyck, Erich. *Bismarck and the German Empire.* N235

Feis, Herbert. *Contest Over Japan.* N466

Feis, Herbert. *The Diplomacy of the Dollar.* N333

Feis, Herbert. *Europe: The World's Banker* 1870-1914. N327

Feis, Herbert. *Three International Episodes: Seen from E. A.* N351

Feis, Herbert. *The Spanish Story.* N339

Ferrero, Guglielmo. *The Reconstruction of Europe.* N208

Ford, Franklin L. *Strasbourg in Transition, 1648-1789.* N321

Glueck, Nelson. *Rivers in the Desert: A History of the Negev.* N431

Gordon, Cyrus H. *The Ancient Near East.* N275

Grantham, Dewey W. *The Democratic South.* N299

Graves, Robert and Alan Hodge. *The Long Week-end: A Social History of Great Britain, 1918-1939.* N217

Green, Fletcher. *Constitutional Development in the South Atlantic States, 1776-1860.* N348

Gulick, Edward Vose. *Europe's Classical Balance of Power.* N413

Halperin, S. William. *Germany Tried Democracy.* N280

Hamilton, Holman. *Prologue to Conflict.* N345

Haring, C. H. *Empire in Brazil.* N386

Harrod, Roy. *The Dollar.* N191

Haskins, Charles Homer. *The Normans in European History.* N342

Herring, Pendleton. *The Politics of Democracy.* N306

Hill, Christopher. *The Century of Revolution 1603-1714.* N365

Himmelfarb, Gertrude. *Darwin and the Darwinian Revolution.* N455

Holmes, George. *The Later Middle Ages, 1272-1485.* N363

Hughes, H. Stuart. *The United States and Italy.* N396

Jolliffe, J. E. A. *The Constitutional History of Medieval England.* N417

Jones, Rufus *The Quakers in the American Colonies.* N356

Keir, David Lindsay. *The Constitutional History of Modern Britain Since 1485.* N405

Kendall, Paul Murray (editor). *Richard III: The Great Debate.* N310

Kennan, George. *Realities of American Foreign Policy.* N320

Kouwenhoven, John A. *The Arts in Modern American Civilization.* N404

Langer, William L. *Our Vichy Gamble.* N379

Leach, Douglass E. *Flintlock and Tomahawk: New England in King Philip's War.* N340

Maddison, Angus. *Economic Growth in the West.* N423

Magrath, C. Peter. *Yazoo: The Case of Fletcher v. Peck.* N418

Maitland, Frederic William. *Domesday Book and Beyond.* N338

Mason, Alpheus Thomas. *The Supreme Court from Taft to Warren.* N257

Mattingly, Harold. *The Man in the Roman Street.* N337

May, Arthur J. *The Hapsburg Monarchy: 1867-1914.* N460.

Morgenthau, Hans J. (editor). *The Crossroad Papers.* N284

Neale, J. E. *Elizabeth I and Her Parliaments,* 2 vols. N359a & N359b

Nef, John U. *War and Human Progress.* N468

Nichols, J. Alden. *Germany After Bismarck.* N463

Noggle, Burl. *Teapot Dome: Oil and Politics in the 1920's.* N297

North, Douglass C. *The Economic Growth of the United States 1790-1860.* N346

Ortega y Gasset, José. *Concord and Liberty.* N124

Ortega y Gasset, José. *History as a System.* N122

Ortega y Gasset, José. *Man and Crisis.* N121

Ortega y Gasset, José. *Man and People.* N123

Ortega y Gasset, José. *Meditations on Quixote.* N125

Ortega y Gasset, José. *Mission of the University.* N127

Ortega y Gasset, José. *The Origin of Philosophy.* N128

Ortega y Gasset, José. *What Is Philosophy?* N126

Pelling, Henry. *Modern Britain, 1885-1955.* N368

Pidal, Ramón Menéndez. *The Spaniards in Their History.* N353

Pocock, J. G. A. *The Ancient Constitution and the Feudal Law.* N387

Pollack, Norman. *The Populist Response to Industrial America.* N295

Pomper, Gerald. *Nominating the President.* N341

Robson, Eric. *The American Revolution, 1763-1783.* N382

Rostow, W. W. *The Process of Economic Growth.* N176

Roth, Cecil. *The Spanish Inquisition.* N255

Rowse, A. L. *Appeasement.* N139

Salvemini, Gaetano. *The French Revolution: 1788-1792.* N179

Silver, James W. *Confederate Morale and Church Propaganda.* N422

Spanier, John W. *The Truman-MacArthur Controversy and the Korean War.* N279

Sykes, Norman. *The Crisis of the Reformation.* N380

Thompson, J. M. *Louis Napoleon and the Second Empire.* N403

Tolles, Frederick B. *Meeting House and Counting House.* N211

Tourtellot, Arthur Bernon. *Lexington and Concord.* N194

Turner, Frederick Jackson. *The United States 1830-1850.* N308

Ward, Barbara. *India and the West.* N246

Ward, Barbara. *The Interplay of East and West.* N162

Warren, Harris Gaylord. *Herbert Hoover and the Great Depression.* N394

Wedgwood, C. V. *William the Silent.* N185

Whitaker, Arthur P. *The United States and the Independence of Latin America.* N271

Whyte, A. J. *The Evolution of Modern Italy.* N298

Wolfers, Arnold. *Britain and France between Two Wars.* N343

Wolff, Robert Lee. *The Balkans in Our Time.* N395

Woodward, C. Vann. *The Battle for Leyte Gulf.* N312

Wright, Benjamin Fletcher. *Consensus and Continuity, 1776-1787.* N402

CPSIA information can be obtained
at www.ICGtesting.com
Printed in the USA
BVHW052256090223
658264BV00001B/45

9 781013 78361